JIMMY O'DEA

The Pride of the Coombe

Philip B Ryan

POOLBEG

Acknowledgements

We extend our sincere thanks to Jimmy's wife, Mrs Ursula O'Dea (Ursula Doyle) and to his only surviving close relative, his sister Miss Rita O'Dea, both of whom gave encouragement, information, and their time in full measure.

The biography would not have been possible without the enthusiastic help of the following people and organisations to whom we are grateful. John Adrian of The Grand Order of Water Rats; Arthur Badrock; Agnes Bernelle; Paddy Behan; Rev Bruce Bradley SJ of Belvedere College, Dublin; Mary Clarke, Dublin City Archivist; Dr Cyril Cusack for his kind assistance, and permission to print his poem "To A Dead Comedian"; Séamus De Búrca, a true and sympathetic man of the theatre; Barbara Durack, RTE Film Archivist; John J Finegan; Rev Sean Farragher, Holy Ghost Fathers, Blackrock College; Sr Mary Bernadette Glennon, Holy Faith Prep School, Kilcoole; Michael Hegarty; Vernon Hayden; David Kelly; Derry O'Donovan; Terry O'Donovan; Mrs Eileen Purcell (Eileen Marmion); James Plunkett; Alan Richardson; Noel Shiels, RTE Sound Archivist; KJ Westmancoat, The British Library; Jeff Walden, Senior Assistant, BBC DATA, Written Archives Centre, Reading; The Secretary, The Marist Fathers College, Dundalk. We have quoted from many conversations, reminiscences, newspapers and journals such as *Hibernia*.

Photographs

We are deeply grateful to the following for the loan of valuable photographs reproduced in the following pages:

John J Finegan, theatre correspondent of the *Evening Herald;* the film director Donald Taylor Black; John Walsh (Editor) and Ursula Curry of the *RTE Guide;* Mrs Eileen Purcell; Mrs Ursula O'Dea; The National Film Archive, London; Vernon Hayden; Derry O'Donovan; Terry O'Donovan; Walt Disney Productions.

If we have inadvertently omitted the name of any person or organisation we shall be happy to rectify the omission in future editions.

THE PRIDE OF THE COOMBE

First published 1990 by
Poolbeg Press Ltd.,
Knocksedan House,
Swords, Co. Dublin, Ireland.

© 1990 Philip B Ryan

ISBN 185371 108X

*For my wife, Christine,
whose help, encouragement and TLC made this book
possible*

Cover design by Pomphrey Associates
Typeset by Typeform Ltd.
Printed by Mackays of Chatham plc

Contents

Plates following pages 32, 128 and 192

REPORTER: *You have become quite a celebrity now, you know.*

MRS MULLIGAN: *Who are yeh tellin'. Them two play-actors Jimmy O'Dea and Harry O'Donovan has me name all over the world and half over Dublin. I went up to the Olympia Theatre one night to complain to Bob Morrison the manager, and a stiff lookin' fella at the door says to me, "Have you got a card lady?" "Card is it?" says I. "If a hundred cards at two and six is the makin's of a lady, then the streets of Dublin must be runnin' with blue blood." I'd take an action for damages against them fellas only for I don't like solicitors.*

(Sketch—"Interviewing Mrs Mulligan"
by Harry O'Donovan, 1931)

Foreword

In theory at least, I am at thirty-three too young to remember Jimmy O'Dea save for his delightful Telefís Éireann series for children *Once Upon a Time*. However the deep love of the theatre in all its many and mysterious forms which has remained with me all my life has as its source a pantomime matinee at Dublin's Gaiety Theatre. I didn't know then, aged about three, that I was watching a comic genius, or that in those his later years he was regarded in some quarters as being somewhat in his decline as an artist. All this impressionable little chisler could be certain of was that this funny-looking man on the stage was absolute magic and that his name was Jimmy—just Jimmy—as it was to adults and children alike all over Ireland.

Apparently there was some difficulty in removing me from the theatre after the performance: I struggled and yelled, not wanting this different new reality to end. My parents retreated to the back of the empty parterre and only the promise by a kindly usherette that the brat could come back "after tea" temporarily quelled the rebellion. Still the bug for which there is no antidote had bitten deep. The passion for the theatre, inherited from my father (the author of this timely biography) and encouraged and abetted by frequent visits to the Gaiety and Theatre Royal, gave me the privileged opportunity to see Jimmy O'Dea a few more times before his death in 1965.

Not that Jimmy confined himself to the theatre—his

old 78 rpm gramophone records seemed to be in every house in Dublin—and I listened happily to Dad's collection of Mrs Mulligan sketches until the records surfaces were worn and I had every line of dialogue off by heart. He could also be seen in the picture-houses, of course, (I remember a surreptitious visit to the old Plaza cinema in Dorset Street to see a revival of *Blarney*) not least when he pooled his magic with Walt Disney's for *Darby O'Gill and the Little People*. And with mixed results he lent his talents to the infant Telefís Éireann.

Nor was his fame confined to Ireland—with his O'D company he was a regular bill-topper on the British variety circuit and he broadcast frequently for the BBC. It could be argued that only his intense dislike of Hollywood prevented his becoming a truly international star. A comic with a "legit" background who was highly estimated by Hilton Edwards and Mícheál MacLiammóir, Jimmy was never the clown with a yearning to play Hamlet although Ian Priestley-Mitchell wrote: "He radiates every attribute necessary to move one in a great and memorable performance of *Hamlet*." Successfully transcending—scorning even—such divisive categories, O'Dea freely incorporated parody, pathos and topicality into his repertoire.

He was a genuinely intriguing and larger than life "character" in Dublin, a city which thrived on characters, and it is not difficult even now to visualise Jimmy O'Dea in his favourite seat in Neary's exchanging pithy remarks with his friend Flann O'Brien, perhaps even inadvertently forming a component of the latter's hilarious creation "The Brother." Often compared to the great and, to my mind, inferior Charles Chaplin, it is now twenty-five years since he took his last curtain call. This remarkable biography more than makes up for the fact that for all that time bookshelves have had to tolerate the absence of such a volume, written in tribute to one of the greatest of Irish artists in this century. *The Pride of the Coombe* traces Jimmy's life and work in a progression from schoolboy to optician, amateur actor to Variety star, low-budget movie to Disney epic.

The author treats his subject with warmth, humour, a keen critical eye, and also with poignancy when the moment calls, but above all with affection. In a book that has been meticulously and thoroughly researched all phases of the life of James Augustine O'Dea are examined and treated with fascinating detail. Of course, no Jimmy O'Dea story would count for much if it did not place its subject in the milieu in which he thrived. This is done beautifully by bringing that most elusive of eras, the day before yesterday, to sparkling vital life, There are evocative pictures of a pre-Lemass Ireland, in particular of Dublin, at a time when in the innocence of our new independence almost anything might just have been possible and many things actually happened.

These days travels with my group The Pogues have meant that I have been fortunate to be able to go to the theatre regularly in the rich pastures of the United States, Australia and Canada as well as in London and other parts of these islands. But when I come home to Dublin I never miss a visit to my first and most cherished playhouse, the still magical Gaiety Theatre. As I pause to admire the bust of Jimmy O'Dea outside the dress circle, the momentary but forlornly impossible hope arises—could it be possible that those twinkling eyes have never really left the place?

Philip Chevron
Muswell Hill
London

Introduction

Christmas in Dublin in 1964 was full of the usual festive spirit with special street lighting, fairy lights and Santa Claus in the shops, carol singing at the GPO and the huge Christmas tree in O'Connell Street, but one familiar figure was missing—Jimmy O'Dea wasn't in panto at the Gaiety.

Jimmy had an almost unbroken run of Christmas shows at the Gaiety Theatre for twenty-seven years and for many years previously at the Queen's and Olympia Theatres. Fathers, mothers and grandparents took their children to see him just as they had been taken by their parents. It became a tradition with scores of families that the children be taken for high tea to one of the brightly decorated restaurants such as the Savoy Cinema Restaurant—which, in addition to being decorated with colourful Christmas trees had its walls covered with boxed-in cut-out scenes from the panto at the Theatre Royal—and afterwards a visit to the Gaiety. It didn't really matter what the panto was called: the purpose of the expedition was "going to see Jimmy."

To many people, including country folk, Dublin at that time was synonymous with three things—Alfie Byrne, who had ten times been Lord Mayor, Nelson's Pillar, which was the city terminus for all the electric trams, and Jimmy O'Dea, who was Ireland's undisputed king of comedy. Now he was ill in hospital and no longer able to laugh his way through the exploits of the Widow Twankey, Sarah the Cook, Dame Biddy Mulligan or perhaps his most lovable creation, Buttons in *Cinderella*.

On the evening of January 7 1965 when the audience had shown its appreciation of the cast of *Sinbad the Sailor* as they took their bows in the grand finale, Jimmy's manager, Vernon Hayden, stepped forward and announced that Jimmy had died at 11 o'clock that morning. Vernon introduced on stage various well-known theatre personalities who reminisced about their dead colleague, each emphasising his great qualities as a person and friend and particularly his status as a comedy actor. Finally, the audience stood silently as the theatre orchestra played his theme music, "Biddy Mulligan, the Pride of the Coombe," to an empty stage and the curtain came slowly down.

Listening to the band, many could visualise the diminutive figure of Jimmy bounding on, neat, dapper and light of foot in a favourite role with great dark eyes sparkling, and whether he was supposed to be Napoleon or Stalin, or Queen Victoria's statue outside Leinster House, a bowler hatted plumber or an out-of-work waiter or musician, his own magnetic magical personality shone through.

Backstage, his partner of many years, Harry O'Donovan, smoked a reflective pipe and recalled that their first pantomime together had been *Sinbad the Sailor*. Harry, the man who wrote Jimmy's scripts and created for him his best loved character, Biddy Mulligan, the Pride of the Coombe, was never to write another line.

BIDDY MULLIGAN
The Pride of the Coombe
(Seamus Kavanagh)

I'm a buxom fine widow, I live in a spot,
In Dublin, they call it the Coombe.
My shops and my stalls are laid out on the street,
And my palace consists of one room.
I sell apples and oranges, nuts and split peas,
Bananas and sugarstick sweet,
On Saturday night I sell second-hand clothes
From the floor of my stall on the street.

CHORUS
You may travel from Clare to the County Kildare,
From Francis Street on to Macroom:
But where would you see a fine widow like me,
Biddy Mulligan, the pride of the Coombe

I sell fish on a Friday set out on a board,
The finest you'd find in the say
But the best is my herrings, fine Dublin Bay herrings,
There's herrings for dinner today.
I have a son Mick, and he's great on the flute
He plays in the Longford Street Band
It would do your heart good to see him march out,
On a Sunday for Dollymount Strand

CHORUS

In the park on a Sunday, I make quite a dash,
The neighbours look on with surprise,
With my Aberdeen shawlie thrun over my head,
I dazzle the sight of their eyes.
At Patrick Street corner for sixty-four years,
I've stood and no one can deny,
That while I stood there, no person would dare
To say black was the white of my eye.

CHORUS

1

Jim

QUEEN'S
THEATRE

Telephone 3016   PEARSE STREET, DUBLIN   Telephone 3016
BOX OFFICE OPEN FROM 11 A.M. TO 3 P.M.

Lessees and Managers · · BOURKE AND WILDE

7-TWICE NIGHTLY-9

COMMENCING MONDAY, 16th APRIL
AND DURING THE WEEK *1928*

FIRST PRODUCTION OF THE NEW REVUE:

WE'RE HERE

Book and Lyrics by HARRY O'DONOVAN
Scenery by The Wilde and Bourke Studios, Dublin
Period Costumes by P. J. Bourke
The Whole Revue produced by JIMMY O'DEA

The strongest combination of Irish Talent yet presented in
Revue, headed by Ireland's Representative Comedian:

JIMMY O'DEA

SUPPORTED BY
FAY SARGENT

MOLLIE DOUGLAS	TOM DUNNE
EILEEN MARMION	LIONEL DAY
CONNIE RYAN	WILLIE O'TOOLE

EILY MURNAGHAN
HARRY O'DONOVAN

Dances arranged by KATHLEEN O'BRIEN, leading
"THE EIGHT JOY-BELLES"

For the first time in Dublin, is offered the best in Irish Talent in
conjunction with an all Irish Management in this Historic Theatre

BOOK EARLY !   **BOOK EARLY !**

GALLERY	UPPER CIRCLE	PARTERRE	DRESS CIRCLE	SEATS IN BOXES
6d.	1/-	1/3	2/-	3/-

ALL ABOVE PRICES INCLUDE AMUSEMENT TAX
THE MANAGEMENT RESERVE THE RIGHT TO REFUSE ADMISSION. NO CHILDREN IN ARMS ADMITTED
CHILDREN HALF-PRICE TO ALL PARTS EXCEPT GALLERY.

CORRIGAN & WILSON, Ltd., Printers, 13 Sackville Place, Dublin

Chapter One

The Coombe of which Biddy Mulligan was the pride is part of the Dublin Liberties in which Jimmy himself was born. The Liberties today has desirable little artisans dwellings, popular with those seeking a trendy townhouse, but in the middle of the nineteenth century when Mrs Kate Kerr ran her little toy shop at 11 Lower Bridge Street it was a place of disease, poverty and squalid tenements. Mrs Kerr, a widow, who was left in debt by the death of her husband Joseph in 1875, was one of the Deas of Kilkenny. Her father, Kyron Dea, was manager of one of the first penny banks in the country, that highest form of financial institution to which an impoverished population could aspire, and he also had connections with a shipping agency. Kyron Dea had another daughter who was a sister in a Dutch order of nuns based in Wales and a son Father Laurence Dea OFM, who was a missionary in India.

Kate Kerr willed her house and shop, solvent and unencumbered, to a second brother, James. He was born in Kilkenny in 1850 and came to Dublin when their father died and found work in an ironmonger's, Messrs Henshaw of Christchurch Place. Mrs Kerr had an assistant Martha O'Gorman who also hailed from Kilkenny and whose father was a painter and decorator. Martha who was born in 1868 left home on the death of her father because she couldn't agree with her stepmother, and became a teacher in a junior school in Dublin. She and her sister, who later became the

Reverend Mother of a High School in Durban, helped their brother Canice financially in his studies to become a priest.

James O'Dea reinstated the 'O,' which had been forbidden under law, into the family name when he became the new proprietor of the toy shop on the death of his sister Kate. In 1894 he married Martha O'Gorman. This was his third marriage. His first wife died of tuberculosis leaving two children, a boy and a girl; the girl Margaret Mary Clare trained as a nurse in St Vincent's Hospital and went to the North of England to tend the wounded from the Somme in 1914, while the boy Ciaran joined his father when the latter went into business for himself. His second wife died in childbirth, leaving three daughters. Two of the girls entered convents and the third, Ann (Nan) got married. Agnes, became Mother Agnes Patrick of the little Sisters of the Assumption, Walton, New York, and May became Mother St. Peter in the Ursuline Convent in Sligo.

James O'Dea and his new wife Martha settled down to making a home over the Dickensian toy shop in Bridge Street and although he was many years her senior they were perfectly compatible and raised a large family. The older step-children were sent away to boarding schools in order that Martha, a very practical woman, could concentrate on running the shop. As the new family arrived a nanny was employed. In addition, Martha's aunt Kate O'Gorman who had been a priest's housekeeper and was a wonderful cook, looked after the household. Great-aunt Kate often spoke to the children about her brother Pat who had a lovely tenor voice and sang with the Moody-Manners Opera Company.

In 1896 James left his employment in Henshaw's and opened in partnership with a man called Gleeson a rival ironmongery shop practically next door to his old employer's at 21 Christchurch Place, trading as Gleeson and O'Dea. When he left Henshaw's James was presented with a silver salver bearing the inscription:

Presented to James O'Dea Esq., by a few friends on his leaving Messrs Henshaw & Co. August 1896

These business friends were the main basis of James's contribution to the new partnership. Gleeson put up most of the money but O'Dea had the contacts especially amongst Catholic concerns which he had built up over the years in the Protestant-controlled Henshaws. Contracts with the South Dublin Union and the Great Western Railway also helped to put the new business on its feet. The partnership was to last until Gleeson died and James was obliged to buy out his interest in the business, which put a strain on the family finances for a time.

Still, the little toy shop prospered and Martha went into the wholesale side of the business, supplying the Henry Street traders with their Christmas fancy goods and mottoes, the most popular of which was, "What Is Home Without A Mother?" Martha must have reflected ruefully on this as she presented James with a family of eight children, six of whom, four boys and two girls, survived. Despite the strong interest in the Church on both sides of the family and with James's older daughters, this new family was more inclined to display an interest in that close ally of the Church in the Middle Ages—the theatre. Although some of them enjoyed the security of what is termed to-day as "the day job," in deference no doubt to their father, they lost no opportunity to appear in the city theatres and later on radio.

Laurence (Lal), because he was the eldest, was obliged to join his father and his step-brother, Ciaran, in the family business which he hated and liquidated some time after his father's death at the age of 82 in 1932. Nell never had any theatrical ambitions and became a happily married woman with a large family which was to include a characteristic sprinkling of religious. James Augustine Jnr, known to the family as Jim, was to write a glorious page in the history of Irish and international comedy. Canice (Ken), was the only one who thought he might become an Augustinian like his namesake Uncle Canice, Martha's brother, who was Uncle Ken to the family, and was at that time connected with John's Lane Church in the Liberties. Ken's mother provided him with all the necessities but he didn't stay long at the monastery, and on his return home announced that he would prefer to be a secular priest. Again, he was fitted out with everything that would be required in a seminary but with growing maturity he decided that he didn't have a vocation after all. Martha accepted this philosophically and with an equal modicum of practicality informed Ken, "Well you can just go out now and get yourself a job"—which he did. in the baby carriage department of Todd Burns. Later he worked with the ESB and played in dance bands at night. His great love, however, was to sing in duets and quartets around the piano, which he played quite brilliantly.

Joseph (Joe) started a printing and stationery concern but this didn't prevent him from taking theatrical engagements ranging from straight plays at the Gate to revue at the Theatre Royal and both he and Lal became members of the Radio Éireann Repertory Company when it was formed in 1950. Joe may be best remembered for his role as the station master in John Ford's film *The Quiet Man*. Rita, the youngest, studied opthalmics but in her younger days she appeared frequently in the Father Matthew Hall under the direction of its best remembered producer JJ Henry and she was also heard on the fledgeling Irish radio station 2RN. It is probable that they were all baptised in St. Audeon's Parish Church, High Street, and it is certain that Jim was baptised there shortly after his birth on 26 April 1899.

Lower Bridge Street in those days ran downhill towards the quays and the river Liffey not far from the site of the "Ford of the Hurdles," Dublin's original settlement. It was a business street to which country folk came, for example to buy lengths of cloth material from Crowe Wilsons. There was a little haberdashery shop down at the corner, a tiny shop in which two people were a crowd. Next door to the O'Dea's was Mullett's pub where the surgical knives were handed out to the Invincibles involved in the Phoenix Park murders and for which Mullett himself served a term of imprisonment as an accessory before the fact. A Fenian to the last, living in an area which had traditionally been the cradle of revolution, Mullet flew the flag of Ireland, a golden harp on a green field, over his pub, when the city was otherwise bedecked with Union Jacks in honour of the visit of Edward VII in 1907. Jim remembered gazing up at this symbol of disaffection with his great-aunt Kate. "More luck to you, Mullett," she said but he was too young fully to understand. The only thing he was certain about in his childish imagination was that the edge of the world was at the top of Camden Street.

On the other side of the street stood The Brazen Head, the oldest tavern in Dublin, notorious for secret meetings and the hatching of plots. It was also noted for a glorious aroma of frying bacon and eggs each morning, at once a source of delight and of sad empty longing to the hungry passers-by who lived in vile poverty in the streets and alleys of tenements above Bridge Street.

The O'Dea children had no garden and were not permitted to play in the area, so they made their own amusement in the nursery, sometimes acting out little playlets which they found in books. In one of these young Jim, aged five, took his first part in pantomime—that of the non-speaking role of Dick Whittington's cat. When the weather was kind, Nanny, wheeling the latest arrival in a pram, took them on the long walk to the Phoenix Park.

An occasional seagull would attempt the hazardous walk along the rounded top of the river wall, a Charlie Chaplin of its kind, while its fellows glided gracefully in the Liffey, on both sides of which the mainly horse-drawn traffic passed noisily along the quays. There were the breathtakingly high bakers bread-vans with the drivers perched precariously on top, from which vantage point they could look down on the coal drays, the heavy Guinness carts filled with huge barrels of porter, trim milk floats usually carrying two large decorative churns complete the brass taps and the more commonplace

farmers carts with their loads of cabbages neatly piled in
a triangle or untidy loads of hay which left evidence of
their passing. There was the occasional strange
conveyance, built for a specific purpose, like the jet-black
narrow carriage which had small grilles instead of
windows; in the front the driver had a small protective
enclosure and the entrance to the conveyance was up
three rail-protected steps at the back. Inside, there was a
long seat on each side, and the purpose of this strange
vehicle was to convey six or eight nuns about their
business as anonymously as possible.

The line of shops along the route was broken at one
point by a large advertising hoarding at which Nanny
would linger to read about the exciting theatrical
offerings displayed on posters that varied from week to
week. On one such week, for example, George
Edwardes' Company from Daly's Theatre in London
were performing at the Gaiety Theatre in a Chinese
Musical Comedy *San Toy*. At the Theatre Royal, Moody-
Manners Opera Company had *Faust*, *Amber Witch*,
Tannhaüser, *Maritana* and *Carmen*. The Queen's Royal
Theatre was presenting a special production of *The
Shaughraun;* George Formby and Vesta Tilley were at
the Empire Palace Theatre, while at the Lyric Bransby
Williams and JW Rickaby were top of the bill. Sometimes
the Lord Lieutenant and his lady, flanked by Hussars,
drove past in stately procession to Dublin Castle. It was a
colourful cavalcade which was appreciated, apparently, by
the populace as gentlemen frequently stopped to raise
their hats to the King's representative.

Jim and Ken, with only a year and a half between
them, could be taken for twins. All the other children
had their father's light eyes and colouring but they had
the dark hair and eyes of their mother. Jim's eyes were
hazel and Rita was to say later that they looked like the
children of gypsies. Both served mass in John's Lane,
often for their uncle Ken (O'Gorman) who was a doctor
of the Church and a brilliant linguist. Later he was a
member of the Holy Roman Rota and but for the death
of Pope Benedict XV might have been favoured with a

cardinal's hat. He served as chaplain to Irish prisoners of war in Germany during the Great War. While he was having a drink in a beer-garden in Frankfurt one morning, a man nearby was pointed out to him as Sir Roger Casement. When Casement was sent for trial for treason evidence was needed to establish his presence on enemy soil in wartime. Dr O'Gorman, to his great relief, narrowly missed having to give evidence against him as he had no desire to advance the cause of Sir Edward Carson. Uncle Ken had a lively sense of humour, and it is likely that he might have been slightly feared by his fellow Augustinians because he was notorious for imitating the voices and gestures of his fellow preachers. Rita claimed that Jim got his talent from the O'Gorman side of the family, adding: "The O'Deas were charming people but a bit stuffy."

This talent began to emerge in the nursery when, having served mass for Uncle Ken, Jim would go through the ritual himself with a giggling Ken as his acolyte and Joe and Rita as the "congregation." His vestments were improvised from towels purloined from the linen cupboard and pinned on at the back and front; the "chalice" was a glass flower vase and the water and wine were contained in egg cups. Jim was very serious as he copied the movements of a priest and glared fiercely at the less than serious Ken who was obliged at the "Sanctus" to strike a chamberpot (the under-delph as Rita put it primly, remembering her days with the nuns at boarding school in Sligo) with a spoon.

At Christmas time Jim's big expressive eyes gazed in wonder at the delights of pantomime as he sat with his parents and the other children at the Gaiety panto. He laughed and jumped in his seat at the antics of the funny men and little did he or anyone else realise that one day he would hold an audience more firmly than any other funny man who ever played that historic theatre, and it would be done with a "quip" as he came to call it, the twinkling of a wicked eye, and a lot of love and sympathy.

Unimpressed by the ordinary toys in their mother's

shop, the children demanded more exciting ones from Santa Claus, so Martha was obliged to write to Germany well in advance of Christmas for more elaborate clockwork and battery-operated toys for her brood. They played with these ingenious creations in the living room above the shop on a large polished table which stood beside the Christmas tree and under the big window behind the red velvet curtains which concealed them from the shabby street and the Dublin night sky. They were privileged, but they cannot have been unaware of the poverty that surrounded them. Often, as they lay in bed at night after the lamplighter had lit the gaslamps in the street, they listened to the horse-cabs trotting along the cobble-stoned quays. Suddenly there would be a fracas outside Mullett's with voices raised in shouts and oaths and the screams of women which often ended with the arrival of the black Maria. Then men and women were taken away suffering injuries inflicted by the batons of the police.

James, to his credit, was painfully aware of the plight of his more unfortunate near neighbours, and after a hard day spent at his business worked tirelessly each evening to alleviate the lot of the less fortunate—to such a degree that Martha fervently hoped that he didn't bring anything else besides himself when he returned home at night. Contagion was rife. His work was practical and he helped to establish in 1912 a free night shelter with 41 beds for homeless men in an old storeroom in Strand Street; this was later transferred to Back Lane in 1915 with a capacity for 200 beds. The size of the problem may be gauged from the fact that during the first year 33,000 homeless men were given shelter and 70,000 free meals were supplied. James always intended more salubrious surroundings for his family, so when in 1908 a premises became available at 162 Capel Street he sold the house and shop in Lower Bridge Street and transferred his business from Christchurch Place to Capel Street.

Chapter Two

Young Jim's first school was the Junior Boys' School, Holy Faith Convent, Dominick Street. The nuns and the Dominican Fathers were renowned for the May Day procession which they organised each year, and spectators came from all over Dublin to witness it. The theme of the procession was the fifteen decades of the rosary, each bead being represented by a little girl dressed as a flower. The *Pater Noster* after every tenth bead was represented by a bigger girl depicting an angel who in turn was preceded by a page-boy. Jim had this role dressed in royal blue velvet slashed at the sleeves and trousers with insets of white satin and a velvet cap. Step-sister Nan had the role of St Michael dressed all in red and with red wings and carrying a large sword. Unfor-tunately, she had been supplied with a genuine and extremely heavy sword so that when she had to draw it and hold it aloft at the elevation during Benediction she very nearly fell over and it took all her puny strength to prevent the sword from crashing to the ground.

When he was about eight Jim was sent as a boarder to the Holy Faith Convent, Kilcoole, Co. Wicklow, which was a preparatory school for the children of business people. There he was remembered as a well-behaved boy who had, even then, a conscious sense of humour. One afternoon he and another small boy were following the stations of the cross in the convent chapel. They had been trained to name each station before prayer and at the sixth station Jim's companion called out: "Jesus meets His Mother." He was promptly corrected by Jim who shouted back, "He does not—He met His Mother down here inside the altar rails; that must be some other one He's meeting now." Years later he and Harry O'Donovan gave a concert in the college and remarked to the Superioress, Sister M Lucy, that they were looking for some quiet accommodation in the area where they could work on a new show they were planning, and she offered them as a haven the empty lodge at the convent gate. The offer was accepted with alacrity.

His next school was Belvedere College, Dublin, where he stayed for a short period around 1910 before going as a boarder to the Marist Fathers College in Dundalk from 1911 to 1912. Again it was typical of him that when he achieved fame he returned to the college in 1930 to lend his support to fund-raising following a fire in the chapel. The reasons for the short spells he spent at his various schools can only be guessed at and his next boarding school was Blackrock College, where he remained from 1912 to 1914. Contemporaries, though in higher grades, were Liam O'Flaherty and Michael Farrell. Dancing and music lessons were part of the curriculum, and for elocution and drama the teacher was the well-known tutor and author McHardy-Flint. It is recorded in the *Freemans Journal* of 28 May 1914 that in the college sports on the previous day the 100 yards sprint (Junior, Third Division) was won by J O'Dea. Jim himself claimed in later life that he also played rugby, and indeed the college account books show that in one quarter, at least his father was billed with £1. 7s. 0d. for games; he was also charged fifteen shillings for "butter at lunch," which bears out the claim that Martha always insisted on the best for her boys. When Jim, inevitably, returned to the college in the 1950s to do a concert in aid of the new church, Merrion Road, he recalled that the concert hall was being built when he was there as a student, adding: "They are still calling it the new hall, and I'm no chicken." He came down from the stage to greet his former dean Fr Peter Meagher, then in his eighties, and was heard to say: "How we hated you when we were here as boys and how we love you now!" He may have been trying to explain that we do not, when we are young, always appreciate what our teachers are trying to do for us but it wasn't said very diplomatically, and didn't go down very well with the college authorities, some of whom noted that it was obvious to all that Jim had not yet recovered from the Christmas festivities!

When his father bought a new family home at 21 Grosvenor Place, Rathmines, Jim transferred to the Blackrock sister college for day-boys, St Mary's, Rathmines, which was a short walk from the new home. The Gogan brothers, Paddy and Tommy, who became prominent in the theatre and cinema world, were fellow students. Col MacNeill was in the same class and he recalled that Jim used to have them in stitches when he mimicked the teachers—in their absence, of course. His favourite target was Fr Tom O'Hanlon the President, who also taught English. Fr O'Hanlon was forgetful about shaving below the level of his Roman collar, with the result that a luxuriant tuft of hair became clearly visible when he emphasised a point. This was most likely to happen on such formal occasions as his presidential address to the school. Jim gave his fellow students an imitation of this by impersonating the good father and at the appropriate moment he would jerk his head like Fr O'Hanlon and reveal a piece of rabbit fur that he had concealed under his collar. Jim's best friend at this time was Jack Lemass, later Taoiseach Sean Lemass. Jim was to be best man at Jack's wedding and their friendship lasted a lifetime. There is a tradition in St. Mary's that the two boys were returning from a walk in the Dublin mountains via St Mary's when they heard about the start of the Easter rising. Eoin MacNeill, whose sons were students at St. Mary's at the time, called to the school in a very distraught state of mind.

The Lemass family had a hatter's shop almost opposite the O'Dea's in Capel Street, which is how the two young friends first met, and one of their first youthful ventures together was to produce an entirely handwritten publication for distribution among their friends. The funny bits and the serial were written by Jim while Jack contributed the serious stuff.

When the time came to decide what Jim would do for a living, he told his father that he would like to go on the stage, to which his father replied: "I'd rather see you in your coffin first." Although Jim quoted this reply on several occasions, his sister Rita doubted that their father would be so crudely forceful and came to the conclusion that Jim made it up probably for dramatic effect. It was a fact that the rather staid James was suspicious of stage folk, a view that may have been influenced by the traditional religious bent in the family and confirmed by the affairs between the Prince of Wales and the lovely "Jersey Lily," Lily Langtry. But he was not immune to being smitten by one of the lovely ladies himself. He once saw a performance of Lehar's *Merry Widow* and was much taken by the "widow," about whom he talked incessantly for days. An amused Martha thereafter supervised James's occasional patronage of the drama. His father's opposition was a blow to Jim at the time but he said many years afterwards that he thought his father had lived to be proud of him. In the meantime he seized the opportunity when brother Ken offered him his first appearance on stage. Ken ran a quartet which appeared in charity shows, and when one of the number fell ill he asked Jim to take his place in order to justify the description of quartet. Jim received strict instructions to just to stand there and move his mouth as Ken did not trust him to sing. After a while Jim gained confidence and started to join in the harmonies, as he thought; Ken became aware of the strange noise and gave Jim a hefty kick on the shins which quickly put him in his place. But, at least, it was a step up from his earliest role in a cat skin.

Because Jim had required some optical attention in his teens it occurred to James and Martha that their son might be well disposed to the oculist profession in which, no doubt, James had contacts. He was consequently apprenticed first to a Mr Kearney, an optician on the Quays, before going to work for Murray and McGrath in Duke Street. In the year 1900 before his partnership with McGrath, Murray was expressing concern in his newspaper advertising for the vision of Dublin's theatre goers:

Persons With Normal Vision
Should be able to See Clearly Everything
that occurs on the stage of
Our Dublin Theatres.
From any part of the house, the various little matters of stage detail and the particular expressions on the actors' faces. Should you not be able to do this your vision needs correction and proper eye glasses will add considerably to your enjoyment. Under proper conditions opera glasses need rarely be carried.
Murray
Optician,
1 Duke Street, Dublin.

Little did Mr Murray realise that his new apprentice would be taking more than a passing interest in matters theatrical apart from concern about the eyesight of Dublin playgoers. From the moment that he began to earn money Jim became a regular patron of the theatres and music halls. He had many to choose from: there was the Gaiety, the Royal, the Empire, the Lyric (which was on the site now occupied by the *Irish Press,* in Burgh Quay, and was later renamed the Tivoli), the Queen's in Pearse St and the new Abbey Theatre. His purpose was not merely to be amused and entertained but to observe the actors and variety turns in order to learn how they got their effects. This search was supplemented by his reading matter which consisted mainly of plays and books on the theatre.

He and Jack Lemass formed a group which they called the Kilronan Players and in 1917 they presented TC Murray's tragedy *Maurice Harte* with Jim in the name part and Jack as Fr Mangan. Brother Joe O'Dea was also in the cast at the Father Mathew Hall. One account relates that there were many tear-filled eyes in the audience when Jim, as the "spoiled priest" appeared in the last act, pale and distraught, mumbling the priestly office. The Capuchin father in charge of the hall at the time commented on the starkness of the play and suggested that they should introduce a little comedy into it, to which Jim took umbrage, feeling that his pride as an actor was being questioned, and furthermore that the suggestion that they would have the cheek to rewrite a famous Abbey play was ridiculous. They also produced William Boyle's *The Mineral Workers,* a comedy which was billed by some not entirely fortuitous misprint as *The Mineral Waters* because the Father Mathew Hall was (and is) a temperance venue. Another production was *The Forge at Clohogue* in which rebels and redcoats, bludgeons and pikes featured heavily.

Jim had in his library a 630-page tome called *Theatre and Stage* edited by Harold Downs which detailed all that the amateur should know about acting and production. This must have been a good investment because when Gabriel Fallon first saw him with the Kilronan Players in the Abbey Theatre on a Sunday night in January 1920 he was playing juvenile lead in Pinero's *Sweet Lavender* which had won the top prize in what was possibly the first attempt to organise an amateur drama festival in Ireland. Gabriel Fallon had, as a man of the theatre, been an actor, director and writer, but his greatest contribution was as a knowledgeable and perceptive critic. In the same year, the Kilronan Players, sponsored by the Irish Dramatic Union to bring better theatre to Dublin, presented Sheridan's *The Rivals* at the Abbey. The cast included Jack Lemass as Sir Lucius O'Trigger; Rona Fanning as Mrs Malaprop; Lal O'Dea as Captain Absolute; Frank Purcell as Faulkland and James A. O'Dea as Bob Acres. Joseph Holloway, the architect of the original Abbey Theatre and celebrated theatre diarist, whose diaries in many volumes are now in the National Library, recorded that he was informed that: "Though small of stature, O'Dea is a regular martinet as a manager, and insists on things being properly done."

This was a characteristic that Jim was to retain until the end of his days.

Later that month he joined the Irish Theatre Company

in the Hardwick Hall, Hardwick Street, just off North
Frederick Street. Hardwick Street was a street of Georgian
houses which, with the Hall has been demolished and
replaced by Corporation flats. Jim had appeared with the
Irish Theatre Company briefly in 1918 in a small role in
Ibsen's *An Enemy Of The People* and a fellow "super" was
PR Gogan, later manager of the Queen's Theatre and
creator with scriptwriters Ernie Murray and Cecil Nash of
the Queen's "Happy Gang," a permanent group of
comics and entertainers which was disbanded only when
the Abbey Theatre was destroyed by fire and the Abbey
Company moved into the Queen's. The Irish Theatre
Company had the patronage of Edward Martyn whose
policy it was to present quality European drama in
contrast to the Abbey Theatre's plays about Ireland.
Martyn's company worked under many disadvantages: the
Hardwick Hall was cold and depressing and very
uncomfortable, with the result that audiences were often
sparse. Despite all this the theatre has been acknowledged
as the forerunner of the Dublin Gate Theatre. The
producer (described nowadays, more accurately, as the
director) was an actor/singer, John MacDonagh, lately
returned from America, whose brother Thomas
MacDonagh was one of the leaders of the Easter Rising.
He cast Jim in Chekhov's *The Cherry Orchard* and he was
acclaimed as "the discovery" of the production, giving a
finished character study of Firs, the old retainer—quite an
achievement for such a young man. Joseph Holloway said
of the company: "They are swelled-headed enough to
think that they are the only intellectual actors in Ireland,
and yet O'Dea goes amongst them a stranger and comes
out on top as an artist."

In November 1920 he appeared again at the Abbey in
the Dublin Drama League's production of Lord
Dunsany's *The Laughter of the Gods.*

All of this play-acting did not escape the notice of
Jim's boss, John Murray, who one day sent for his
apprentice and with a great flourish produced Jim's
indentures—the legal document first drawn up centuries
ago which apprentices were required to sign though few

if any ever read them. Murray's finger came down on a clause which he made Jim read aloud and which said in effect: that it was forbidden for an apprentice to frequent ale houses or enter into playhouses. He had broken his agreement. Murray looked at him; he looked at Murray—and all he could do was laugh. He was coming towards the end of his time and John Murray suggested that he should get some experience abroad, so it was arranged that he would go for six months to Murray's brother at 100 Lothian Street, Edinburgh. Jim didn't like Scotland at that time (in later years he was a welcome visitor there); he had digs with a family of Plymouth Brethren who not only frowned on his frequent visits to the theatres but also forbade him to whistle on a Sunday.

On his return to Dublin in 1921, his association with Murray at an end, James A. O'Dea, Optician, opened his first premises in South Frederick Street, where he performed "all optical work accurately and scientifically under personal supervision." In September Madame Kirkwood Hackett presented Shaw's *You Never Can Tell* at the Abbey with James A O'Dea as Finch McComas. Another member of the cast, playing Boon, was a young man called Harry O'Donovan.

In the last weeks of the year Jim appeared in the play that was to bring him to the attention of a wider public, and significantly the role was a comedy one, that of Councillor Woods in John MacDonagh's new play, *The Irish Jew,* at the Empire Theatre.The play was set in Dublin prior to 1916 and MacDonagh said he had been working on it for seven years, even during the period when he had been director with the Irish Theatre Company. The curfew enforced during 1921 had been a blessing in disguise for he filled in the long evenings by writing. The idea for *The Irish Jew,* which had been simmering all those years, suddenly boiled over and spread itself over four children's copybooks. The plot of the satire had some curious echoes of events in the Dublin of the time. Alderman Abraham Golder, Jewish Lord Mayor of Dublin, shocks both Unionists and

Mrs Martha O'Dea with her three sons about 1901. *Left to right:* Ken, Jimmy and Lawrence.

Jimmy O'Dea the film actor around 1930.

Harry O'Donovan, Jimmy's partner and scriptwriter.

Jimmy O'Dea (on left) as the rightful heir in *The Casey Millions*.

From left: Fred Jeffs, Jimmy O'Dea and Nan Fitzgerald in *The Casey Millions*.

Jimmy O'Dea in a characteristic female role in a 1930s Olympia Theatre Show.

Jimmy O'Dea as Buttons from a Gaiety Theatre production of
Cinderella.

Jimmy O'Dea, Noel Purcell and Harry O'Donovan in the film
Jimmy Boy, 1935.

Jimmy in blackface for the film *Jimmy Boy*.

Betty Driver (now of *Coronation Street*), Edmund Gwenn and Jimmy O'Dea in *Penny Paradise*, 1938.

Jimmy O'Dea with Nova Pilbeam in the film *Cheer, Boys, Cheer*, 1939.

Jimmy O'Dea with Graham Moffatt (left) and Moore Marriott (right) in *Cheer, Boys, Cheer*.

Jimmy O'Dea as Napoleon in *Cheer, Boys, Cheer.*

Betty Driver and Jimmy O'Dea in *Let's Be Famous,* 1939.

Caricature by David Kelly.

Jimmy O'Dea the matinee idol.

"Don't-rock-the-boat" Nationalists on the city council when he announces his intention to attend a banquet dressed as Robert Emmet and recite Emmet's speech from the dock. The Unionists attempt to buy him off with the promise of a knighthood while the Nationalists offer to buy his picture-house as the site for a municipal art gallery. Golder refuses both factions and the Nationalists incite a mob to burn down his cinema. This reflects the 1913 controversy as to whether Dublin Corporation should accept the Sir Hugh Lane Bequest on the condition that they must build a municipal gallery of modern art. Lorcan Sherlock, then Jewish Lord Mayor of the city, favoured such an acquisition, and not only that, he was managing director not of a cinema but of a music hall, the Coliseum in Henry Street, which was destroyed by fire in the rising of 1916. Although the publicity material stated that the public were requested to note that all the characters in the play were purely fictitious, and had no reference to any living personage, *The Freeman's Journal* of 13 December noted: "The make-up in some cases were remarkable accidents," and *The Evening Herald* of 14 February 1922 reported: "Mr MacDonagh exercises an author's rights. And we of the audience, also with rights, exercise our minds. Memories crowd. What was it that the Dublin Corporation of the 'we hereby resolve' days used to be called. Now we remember—'An Augean stable'; 'a sink of iniquity'; 'a nest of crooks' 'a conspiracy of jobbery' et cetera. Golder put up his fight to the finish against the job gangsters opposed to him."

The play was in four acts, the first three set in a room at the Mansion House, and the fourth in the Corporation Council Chamber. The cast included Paul Farrell (Pól O'Fearghall), who was outstanding as the Lord Mayor. Fay Sargent played his wife, Mrs Golder, whose make-up had the pale creamy pallor of a Jewess, and whose favourite line, recited every time her husband paused for breath after a long impassioned harangue, was: "My mother always said I married a fool." Her confusion of "Chous" with the name of a guest

sounds intriguing until Councillor Woods spells out
C-H-A-O-S. The cast also included Frank Fay as Sir
Alfred Peel who intrigues with Castle hacks and jabbers
about high art; Jim's brother Lal played the cinema
manager, and the name of Harry O'Donovan cropped
up once again, this time playing Alderman Dan Barry,
the main villain and chief party boss. At one point in the
play after a banquet he asks Jim (playing Councillor
Woods and dressed in a loud check suit and bowler hat),
"What are you going to do now, Councillor?" Jim
removed his hat and holding it before him like a basin
replies: "I think I'm going to be sick in a minute."
MacDonagh was delighted with his performance and
that night rewrote and extended the role of Woods. The
character comedian, Jimmy O'Dea, was appearing on the
horizon. There can be no doubt that the part of
Councillor Woods was a turning point in his career. It
was as if Jim had looked into a mirror and saw in Woods,
the comical Dublin character, aspects of his own
humorous nature and outlook on life. And seen beyond
Woods in the mirror were countless other dimly
delineated essentially Dublin characters.

The play was revived in February of the following year
and again in February 1923 at the Queen's Theatre with
John MacDonagh himself as Abraham Golder. By this
time Jim was being billed and referred to in the press as
Jimmy O'Dea, which is what the public were calling him
in any case, although his name still appeared in theatre
programmes as James A O'Dea. (A revival of the play
was planned in the 1950s when Robert Briscoe became
Jewish Lord Mayor of Dublin but the idea was
abandoned when Briscoe left office.

In the meantime in January 1922 Jim appeared once
again with the Dublin Drama League at the Abbey in a
season of one act plays: Wilde's *A Florentine Tragedy*
with Paul Farrell; Arthur Schnitzler's *Festival of Bacchus*
with Norman Reddin and Chekhov's *The Bear* with Paul
Farrell and Katherine MacCormick. In March,
MacDonagh again cast him in a playlet, *The Pride
Of Petravore*, which was included in a variety bill

at the Empire. MacDonagh had offered the play to the Abbey directors in 1916 but they rejected it. It was an amusing lightweight piece about a widow Eileen O'Brien who is on trial for violating the licensing laws that forbid a woman on her own to run a public house. She is acquitted when PJ Mullarkey JP UDC (James A O'Dea) offers marriage and is accepted. Harry O'Donovan played an R.I.C. sergeant.

Jim hadn't broken all ties with the Kilronan Players and he still regarded himself as an amateur. A small group of them including Jack Lemass, Rona Fanning and Kathleen Walshe used to take a hackney-car to Skerries on Sundays in the summer. This could be a hazardous journey as there was always the possibility of running into an ambush. Skerries was well known as a resort to the O'Dea family as they took their summer holidays there for years. Jim and his friends performed there as a concert-party, calling themselves "The Sand Dabs" after small flat fish found at low tide on the sea shore at Skerries. Jim and Jack sang "The Vicar and I" and Louis Tierney recited some of his amusing monologues, several of which Jim was to record on gramophone records when he became a professional. Martha O'Dea, who must have had some latent talent as a performer, used to recite one of Louis' recitations at the occasional Sunday night parties in Rathmines. Her favourite was "Bluebeard":

> She used to talk of Bluebeard who had so many wives,
> They nearly drove him looney, so he had to take their
> > lives,
> He'd chop their heads off, every one. Oh gawney
> > what a sight!
> And put them in a certing room upon a certing night.
> Then he married someone else but I'm certain she
> > kicked out too,
> Because Bluebeard was a tough oul' nut with nothing
> > else to do.

Madame Kirkwood Hackett presented a repertory

season in the Abbey in May of that year. During the first week Jim took the Cockney role of Drinkwater in Shaw's *Captain Brassbound's Conversion*. In the second week there was a drama by Anthony P Wharton (born in Ireland 1877), *Irene Wycherley*, in which Jim played Sir Peter Wycherley. Shelagh Richards was also in the cast. An advertised production of Wilde's *The Importance Of Being Earnest* had to be cancelled due to performing rights difficulties and the final week saw the first production of *The Tangle*, a psychic play by Irish-born Dr WM Crofton in which Jim played Dr Serpi-Brine This play too featured Harry O'Donovan.

The year ended with the screening of two silent films in which Jim appeared. They were made by the Irish Photoplay Co. whose directors included K Baron Hartley, CE McConnell, JJ Walsh, George Nesbitt, R B O'Rourke, Daniel Harrigan, JJ Bradshaw and Ald Joseph MacDonagh. They had capital of £10,000. The films, of which there were three in all and the first to be made in the new Irish Free State, were produced by Norman Whitten, written and directed by John MacDonagh and photographed by Alfred H Moise. Far down on the list of credits was the name of Harry O'Donovan, who acted as property master.

The chairman of the company Mr Charlie McConnell who became head of the well-known McConnell Advertising Agency recalled the early Irish film venture for author Gus Smith in 1965: "We didn't make money from them," he said "but we did cover ourselves. The stars of the films, as we liked to call them, were paid peanuts compared with even the small-time player of to-day. The 'extras' were delighted to work just for the thrill of being in the film. I remember Jimmy O'Dea quite well. He was very young then. You could say shy, I suppose. He mostly played straight parts as in *The Casey Millions* when he was the romantic male lead. He revealed great talent even at that early stage. I thought at the time, and I was later proved correct that he had a big future in films. People always seemed to like him on the sets and on location of films. I didn't see in him then the great comedian he was later to be but he had always a lively and lovable sense of humour." Mr McConnell said that at the time they looked upon the venture as good fun but he realised at the time as he did now that this small country could not compete with the film-makers of Britain and America with all their millions. But their little films—they ran for about an hour—were a success on the cinema circuit in Ireland and were actually shown in America.

Kevin Rockett, writing in "Cinema and Ireland" was to say: "They were unlikely to serve as a challenge to the increasingly sophisticated films which already dominated Irish screens, and were far removed from the previous decade" This change in taste is explained by Brian McIlroy in his *Irish Cinema*—"As the civil war began to take root, one production company inspired by Charles McConnell, Irish Photo Plays Ltd. embarked on the path of light comedy; as violence between Irish people increased, the general populace's hunger for entertainment prevailed over ideological arguments".

The first of these films, *The Casey Millions* was first shown at the La Scala, Dublin in the week commencing 22 October 1922. The story is set in the sleepy village of Killcasey which is roused by the advent of two broken-down actors, Professor Alfresco ("the worst Hamlet since the flood" played by Barrett McDonnell), and his side kick, Jerry (Chris Silvester) who have been ejected from their previous engagement by an infuriated audience. Realising that their drama does not pay in that part of Ireland they turn lawyers, having read in a scrap of old newspaper that the Casey Millions, left by Patrick Casey of Lockjaw, Kentucky, USA awaited a claimant. The two thespians act their parts so well as beneficent lawyers that the very many Caseys of Killcasey are completely taken in. The skull, which was formerly that of Yorick (a stage prop), now proves to be that of the late lamented Patrick Casey, and the Casey claimants are assured—after they have parted with ten and sixpence each—that should their bumps compare favourably with those of the skull they will be assured of the fortune.

The "lawyer's" host, Bart Casey (Fred Jeffs) has designs on them for the hand of his daughter Peg (played by the Limerick actress, Nan FitzGerald) to the chagrin of the farm hand, Luke (James O'Dea) who is her lover. Luke is shown the door in no uncertain fashion until he is found by Dublin solicitors to be the rightful heir to the fortune. The *Irish Times* said: "Not one person (at the trade show) yesterday morning, expert or otherwise, failed to find in it interest and entertainment and great promise for its future."

Wicklow Gold, the second film, was screened on 20 November in the Empire Theatre. It was a matchmaking story in which a Wicklow farmer, Ned O'Toole (Chris Silvester), who believes that some of the rivers of Wicklow are filled with gold, objects to his son, Larry (James O'Dea) marrying, Kitty (Ria Mooney), the daughter of Widow O'Byrne (Kathleen Carr). They trick the old man into believing that there is gold in the river running through the widow's land. The cast also included Frank Fay and Val Vousden.

The *Irish Independent* described it as: "A series of excellent and highly amusing pictures."

The *Irish Times* thought that: "The humour is more enjoyable because it is native and the acting is certainly clever."

Séamus de Búrca who saw both films in the old picture house in Dorset Street said that they were every bit as good as anything that was then being screened from abroad.

Chapter Three

In January of the new year, 1923, Jim appeared with Fred Jeffs and Barrett McDonnell in *The Wooing Of Julia Elizabeth,* a cameo of Dublin tenement life by James Stephens as part of a variety bill at the Queen's Theatre. It is very likely that by this time Jim regarded himself as a semi-professional. *The King Of Dublin,* a musical comedy with book by Edward McNulty and music by Tom Madden, followed at the Queen's. It took the form of historical tableaux recalling a period of over 1,400 years, starting with the court of the King of Dublin in AD 450, and ending on O'Connell Bridge in 1923. Harry O'Donovan was the king (afterwards a barrister) and Eileen Hayden was his queen (later a street-singer); Tom Dunne, an important foil to Jimmy later on, was Chief of the Household Guards, (afterwards a policeman) and James O'Dea was Master of Ceremonies, (later a burglar).

Melodrama followed in May with *A Broken Heart,* in which May Craig, Val Vousden and Ira Allen appeared with Jim contributing the humorous element in a character comedy role. He was featured in June as Matt Ruddock in "a powerful domestic drama" called *A Mother's Love* by an unnamed author—it seemed to be sufficient to bill it as being by the author of *The Prodigal Parson.* In addition to Charles L. Keogh and Tom Moran the cast included May Craig and Ira Allen.

Jim was constantly in demand for concerts, benefits and smoking concerts, and in October he appeared as a variety turn between playlets for Harry O'Donovan's brother, Frank, whose touring company would become famous all over Ireland. The venue was the National Theatre in the Rotunda Buildings in Cavendish Row, which had previously been known as The Everyman and would eventually become world-famous as Hilton Edward's and Micheál MacLiammóir's Dublin Gate Theatre. Frank O'Donovan's company was as self-sufficient as it was possible to be and watching Frank in a dressing-room one morning strenuously setting out a large poster for the show, Jim remarked: "If you fellows put as much energy into a real business as you do into your theatricals you would make a fortune." That *he* wasn't neglecting his own real business is illustrated by the fact that the newspapers carrying the advertisements for the Frank O'Donovan show in which Jim figured so prominently also carried advertisements in which he announced that "owing to increase of business James A. O'Dea—Optician, has moved from South Frederick Street to larger and more suitable premises at 7 Nassau Street." As usual, customers were still assured that all optical work would be accurately and scientifically fulfilled under personal supervision. Also in October 1923, because of his profession of optician, Jim was called upon to perform a sad duty as a professional witness. His old friend Jack Lemass had a brother Noel who had been involved in the Civil War and he was missing for a long period until a badly decomposed body was found in the Dublin mountains which was thought to be that of Noel Lemass. Jim was obliged to attend the inquest and his evidence proved positive identification of the body. Jim was able to say that he personally had made the spectacles worn by the deceased for his friend Noel Lemass.

This was Jim's second brush with unnatural death. His first experience occurred in Skerries, and details of the tragedy were related to Séamus de Búrca by Ina Connolly. Ina was sitting on the beach one afternoon in 1917 with Muriel MacDonagh, widow of the executed signatory of the 1916 Proclamation, Thomas

MacDonagh. Her children Donagh and Barbara were playing on the beach and Muriel asked Ina to keep an eye on them as she removed her engagement ring and handed it to Ina preparatory to going in for a swim. When the poor lady got into difficulties and was accidentally drowned, the alarm was raised, and it was Jim and Jack Lemass who both ran for the police."

That Christmas of 1923 Jim made his debut in pantomime at the Queen's Theatre as Buttons in *Cinderella*. He was given no script and had to make his own laughs. Jim said later: "It may have developed my spontaneity but it was certainly a tough experience and I don't think I was very funny." Older theatre-goers who remembered the panto recalled Jim with affection, for his sympathetic performance as "Buttons."

Séamus de Búrca, who was then a schoolboy, remembers seeing one of the matinees and thought that one of the highlights of the show was Jim singing Tom Madden's song "Bridget Donohue" in the ballroom scene. When he finished the song he went to the wings and little Florence Sullivan, the daughter of the theatre manager, Jack Sullivan, was led on by the hand and they sang the song together. Jim and the little girl were very appealing and charmed the critics who also commented on the "King Bruce and the spider" routine between Jim and Billy Irving (as Baron Popitoff) "...which made boxes and circles, pit and gallery alike laugh consumedly." The panto ran for a record-breaking 98 performances.

In the following February John MacDonagh turned his attention to the comparatively new form of entertainment called revue. His *Dublin Tonight* was the first Irish show of this type and was completely different to the usual cross-channel variety bill that was served up each week, with every likelihood that the same acts would be booked for the same week a year hence. MacDonagh and the Queen's management gambled on the patrons' acceptance of this new form of entertainment. The *Evening Herald* welcomed the show with an extraordinary effusion of prudery:

It provides demonstration that variety entertainment
in the form of what is commonly called revue can be
made topical and served up in Dublin for local
consumption. *Dublin Tonight* is wholesome fare after
some of the shows presented to audiences— shows in
which half naked women in clothing that could not in
decency be made scantier were presented on the stage
suggesting rows of hooked meat hanging outside
butchers' stalls. Only the butchers' display is more
healthy to look at.

Judging from photographs of dancing troupes of all
nationalities of the period it is only too apparent that the
writer of that review would have been scandalised by the
modern mini-skirt.

The revue was written and directed by MacDonagh
and starred Jimmy O'Dea. The show opened with a
glimpse of a queue outside the gallery door, complete
with orange seller, street singer and the queue-breaker
(Jimmy) who later in the show makes appropriate
comments on the performers from his seat in the gods.
(A favourite ruse down at the Tivoli Theatre, which
faced on to the Liffey, sometimes occurred when there
was an unusually large queue for early doors at the
gallery entrance. Naturally those at the head of the
queue could expect to obtain the best seats at the front
of the gallery but there might be a sudden cry of "Help,
quick, there's a man in the river," and the entire queue
would rush to the river wall only to witness nothing
more than a seagull drifting on the tide. In the
meantime, of course, the perpetrators of the scare would
have taken up positions at the head of the queue.) There
was a bar scene with Jimmy as the customer who pays,
and Dick Smith as the customer who doesn't. Fay
Sargent was the barmaid, and according to the critics:
"...it caused a good deal of laughter on account of its
vivid truth to life." Harry O'Donovan sang "Duffy"
with the Lennox troupe of dancers, and appeared later as
the General in a typical MacDonagh touch of seriousness

called "A Night In Dublin," of which the *Freeman's Journal* said:

> The most interesting part of the performance is perhaps the dramatic sketch, introducing a raid by a party of Black and Tans in pursuit of General MacDermot, the rebel, and in which the central figure is the general's sweetheart, a part which is ably filled by Ria Mooney. An amusing duet entitled "Dublin Tonight," reciting many of our existing woes (touching on the forthcoming Tailteann Games, Dublin mud, Dún Laoghaire versus Kingstown etc) was sung in great style by Jimmy O'Dea and John MacDonagh.

The *Irish Times* reported: "The principal comedian is Jimmy O'Dea who certainly knows how to extract the utmost from each scene."

Despite the fact that the first three nights were a nightmare when everything went wrong from start to finish—lights went out, scenery crashed, curtains came down and went up again indiscriminately—and this drew the remark from one commentator that, "what the show needed badly was a bad-tempered producer who would make the performers sweat at rehearsals," the show ran for two weeks and Jim claimed that those involved learned one thing—that revue is the hardest thing to get across but once you learn the tricks it's the easiest.

MacDonagh followed this up in April with another revue, *Next Stop Dublin*, at the Olympia Theatre. (In deference to the national fervour in the new Irish Free State, the Empire had been renamed the Olympia in January 1923.) "There are many well-known favourites in the cast," reported the *Evening Herald;* "the leader is Jimmy O'Dea, a local comedian who has already won his way to popularity. He appears in most of the scenes presented and, whether as a country yokel, the tipsy son-in-law, the 'American lecturer,' or the captain of the fire brigade who trades in holocausts or spontaneous combustions, he is equally successful. His was certainly a brilliant performance."

In June John MacDonagh presented his new four-act play, *Brains*, at the Olympia. It was described as "a grey matter comedy," and in presenting it MacDonagh claimed that he was trying to find out exactly what Dublin audiences wanted. He said that the directors of the theatre had given him a free hand and he could, and perhaps should, have produced one of his revues, which had been so well supported. Instead, he was putting on a "legitimate" comedy, and could, at least, look his accusers in the eye next time they charged him with having gone over to "bare legs." Millions had been lost trying to gauge the public taste, and yet every season in the producing centres of the world the "sure thing" of the experts flops while the "not a ghost of a chance" romps home. "Within the past ten years," he continued, "a big change has taken place in the theatre and we are told most of the blame rests with the Pictures. There are no great plays, and consequently no great actors because the public are doped by swiftly-changing pictures specially prepared to please every intellect i.e. the meanest. This doping paralyses the mental faculties, and so a play requiring the exercise of any intelligent interest on the part of the audience is doomed on the principle that you can't get juice out of a squeezed lemon. Well, be that as it may, there is in Dublin, I hold the hope," continued Mr MacDonagh, "a chance for plays requiring grey matter, both before and behind the footlights."

In England, he further averred, this apathy is also attributed to post-war mental lassitude, and the thoughts of theatrical purveyors are turning back in despair to the grand manner of the old school in hopes that the thundering voice, the rolling eye and the majestic gesture may make the tired business man again sit up and take notice. " 'I go to the theatre to be amused' one hears repeatedly," and he personally applauded the sentiment because he found that the standard must be raised to meet this demand and not lowered as is erroneously supposed. "It is comforting for us to pretend that the standard of theatrical taste in Dublin is high, though sometimes our pride should be jarred somewhat by the quality of the goods presented for our amusement." The previous year in London a theatrical manager had informed him that a play produced in say, Chortley-Cum-Puddle would stand infinitely a better chance of consideration from London's point of view than one produced in Dublin, but why should Dublin share this point of view? "I am not pleading for any preferential tariff in favour of 'home produce'; I would have the home article stand every test of comparison with the foreign one in the matter of presentation and general efficiency. For my own productions I try to secure the best available artists." (MacDonagh's denigration of "the Pictures" is surprising especially in view of the fact that he was himself responsible for writing and directing several films.)

The plot of *Brains* dealt with the grafting of a fragment of one brain to another, and the extraordinary result shows the bewildering complications that might follow in the march of science were such operations possible. Jimmy, as he was by now generally known, headed the cast in the dual role of the Hon. Reginald Wye and a music hall performer. He got good notices but, according to the *Evening Herald* : "The play was disappointing to many. There is too much talk and too little action, and it could easily be cut down to three acts."

Some good performances were noted from Val Vousden (who would in later years delight listeners to Radio Éireann with his own monologues), Frank Fay, Paul Farrell, Madame Kirkwood-Hackett, Mabel Home and Kathleen Drago, who was brought over especially from London for the production and who would have later associations with Jimmy for his gramophone recordings. But the play is of greatest interest to the theatre historian because it brought together for one occasion Ireland's greatest comedian and the greatest of the Abbey Theatre actors—FJ McCormick—in a comedy role, though of much less consequence than his great

creations of the O'Casey characters, Joxer Daly and
Fluther Good.

There was a revival of *Dublin Tonight* at the Olympia
in August. The Tailteann Games had opened on August
2 so a new sketch called "Our Visitors" was included.
This was about an accommodating landlady who gives
up a room, already occupied, to four visitors—an
Englishman, an American, a Chinaman, and finally a
black. A boisterous night in the room ends happily with
the singing of "The Star Spangled Banner"; "God Save
The King," and an Irish song. The landlady was played
by Jimmy in his first dame role. When "she" had all her
boarders snugly tucked up in one bed she cast a
deliberate glance underneath and remarked: "Well I
think yez have everything"—a foretaste of his great
character Biddy Mulligan. Sister Rita (as Rita Day) and
brother Lal also appeared in the show. The *Irish Times*
said: "Jimmy O'Dea appeared as the landlady...and he
excelled in the part."

The *Evening Mail* critic reporting on the next revue
All The Best in November said: "The talented Jimmy
O'Dea has only to gesticulate to cause laughter, and to
say the least, on his witty interpretation last night, he
shone with unusual brilliance."

True to the early genuine revue format these shows
had a story line or theme. *What A Life*, for instance,
which was presented at the Olympia in February 1925,
was about the voyage of a canal boat the *Nancy Hands*
skippered by Jimmy O'Dea, which leaves Portobello
Harbour with a pantomime company on board in search
of fresh towns and sure salaries. The company makes
merry on board until the craft is wrecked on the rocks
of Ireland's Eye, where the the cast dressed in their
pantomime attire continue their antics on their "desert
isle" until the arrival of the skipper's wife nips the fun
and a romance in the bud.

Romance may have been a big factor of the trips
made by "The Sand Dabs" to Skerries a few years earlier
where, besides reciting "Little Orphan Annie," Jim had
regular meetings with Bernadette Fagan of St. Etna's,

Skerries. Bernadette was one of the large family of
Bernard Fagan, merchant and proprietor of The Red
Lion public house in George's Street, Dublin. Jim and
Bernadette were married in Skerries on 15 April 1925.
His best man was his brother Joe and the matron of
honour was Frances Fagan. The couple went to live in a
flat at 1 Fitzwilliam Square where in the flat below lived
a Mrs Ball who was extremely kind to the newly-weds
and often had breakfast ready for them when they
returned from Sunday mass. Unfortunately, Jim was to
have his third brush with unnatural death there when it
was discovered that Mrs Ball had been murdered by her
son who was an actor.

The third and least successful of the Irish Photoplay
films was released around this time. It appears to have
received a trade showing in the Shaftesbury Pavilion
London at the end of November 1924. *The Bioscope* said
that the title *The Cruiskeen Lawn* was uninspired and
could be improved upon, an understandable criticism
from an English trade paper. "The action," it continued
"consists mainly in trivial incidents of very mild humour
and told at unnecessary length."

The Cruiskeen Lawn of the story is a retired
racehorse, the property of Boyle Roche (Tom Moran)
the impecunious owner of a dilapidated mansion, who is
in love with Nora Blake (Kathleen Armstrong) whose
father Dick Blake (Fred Jeffs) is heavily in debt to an
opportunist called Samuel Silke (played by Jimmy
O'Dea complete with heavy black moustache, giving
him every appearance of the old-fashioned melodramatic
hard-hearted villain). When Darby (Chris Silvester), the
Roches' stable-hand, buys a bottle of medicine for his
rheumatics from a quack known as Dublin Dan (Barrett
MacDonnell), the horse accidentally drinks "the elixir of
life" and is rejuvenated. Boyle decides to run him once
more in the Callaghan Cup and arranges with Silke a bet
of £10,000 to £500 that the Cruiskeen will win.
Unfortunately, the effects of the elixir wear off as
suddenly as they took effect, and a frantic effort is made
to find Dublin Dan to secure a fresh bottle.

Apart from taking part in the MacDonagh revues at the Olympia, Jimmy found himself that year playing his first pantomime dame at the Queen's. He was Martha the coo2k in *Dick Whittington* with Tommy Mostel (who also produced as Idle Jack) and his wife Ray Zack as Dick. According to *The Era:* "Jimmy O'Dea added much to the success of the production, his topical gags and amusing cross-talk with the Baron being very droll."

The opening of the Free State radio station 2RN in 1926 was reflected in a sketch that Jimmy performed in the MacDonagh show *An Easter Egg* at the Olympia, called "How To Broadcast A Play." From May of that year Jimmy became a regular broadcaster himself; he took part in an exchange broadcast with Belfast, singing a nonsense song, "How can a guinea pig show it's pleased, when it has no tail to wag?" As Maurice Gorham wrote (in *Forty Years of Irish Broadcasting):* "A regular GAA commentator, "Carberry" (PD Mehigan) had a great following on 2RN and as early as October 1926 a reader of the *Irish Independent* wrote in to complain abut the irreverence of a parody of his style in a broadcast by Jimmy O'Dea."

In December he was back at the Olympia as Silly Billy in John MacDonagh's original pantomime *Jack and the Beanstalk*. It was announced that the author intended to give the public everything new but the title. Tom Dunne was Dame Dumpling and the cast included Eily Murnaghan.

The theatre critic of *The Crystal* noted:

It is hard to believe that Jimmy O'Dea's gift for nonsense and laughter-making absurdity would not make a fortune abroad. His sense of fun is as spontaneous as that of a six year old child. And he has something of a child's pathos, as those who have been moved by his sobs and tears know well. Between them—the one as author, the other as actor—Mr MacDonagh and he have given Dublin revues as distinctively Irish as the peasant plays of the Abbey.

The reference to the peasant plays of the Abbey was

ominous because in 1927 the exportability of the revues was severely tested. In April they made an exploratory foray to the famous Argyle Theatre in Birkenhead where Jimmy O'Dea and Company were prominent on the bill in a sketch called, "A Slice Of Life." *The Liverpool Echo* noted merely that: "Jimmy O'Dea was well to the fore," while the *Liverpool Post And Mercury* remarked that: "...he brings out the delightful wit of Ireland." Joseph Holloway noted in his diary for Sunday 24 April 1927:

The Drama League produced *The Cradle Song* by Sierra at the Abbey—a beautiful play, beautifully played. I nearly clapped my hands off. [Gabriel] Fallon and Jimmy O'Dea did likewise. I sat between them. O'Dea (just back from Birkenhead) told me that the audience he played to at Birkenhead liked their effects broadened, it was easy to extract laughter from them if you simply played for laughs.

This suggests that Jimmy favoured some thought and meaning or purpose behind his comedy rather than the mere empty routine of cracking jokes. It is significant that this was his outlook on his work virtually from the beginning. Heartened by the initial success, although the response was not entirely to Jimmy's satisfaction, a full-scale revue was planned to tour the North of England in August.

Jim employed a qualified practitioner to work in the shop in Nassau St., which was to be managed by his sister Rita who was studying for her state degree. Jim's final departure from the premises was a great relief to Rita. She regarded her brother's handling of the business as most unbusinesslike. Customers coming to have their eyes tested or some related service were likely to be startled by the sounds of theatrical activity coming from the recesses of the shop as Jim and his friends warbled comic songs or argued loudly about the possibility of getting a laugh from a particular line when they rehearsed a new sketch. The severely competent Rita was greatly relieved when Jimmy O'Dea, professional comedian, was ready to take England by storm.

The revue, called, appropriately, *Irish Stew,* was a fiasco, and Jimmy was to say of it later: "I'm afraid it was so Irish that they [the English] didn't know what we were talking about although it was in the English language." The show had been a success in Dublin where audiences were accustomed to MacDonagh's injections of serious or literary material and the comedy was localised and topical but what could an English audience make of a show which according to the *Lancashire Daily Post* reviewing the show at the Preston Hippodrome: "...is a remarkable collection of Ireland's songs and odds and ends of her early history, particularly in the times of martial law, and the potato famine."

Jimmy appeared as a country boy on his honeymoon, a female hypochondriac in a dispensary, a tourist in Spain, a piano tuner mistaken for a doctor, a tripper looking for a bath in a hotel and a slum denizen confined to bed because his trousers are in pawn. All laughter- provoking situations one would have thought, but the scripts lacked universality and MacDonagh, in an effort to save the show, brought in a red nose comic to augment the cast instead of rewriting the material. Jimmy, rightly, took umbrage and the show was disbanded. It was the end of a remarkable collaboration. Jimmy said sadly:

> The tour folded up at Birkenhead. The English wouldn't have the Irish at any price—at least they wouldn't have us. The company trooped back to Ireland, but the wife and myself we thought we'd stay on and in Birkenhead of all places. Stay on in the hope, if you please, that something would turn up. There we were just round the corner from Liverpool, and down to our last half dollar. Why didn't we go back to Ireland? I'll be quite honest with you we were too proud, but eventually we sailed back to Dublin broke to the wide.

Very probably he wired Rita in Nassau Street for the cash to pay expenses.

That Christmas Jimmy bounced back to appear with his old friends Tommy Mostel and Ray Zack as Simple Simon in *Dick Whittington* at the Theatre Royal, Portsmouth, where he was described by *The Portsmouth and Hampshire County Times* as: "A quaint comedian with an irresistible manner and a host of novel humorous quips."

After Birkenhead Jimmy was at a crossroads in the career which he had only recently embraced wholeheartedly as a professional, and a return to his optical business would have been an admission of failure. But circumstances and personal associations had changed radically; the association with MacDonagh, although it wasn't a partnership, had been an anchor: he was assured of his comedy material written by a man who understood his capabilities if not his full potential. Here was a comedian without a scriptwriter, but over in Dublin, unknown to Jimmy, there happened to be a scriptwriter without a comedian!

2

Jimmy

THE LONDON COLISEUM
CHARING CROSS

Licensed by the Lord Chamberlain to SIR OSWALD STOLL. Chairman and Managing Director. The Coliseum Synonde Ltd. Coliseum Buildings, W.C.

Managing Director . . . . Sir OSWALD STOLL.

Manager . . . . WILLIAM AGNEW.

NOVEMBER 10TH
AND DAILY AT

2·15 P.M. | **5·15 P.M.** | **8·15 P.M.**

THE CELEBRATED LIGHT OPERA AND MUSICAL COMEDY STARS

WINNIE MELVILLE
& DEREK OLDHAM
IN SONGS AND DUETS.
CONDUCTOR - MAURICE BESLY.

TEDDY BROWN
THE WORLD'S GREATEST XYLOPHONIST.

GEORGE LACY
THE NEW COMEDIAN.

PREMIÈRE DANSEUSE AND SINGER FROM 'THE THREE MUSKETEERS'

ULA SHARON

BILLY BENNETT
"ALMOST A GENTLEMAN."

MUSICAL COMEDY SINGER & DANCER.
CORA GOFFIN

"THE IRISH DAN LENO." *Daily Mail.*
JIMMY O'DEA
AND COMPANY—IN
"MICKY TRIES MATRIMONY"
BY HARRY O'DONOVAN.
COMPANY INCLUDES
LITTLE EILEEN MARMION
IRELAND'S JUVENILE STAR.

THE
SENSATIONAL CHINESE
HAI-YUNG
FAMILY
THE WORLD'S MOST MARVELLOUS ACROBATS, JUGGLERS, CONTORTIONISTS TOP SPINNERS, BALANCERS AND HAIR RAISERS, IN A GORGEOUSLY MOUNTED SETTING OF ORIENTAL SPLENDOUR.

DELIGHTFUL DANCER
ELSA D'ARCY

A WELSH SINGER.
TREVOR WATKINS

GEDDES BROTHERS
THE MUSICAL SCOTS.

BRITISH MOVIETONE NEWS
TWO EDITIONS CHANGED ON THURSDAY.

OR WHEELS FOR LAUGHTER PURPOSES ONLY.
FOUR DAIMLERS

Musical Director - ALFRED DOVE & GEORGE SAKER. Assistant Manager - F. H. GRITTEN. Stage Manager - N. CROCKER. Box Office Manager - S. HARBOUR.

PRICES AS USUAL. **Telephone Booking Office Temple Bar 3161**

CHILDREN UNDER TWELVE HALF-PRICE TO SEATS AT 2/4 AND UPWARDS AT 2·15 & 5·15 PERFORMANCES, HOLIDAYS EXCEPTED. Children in arms not admitted.

THE MANAGEMENT RESERVE TO THEMSELVES THE RIGHT TO CHANGE OR VARY ANY PART OF THE PROGRAMME WITHOUT PREVIOUS NOTICE. JAMES UPTON Ltd., Printers, London and Birmingham.

Chapter Four

Already by the late 1920s Harry O'Donovan was an experienced man of the theatre. He had appeared in variety, revue, straight drama and even as a member of a balancing act in a circus—in addition to a brief spell as a challenger in a boxing booth. He started his stage career in 1908 when at the age of eighteen he threw up his apprenticeship in the painting and decorating trade to join the Eddie Mac touring company.

Life in the "fit-ups" was a tough training ground and Harry was called upon to perform every sort of job connected with the running of a show. His stage speciality at that time was a dancing act executed on roller skates, and this was many years before Gene Kelly performed a similar act in films. George Burns claims to have had a tap dance on roller skates when he was in vaudeville and that the secret behind the act was to lock the back wheels of the skates.

Harry was born Henry Donovan on 7 February 1890 at 3 St James's Terrace, Botanic Road, Glasnevin, Dublin. He adopted the stage name Harry O'Donovan later and had the "O" restored to the family name by deed poll. His father, Michael Donovan, was a paper-keeper in the G.P.O. who was often called upon as a handwriting expert to decipher badly addressed mail. His mother, Elizabeth Maley, was of Protestant stock from Boston, USA, who became a convert to Catholicism in order to marry Michael. Harry's paternal grandfather, also Michael Donovan, was a sergeant in the R.I.C. in Cork who was transferred in Dublin in 1830, where he was known around the infamous Mud Island area as "the rowdy sergeant."

There were four children in the family apart from Harry. His equally well-known brother Frank became a famous performer all over Ireland with his touring show which he ran with his wife, Kitty McMahon. When TV killed off all the variety companies Frank infiltrated the enemy camp and started a second career as Batty Brennan in the long running series *The Riordans.* Another brother Kevin was at one period managing director of the Pavilion Theatre, Cork. A third brother Philip died in the black flu epidemic of 1918. The only sister, Aileen, married and had five children. Her first husband, Malony, died and she married Joseph Kennedy.

When the Donovan family was very young they moved house to 6 Millbourne Avenue, Drumcondra, and it is possible that their neighbours in No 2 could have been James Joyce's family who lived there for a short period in 1894. It is likely that the young Donovans received their schooling in the nearby St. Patrick's National School—not that Harry was very much interested in school. He spent as much time playing truant as he did in the classroom. When theatre engagements were scarce Harry became involved in a short-lived apprenticeship at a Summerhill garage which served some of the cars which took part in the first motor races in the Phoenix Park.

In 1920 he started to earn money as a writer with newspaper articles at first but he had yet to discover his true metier. In the meantime he took his own show on the road, but the Anglo-Irish war killed off most of the touring companies, including Harry's, and in the winter of 1921 he was forced to pay off his cast and return to Dublin where he had to borrow the money to transport his scenery, costumes and props from the railway station.

He managed the old Grand Central Cinema in Dublin for a spell but he continued to make frequent appearances in concerts around the city. Thus it was that he met two sisters Eileen and Eva Hayden from Sandyford.

Eva worked for the then familiar firm of Valentine which published greeting- and postcards. She composed appropriate verses for the cards. Many years later, as Eva Brennan, she would write and compose songs like "The Charladies' Ball" and "Sweet Daffodil Mulligan" for Jimmy O'Dea. Eileen was a well-known operatic soprano who had studied with Dr Vincent O'Brien and sang with the Brysan Opera Company. She later became a member of the Dublin Operatic Society. She and Harry married in 1924 and they had one son Terence (Terry), who was to become a brilliant pianist and the composer of many of the songs in his father's revues.

Eva married a man called Brennan who died leaving a family—Denis, Paddy and Joyce (Joy). Joy was to become a well-known member of the Cecil Sheridan company and Denis had a distinguished career as a straight actor. It was typical of Harry that he took responsibility to a great extent for the young Brennan family and helped to rear and educate them. When 2RN began broadcasting in 1926 the station authorities were searching for suitable radio scripts and Harry sent them one which was accepted. After a second and a third they asked for more and Harry began to supply the station regularly. A particularly successful one was called "A Trip To The Planets." Encouraged by Harry's success his sister-in-law Eva Brennan also began to submit scripts, among them being one of note called "The Ginger Twins." Harry himself became well-known on the air and in 1927 he went into management again and produced two revues at the Olympia with music by Tom Madden. The first show *Dublin Pie* was presented in February, followed by *Pleasure Island* in May. These shows contained sketches that he would use again in the future. He took a show in the revue format on the road with disastrous results. Audiences just wouldn't accept it; country audiences were accustomed to seeing a play (preferably a melodrama) and a light comedy piece followed by a variety concert, and the new revue format was alien to them and tantamount to false pretences. Apart from that, unlike John MacDonagh, Harry didn't have a comedian of high calibre despite the fact that his comedy material was first rate. In fact some of the sketches from the two Olympia revues were later performed (and transformed) by Jimmy O'Dea and indeed became bestselling gramophone records. Before this, Jimmy had asked Harry to write material for him but nothing ever came of it.

It is possible that Harry didn't want to encroach on John MacDonagh's territory but Harry's son Terry recalls his father speaking about a dame act that he wrote for Jimmy, circa 1923, which received a standing ovation when it was performed, possibly in the Father Matthew Hall. If this account is accurate it would pre-date Jimmy's first documented appearance as a dame character by several years; it would also have been the precedent for MacDonagh's decision to cast him in a dame role in *Dublin Tonight*. Accounts of the fateful meeting that led to the formation of the O'Dea/ O'Donovan partnership in 1927 vary according to different newspaper articles or radio interviews. Jimmy and Harry are supposed to have met by chance in Henry Street, Pembroke Street or Merrion Row and the ensuing conversation led to the formation of O'D Productions. What is certain is that they had both just experienced humiliating flops. Harry had abandoned his Irish tour and audiences had abandoned Jimmy's English tour.

In a TV interview with Joe Linnane after Jimmy's death Harry gave a different version. Harry related that he had been performing in London:

> When I came back from London I put up a show myself at the Olympia, so Jimmy came up to me after the show was over and he said, 'I like the material you write' in his direct down-to-earth way. He said, 'You've got very good material, Harry, but you haven't got the right comedian.' So I said, 'Well, I think the right comedian is not standing very far away from me'. Then he said, 'Well, Harry, let the two of up put up a show together.' So there you are; we did,

and that's the only partnership we ever had—nothing in writing, just a verbal contract.

So it was settled with a handshake over a couple of bottles of stout. The new partners always boasted that they never had, or required, a legal contract and that their association was always friendly and amicable. This was probably good as a publicity gimmick for their public image but their relationship was not always trouble-free.

The true story of the formation of O'D Productions is probably a mixture of the different versions. After their first business encounter nothing seems to have happened for some time: Jimmy honoured his contract to appear in pantomime in Plymouth and on his return the new partners seem to have been engaged in concert appearances. For instance, they appeared together in a concert in the St Vincent de Paul Hall, Kells, on Sunday 18 March 1928 when they performed what was to become their most famous sketch: "Sixpence Each Way." Jimmy is an undecided female punter who constantly changes her bet and informs the harassed bookie's clerk that she will report him to his boss with the immortal observation: "It's the likes o' me that keeps the likes of you, keeping the likes of him walking about in his Rolls-Royce." This sketch was not, as has been supposed, a Biddy Mulligan creation; it was written long before the advent of Biddy, and was first performed in Harry's show *Pleasure Island* in 1927 with Joe Masterson in the dame role. Much of the material that Harry provided early on for Jimmy was written before they became partners.

In April, 1928 they planned their first revue which was to be presented at the Queen's. The formation of O'D Productions, which would in time become a limited company, was an act of faith in the future of variety. The new partners must have been aware of the growing threat to live shows from Hollywood. Sound films had just been introduced and no variety company could compete with the lavish "all-talking, all-singing, all-dancing" musical films to which audiences were flocking.

Social conditions were not good either: the effects of the
Wall Street crash had repercussions all over Britain and
Ireland resulting in the Depression and widescale
unemployment. Everywhere the proprietors of the
Empires and the Hippodromes hedged their bets and
had their theatres wired for sound to accommodate the
new talking films, in case it should be necessary to
change over to the new marvel. In the end many
compromised with a mixture of film and live show called
Cine-Variety. Radio, too, was taking its toll as for the first
time potential audiences found it to be unnecessary to
leave their own homes in order to be entertained. By the
mid-thirties the top of a variety bill, which might be a
dance-band, would have its roots more firmly in steam
radio than in the theatre. Alfred Black, son of impresario
George Black who ran the Palladium, said of his father's
inclusion on the bill of Christopher Stone, the first radio
"disc-jockey": "The cheekiest thing Dad ever did was to
put on Christopher Stone at the Palladium. Stone would
come on and say, 'I'm now going to play you a very nice
record, I hope you enjoy it, and he'd sit there and put a
record on, and the audience sat there like lemons and
listened to it!"

Music-hall had come a long way since its first formal
home in the Canterbury Hall which was opened by
Charles Morton in Lambeth in May 1852. The original,
old-style music-hall lasted only about sixty years and
many commentators date its demise from before the first
Royal Command performance given at the Palace
Theatre, London in 1912. After that an artist's time on
the bill was shortened from as long as thirty minutes or
more to eight or ten minutes, with the result that what
became known as Variety had more pace and liveliness.
The early music-hall with its satirical songs and patter had
reflected the hard life of the times but the new breed of
comics in variety generally wore grotesque make-up and
sang nonsense songs and they had a fondness for props of
every description. The O'D partnership had no use for
extraneous stage props or gimmicks and their comedy
was based on sharp observation of real life situations. The

variety theatres in Dublin weathered the storm pretty
well, the only casualty being the Tivoli, until in the
1960s television caused the demise of the mammoth
Theatre Royal and the Capitol. But this time scores of
cinemas closed their doors with them. It was evident that
their sites were more profitable as office blocks,
department stores and supermarkets.

Still back in 1928, Harry and Jimmy planned their
first big show. The legend, perpetuated by both of them,
is that they were flat broke and again, accounts vary as to
how they secured the capital for their first venture.
According to one version Harry is supposed to have sold
his piano and Jimmy discovers an old Post Office book
showing £9 to his credit. Both were married at the time
and must have had secure incomes. Jimmy especially
must have had an income from his optical business.
Besides it is unimaginable that they managed to secure
the Queen's for £9 and the proceeds from the sale of a
piano. In a broadcast from Manchester in 1945 Jimmy
said: "Four days before the first production I
remembered I hadn't given Harry any money. He said
'Well, I only spent £9 up to now.' We took over £700 in
the first week."

The show was called *We're Here* and the cast contained the nucleus of what was to become the O'D
company. The O'Dea name was well to the fore in the
Dublin theatres that week as Ken O'Dea was appearing
at the Theatre Royal doing songs at the piano with
Norman Redmond. The Queen's show was an instant
success and featured Jimmy in "The Truth About
Napoleon," which showed the human side of the
little corporal's character. There was also "The
Sneezicoughskis"—the only Russian quartet in captivity,
led, of course, by Jimmy who later joined Harry in a
satirical topical song "The Two TDs" which was sung to
the air of "Let The Jug Pass" from Richard Brinsley
Sheridan's *The School For Scandal*. Taking part in the
sketches were O'D stalwarts Tom Dunne, Fay Sargent,
Mollie Douglas, Lionel Day (Lal O'Dea) and Connie
Ryan; songs were by Eily Murnaghan, Willie O'Toole

and Eileen Marmion who had been a star attraction in Harry's independent shows. Kathleen O'Brien led the "Eight Joy Belles" whose number was increased to ten by the time the show reached Belfast. The show ran a second week before touring to the other major Irish dates. The critic of a Belfast newspaper was to say: "In the hands of Jimmy O'Dea, the humorous side takes on a sparkle which transforms every word and action into a huge joke, and everyone of his comedy scenes becomes a burst of laughter."

When they played the Palace Theatre, Cork, the "house full" cards were displayed outside and the local critic was to observe that *We're Here,* "affords a feast of excellent singing and dancing, and a great deal of happy comedy none of which bears a trace of vulgarity."

They were back in the Queen's in June and again in August with two more shows. Séamus de Búrca was at that time property master in the Queen's and he remembers that Jimmy was, to use Séamus's own words "a very cranky producer." In one sketch a telephone was supposed to ring and when it failed to do so one night Jimmy tore strips off Séamus who made sure from then on that the had a second bell, revolver shot or whatever to fall back on in case the first one failed. Jimmy was a tough taskmaster in matters relating to his shows and he had no time for sloppiness or second best but to his credit it must be said, and many have affirmed it, when Jimmy told you off and saw that you got his message he held nothing against you afterwards and that was the end of the matter.

In October they changed venue and opened at the Olympia with a show appropriately called *Now We're Here.* However the next logical step was to produce a pantomime so, in answer to an advertisement in *The Stage* which offered scenery for all pantomime subjects, they went to England to select their subject. As it turned out they were faced with Hobson's choice. In the dimly lit scenery warehouse all they could clearly discern were hundreds of thousands of sequins and spangles glittering in the semi-darkness. "This," said the dealer proudly "was the Diamond Valley scene from *Sinbad The Sailor* and no, he didn't have anything suitable for *Aladdin* or *Babes In The Wood*. In the face of this blatantly misleading piece of advertising, *Sinbad* it had to be! An important point in its favour was that it hadn't been seen in Dublin for some years and it was well received when it opened at the Olympia on Christmas Eve 1928. Harry ensured that the comedy was derived from the working out of the story and not, as was the custom then, from a series of interpolated "gags" which had no bearing on the plot. Jimmy was Toobad the Tailor from Tipperary and Tom Dunne was the Dame Widow Snatchem. Tom was a fine performer and an excellent foil to Jimmy. His family had a paint and wallpaper shop in Dublin, in whose window a notice proclaimed: "Our Wallpaper Deserves Hanging." Harry's son Terry was born on the Sunday before the first performance of *Sinbad* and was the youngest member of the audience present on that Christmas Eve.

In April of the following year, 1929, they were back at the Queens with *April Fooling*. Billy Scott Coomber made his first revue appearance in this production which was notable also for the appearance of Harry O'Donovan and twelve year old Eileen Marmion in "Betty, the Breaker of Hearts." It was an old routine from one of Harry's earlier shows in which little Eileen dressed in a short tutu emerged from a large chocolate box in the centre of the stage and sang her song with Harry. At the end of it he carried her off perched on his shoulder. When they did this act in a variety show in Cork two years previously an irate patron wrote to the theatre management to complain about a dirty show with particular reference to the fact that Harry "carried a naked woman off the stage." There were to be no quibbles or moral outrage of this nature when the show, having visited Limerick and Waterford, played to full houses in Cork and the Civic Guards had a strenuous time regulating the queues of people seeking admission.

In May Jimmy repeated his Napoleon sketch in an Olympia show in aid of Jervis Street Hospital and also on the bill from the Capitol Theatre (known previously as the La Scala and on whose namesake in Milan it was supposed to have been modelled), were the Tiller Girls, one of the famous John Tiller troupes, and a Peg Tisdall, daughter of a Dublin musician who was herself an accomplished pianist and vocalist, who had started her career by playing and singing sheet music selected by prospective buyers in Woolworth's of Henry Street. Peg eventually achieved real fame all over Britain on radio, stage and records with the Roy Fox and Jack Hylton bands as leading vocalist, Peggy Dell.

A season of Cine-Variety at the Queen's followed, in which Jimmy appeared in a series of character sketches which had been made into gramophone records. Radio was a comparatively new phenomenon in 1929 and the public were still accustomed to deriving entertainment from the gramophone with the large horn speaker. This had all but replaced the old reliable piano in the parlour which for so many years had been the centre of home-based entertainment on Sunday evenings in countless homes when many budding tenors invited Maud into the garden.

Jimmy had cut his first records for C & J Henecy of 18 Crowe Street, Dublin. Henecy's carried large stocks of gramophones and records of all the leading companies and also records of local entertainers, singers and musicians on their own green and gold Henecy label. These were recorded and pressed by the English Edison Bell Record Company. Jimmy's earliest recordings were of pieces by Louis Tierney: monologues like "Mrs Maher's Little Shop" or "Cinderella Up-to-date" and material from John MacDonagh's revues such as "The Ballad of the Medical Student" or "Parody on Dublin Bay." The Henecy recordings were made in September 1926 and in April 1929 Jimmy and Harry cut two records for the short-lived Dominion label but in the following July they secured a valuable contract with

Parlophone records who were then in Dublin recording Irish solo artists bands and choirs. The first of the two records in their first session was of Jimmy singing "Bridget Donohue" with Harry on the reverse side with "I'll Slip Out The Back," but it was the second record that was to establish them as front-rank artists whose records were sought in Britain and even the USA and Australia. This was "Sixpence Each Way" which, already a stage success, became one of Parlophone's best sellers in the 1930's, ranking No 3 in their list of money makers. There were several other classics in their output which certainly added to their reputations in Ireland and in England. In the average home in Ireland, where the favourite records included those of John McCormack, Fritz Kreisler, Peter Dawson and Caruso, there was always room to be found for several Jimmy O'Dea records in the record rack to lighten the Sunday evening recital and literally thousands of people all over the country knew his recorded sketches off by heart; indeed some favourite lines became part of the vernacular.

Despite their huge success, and Jimmy was to be congratulated for partly overcoming the difficulties, the records were pale shadows of the stage star. Jimmy was essentially a live performer who was at his best with a live audience to bounce off, and he couldn't do that on a record. He was to experience the same difficulty, to a great extent, later on in films. Besides this his performance relied on much more than his voice; there were the visual impact of his gestures, the quicksilver movements of his feet and above all the facial expressions, with the remarkable eyes, and the fluid mouth and lips which seemed to come alive when powered by a witty flow of Dublinese. Today, although they retain their inherent shortcomings, his records do provide a clue to his artistry.

"How the hell can I be funny into a funnel?" asked one perplexed performer in 1900 when confronted by the recording horn; that Jimmy overcame the difficulty, to some degree, was due in no short measure to the scripts that Harry wrote for him. The most successful were those featuring the essentially genuine Biddy Mulligan; others were very often abbreviated and adapted versions of stage performances which do not appear to be particularly funny in typescript but that Jimmy's interpretation brought alive. Each was a little playlet, complete in itself, and many of the devices he used on the records in order to reach a quick denouement in the limited time available on a record stretched credibility to the limit. For instance, telegrams would be delivered in the most unlikely places in the most unbelievably short timespan, from the most unbelievable people—just in the nick of time. His subjects, too, could be rather repetitive; the border and partition were regular topics but Harry's favourite subject was the Irish Sweepstake. He wrote the script for at least five or six records on this theme. (He actually called one of their 1934 revues *£30,000*, which was then the top prize in the sweep). The best of the records display a fine style, observant and exact, with a sense of pace and an ear for the unusual phrase. When Harry's script provided Jimmy with the opportunity to shine, the result was a classic like "The Irish Jaunting Car," which was recorded in their second session in October 1929. The partners, as far as was possible, did all the voices on their records, with ladies' roles being taken by Connie Ryan and later by Kathleen Drago. Tom Dunne and Noel Purcell too were occasional contributors. The former is the irate gent in "Mrs Mulligan In The Tram" and the latter had a dame role in "Fresh Fish." There are four characters in "The Irish Jaunting Car": an American looking for a ride on an Irish jaunting car, Billy Waters, a weedy little hotel porter from the North, and Barney Higgins, a gruff Dublin jarvey; in addition there is a one-line role for a Dublin shawlie. Harry played the American and Jimmy played the other three characters, giving each a fully delineated character in an amazing display of virtuosity. In those days, of course, the jaunting car was not the sole prerogative of the jarveys in Killarney.

(Excerpt from "The Irish Jaunting Car")

AMERICAN: So this is an Irish jaunting car?

BARNEY: The real thing sir; I've driven it myself for thirty years.

AMERICAN: What! The same car?

BILLY: Yes sir, and the same horse too.

BARNEY: You're a liar where you stand, Billy Waters, I'll have you up for libel.

BILLY: Libel is it? If you brought that animal into court as exhibit "A" you'd be summonsed for robbing the museum.

BARNEY: Don't mind him, sir, don't mind him; I only bought that mare last year.

BILLY: Last year. That aul' nag is one of the original string that went into the Ark.

BARNEY: Billy Waters, if there was a train going to a certain warm spot that was not on this earth, I'd drive you there meself free of charge to the station so that you wouldn't miss it. Listen to him, sir, running down the Irish jaunting car that's as much an institution of the country as round towers, Guinness' stout and wet weather.

AMERICAN: Well I think we'd better make a start. Will you give me a hand up.

BARNEY: Give me your hand sir, Put your foot in the step. Up you come me lad.

BILLY: That aul' yoke'll break under you sir. Better let me call you a taxi.

BARNEY: If you don't go in outa that Billy Waters, the next call that you'll hear is one that an angel is going to blow on a trumpet. (CRASH) What's that?

BILLY: One of your lamps is after fallin' off.

BARNEY: Is it the one with the bit of candle in it? Go in for the love of Mike and take your evil eye off me horse before she drops dead. Come on Jenny. Off we go sir. Come up me gerrel...Hey missus, will you take that perambulator full of fish from under me horse's nose.

SHAWLIE: Sure I'm waitin' for the polis man to give me the signal.

BARNEY: Hasn't the poor man enough to do with his hands without giving the "come-on" signal to a perambulator full of Dublin Bay herrings.

The first Mrs Mulligan records were also made in the October session. These were "At the Telephone" and "At the Pawnshop." In the latter Mrs Mulligan is asked by the assistant: "Show me Napoleon's crest on that jug."

MRS. MULLIGAN: There it is on the bottom. EPNS, the "N" is for Napoleon.
ASSISTANT: What's the EP for?
MRS. MULLIGAN: His confirmation name, Edward Percy.
ASSISTANT: And what's the "S" for?
MRS. MULLIGAN: That's just to make it hard.

It is very possible that the character of Biddy Mulligan was devised primarily to give Jimmy a definite *persona* on gramophone records and in turn their success created a demand for her on stage. Certainly her theatre appearances do not predate the records. In fact, one of the first dame roles that Jimmy played with O'D productions was in a sketch called "Marrying Mary" in the Queen's Theatre in 1930 and the character was called Mrs Brady, with a husband and daughter.

In Britain there were many precedents for creating characters exclusively for records and the practice extended to Irish artists and others like Michael Casey whose true name was Russell Hunting. He was a Boston actor with no Irish connections, who was very successful on Regal records with a character called Casey who had escapades at the dentist's, at a wake, as a judge and as a doctor. Another such was Dick Forbes, the Cork comedian and script-writer, who made records for Parlophone as a character called Mulcahy.

The Mrs Mulligan records, as a collection, vie with Joyce's *Ulysses* for the frequency of their reference to Dublin streets from the Liberties to Grafton Street; to characters ranging from well-known bookies to Alfie Byrne and now defunct institutions such as the Royal Iris and Williams and Woods. Some of the references, such as "the Noblett's Corner look," are now rather obscure. Noblett's was a sweet shop but the meaning of "the look" must be lost as a mystery of the 30s. Harry's Mrs Mulligan sketches worked best when he used the song "Biddy Mulligan" as a guide to the character but later he became inconsistent: Mrs Mulligan was supposed to be a widow but Harry gave her a husband; her son Mick who played the flute in the Longford Street band never once appeared on stage or record. Instead Harry gave her a daughter and their address varied. Sometimes as in the song she sold fish laid out on the street but at other times she had a sweet shop. Names varied also: her husband was called Larry on the records and Mick on the stage. And her own name was variously Julia, Maggie and Bedelia on the records. Ideally, the classic Mrs Mulligan sketch is the one in which we can visualise the tired little widow in her bonnet and shawl (black as they usually were in those days) hurrying home after a busy morning of walking and haggling over the price of her dinner, slightly bad-tempered and loath to suffer fools gladly, especially in the tram.

(Excerpt from "Mrs Mulligan In The Tram")

MRS MULLIGAN: Wait a minute conductor.

CONDUCTOR: Come one—give me your hand.

MRS MULLIGAN: I can't. If if let go the parcel of tripe I'm ruined.

CONDUCTOR: Well 'pon my soul it's a special car we'd want for you. Come on, up you go.

MRS MULLIGAN: I wish you'd run a special tram to York Street, and not be forcing me to fraternise with the eleetey of Terenure. Hey! mind, the fish it's coming through the paper already.

CONDUCTOR: There's a corner seat for you.

MRS MULLIGAN: Not that I'm not as good as anyone from Terenure or Rathmines. There's none of your Russian boots and no breakfast about me. Excuse me sir, is my tripe leaking on your spats?

IRATE MAN: Conductor, couldn't this woman leave her parcels outside; there's an abominable odour.

MRS MULLIGAN: Are you addressing your remarks to me, Colonel Bogey?

CONDUCTOR: The gentleman objects to the smell of that tripe.

MRS MULLIGAN: Much about him. Let him take a walk down Moore Street and get his nose educated.

Equally successful were recorded versions of stage sketches with Jimmy as Mr Quiggelley, the tenor from the Coombe and Kevin Street Musical Society, who when asked by the conductor "What are the medals for on the lapel of your dinner jacket?" replies. "I haven't the slightest idea; they were sown on the coat when I bought it."

In "Buying the Furniture," Jimmy as the country lad with his new bride is asked by the furniture salesman: "Perhaps you would like twin beds?"

JIMMY: Like what! Mary Jo, come out of this, we'll make our own arrangements, thank you.

MARY JO: What he means is two beds.

JIMMY: Why so? I've only one wife.

One song recorded by Jimmy in 1934 called "Everybody wants to win the Sweep" throws an extraordinary light on people's ignorance of Hitler's pogroms and on what was then considered funny:

If Mr Hitler won it would he stand himself a wet?
Would he send it to the Kaiser or pay off the
German debt?
Would he hire a lot of liners, fully manned with
German crews
And send off to Dublin with 100,000 Jews?

Such a verse sung around the time that a liner full of
Jews was searching for sanctuary in any friendly port
must say something for the insular outlook of the Irish
at the time.

The character of Biddy Mulligan was inspired by an
old song written before Jimmy himself was born. Called
"Queen of the Coombe," it was specially written by W S
North for a Gaiety Theatre pantomime *Taladoin, or The
Scamp With The Lamp,* which opened on Thursday,
December 26, 1889. The song was sung by Richard
Purdon who played the part of the Widow Twankey.
The words were printed in the programme as was the
custom then in order to establish copyright.

THE QUEEN OF THE COOMBE

I'm a dashing young widow that lives in a spot
That is christened the Dublin Coombe,
Where the shops and the stalls are all out on the
street,
And my palace consists of a room.
At Plunkett Street corner for forty-five years
I've stood at my stall, 'tis no lie
And during them years there's not one could be
found
To say black was the white of my eye.

Chorus:
You may ramble through Clare, and the County
Kildare,
And from Drogheda down to Macroom,
But you never will see a widow like me
Mrs Twankey the Queen of the Coombe.

I sell apples and oranges, pears and split peas,
I sell bulls eyes and sugar stick sweet;
On Saturday night I sell second hand clothes
From my stall on the floor of the street,
I sell fish on a Friday spread out on a board
Fresh cod fish from out of the say,
Haddocks and mackerel and herring so sweet,
The herrings of famed Dublin Bay.
(Chorus)

Seamus Kavanagh later adapted it, calling it "Biddy Mulligan the Pride of the Coombe" and it was sung by several Dublin performers like Tony Reddin, who apart from performing and recording was the manager and producer of the shows at the La Scala Theatre. It was recorded on the Eclipse label (inexpensive, seven-inch records sold mainly by Woolworth's) by a Dublin comedian Patrick Kavanagh, around the period that Jimmy recorded it for Parlophone and made it his own; it was to serve as his theme music throughout his career. It is of interest to note in passing that although Seamus Kavanagh's newer version includes the line "From Francis Street on to Macroom" in the chorus the line from the older original version "And from Drogheda down to Macroom" is often heard today at Dublin party sing-songs.

Jimmy and Harry, influenced, no doubt, by the success of the dame punter in "Sixpence Each Way" adopted the character as the perfect vehicle for Jimmy's particular talent as a dame comedian. Leading British comedians from Dan Leno, George Robey and Wilkie Bard to Douglas Byng, Arthur Askey and Frankie Howard had a tradition of appearing as dames at pantomime time and these were often over-rouged caricatures of women (or harridans) with exaggeratedly big, blowsy bosoms which took on a life of their own when they were hoisted up with navvy-like folded arms. Norman Evans introduced his "Auntie Doleful" in variety programmes with his "Over the Garden Wall" act around the end of the 1920s, but again the portrayal depended upon exaggeration. The most outrageous of them all was Arthur Lucan as the Irish washerwoman Old Mother Riley. Arthur Lucan's first appearance as a dame was as Mrs Kelly, with Kitty McShane as her daughter in a sketch called "The Come Over," which received its first production in a Jim Jonson show at the Tivoli Theatre, Dublin in 1913 and which then toured Ireland. Paddy Kenny and Con West, the script-writers, gave Lucan the name Old Mother Riley in his first film. She was a grotesque character much given to jumping about in a rage with arms weaving preparatory to throwing the contents of a dresser full of delph all over the stage.

Many theatre-goers, predominantly men, had an aversion to men dressing up in women's clothes on stage. Even today there is some resistance to Danny La Rue and his trunkful of gorgeous creations. Danny, incidentally, saw Jimmy in *Mother Goose* in his native Cork in 1934 and wrote later: "I was in awe of this great Irish comedian playing dame and I scarcely took my eyes off him through the performance. He mesmerized me...and obviously influenced me tremendously." Arthur Sinclair, the great Abbey Theatre actor of the early years, speaking to Joseph Holloway, "wondered why O'Dea played female parts and thought it disgusting for a man to do so."

Jimmy's Biddy Mulligan was a closely observed character study without any exaggerations. She was meticulously clean and neat with shining black hair parted in the centre, tightly combed into little curls over the ears, and crowned with a fussy little hat. She had a long skirt and apron and a checked shawl over her shoulders. Her blouse and shawl changed over the years according to the dictates of fashion but that was her basic costume which was completed by black elastic-sided bootees which were, like the wigs and the clothes, specially made. Although she never displayed them under any circumstances she wore long old fashioned bloomers underneath (a sure laugh for lesser comics). Asked by Vernon Hayden why he went to the trouble to complete the costume with bloomers that nobody knew about, Jimmy, the perfectionist, replied "I know!" The character he portrayed was the typical Dublin shawlie, witty and sharp-tongued though she could assume an air of gentility with a quasi-refined accent until, goaded by her errant husband, Mick, her mood and accent suddenly changed and she poured on him a torrent of restrained invective. She had a genuine dignity in the face of adversity and was ever optimistic. Much of the material in the Mulligan sketches was true to life, and both Jimmy and Harry frequented the pubs used by their models and listened in on the conversations of the shawlies. In fact, Jimmy always drank in the public bar for preference in whatever pub he might find himself. To Jimmy, Biddy Mulligan was a real character, in the theatrical sense, and rather than give the usual superficial performance of a dame comedian he played her as a real woman, drawing on the reserves of the femininity in his own nature. And he drew a fine line between a recognisable comic creation and the overblown reality of the real thing. Jimmy was aware of the trap of being too perfect and never lost touch with his own personality.

When he visited Canada in 1961 the critic of the *Toronto Daily Star* was to write:

> His appearance as Mrs Mulligan—a woman from the fish market of Dublin entertaining an American visitor—was hilarious and excellently worked out. His movements and intonation were so genuinely feminine that for a while, not having been able to consult the programme in the dark, I assumed that his supporting cast included a low voiced and boisterous actress.

Jimmy had the knack of turning laughter into tears and many compared him in that respect to Chaplin and, while it is true that many of his sketches have a Chaplinesque twist in them, mingling pathos with comedy, the comparison is not a completely satisfactory one. Granted that both men often achieved similar effects, the means by which they arrived at them were completely dissimilar. A possible exception to this is the sketch "Buying A Turkey," in which the important detail depends upon action rather than dialogue as in Chaplin's silent films. In the sketch Mrs Mulligan is forced by penury to buy a thin, famished turkey for her Christmas dinner. Due to a mix-up with identifying labels, a messenger boy, on his way to deliver of a fine plump bird to a well-heeled customer, puts the wrong label on Mrs Mulligan's bird and takes it for delivery by mistake, leaving the big bird on the counter. The stage directions read:

> Mulligan is about to call him back. He is off. Music plays softly. She moves towards the turkey. Puts out a hand gingerly and takes it. Turns slowly and walks a couple of slow steps...suddenly makes a dash and runs off. (Blackout)

Audiences silently watching this sketch were consciously sympathetic to the poverty-stricken Mrs Mulligan, and anxiously willed her to take the fine fat turkey. Gabriel Fallon described it as comparable to the Fall.

Chapter Five

One morning in College Green, Jimmy and Harry, after rehearsals in the Olympia, met Micheál MacLiammóir and Hilton Edwards who had just been at rehearsals in their new Dublin Gate Theatre. Michael remembered:

> The normal civilities passed. The same desultory mutual questions and answers about each other's work, then a few phrases more—odd, half-loving, half-cynical phrases of the ancient freemasonry of the theatre.
> "They are the first pros I have met since we left McMaster," Hilton said, "What did you say their names...?"
> " O' Donovan and O'Dea."
> "Which is the little fellow?"
> "O'Dea. Jimmy O'Dea."
> "He's a great comic," Hilton said.
> "He's the greatest in this country," I told him
> "He looks and he sounds like one of the greatest in the world," my partner murmured.
> A great comic...carries with him visibly and audibly, a sort of exorable grandeur, a kind of ludicrous, luminous aura."

One of the greatest in the world! Soon Jimmy would be exposed to the opinion of audiences in one of the great world showplaces at that time the Mecca of every hopeful performer seeking the approval and fame of London's West End—the London Coliseum.

It was 1929 and for the moment they had a panto to do in the Queen's. It was *Little Red Riding Hood*, which was notable for the appearance of the six-foot-four Noel Purcell as Dame Longshanks in his first professional role. Noel, as Dublin as the Liffey with a distinctively clear Dublin accent, was a year younger than Jimmy. He was born in Mercer Street and his widowed mother ran an antique shop in Camden Street. He served his time as a cabinet maker but spent most of his spare time doing amateur shows around the city. A kindly, helpful and cheerful man to whom everyone was "me aul' brown son" he rose to stardom in his own right and appeared in many first-rate British and Hollywood films. As the crowning accolade to his career and as mark of the esteem in which his fellow Dubliners held him he was made a Freeman of the City of Dublin a few years before his death in 1984.

Sitting in the panto audience one evening DJ Clarke, the shrewd manager of the Argyle Theatre, Birkenhead, found he was enjoying the show and was impressed by Jimmy as Weary Jimmy partnered by Tom Dunne as Tired Tom. The cast also included the Ennis entertainer Mike Nono, and Eileen Marmion as Red Riding Hood was "so sweet, pretty and petite that she made a wonderful contrast to Dame Longshanks." It was in this panto that Jimmy introduced the catch-phrase that he was to use for many years—"You can't puzzle Jimmy." DJ Clarke had a legendary eye for talent, and was reputed to have booked promising young newcomers for years in advance at a fixed salary, with the result that he had performers like Sir Harry Lauder working a week for him regularly every year at a fraction of their worth after they became famous. Still, Clarke wasn't as unfair and tightfisted as might be imagined; expensive gifts changed hands instead of a big salary. When he returned to England he recommended the O'D company to Sir Oswald Stoll, chairman of the number one Stoll circuit.

When the panto played Cork the company stayed on

a second week in a new revue called *Irish Smiles*. This show was seen by a representative of the Stoll organization, who had crossed over to Ireland on the recommendation of DJ Clarke, and on the following morning he interrupted Jimmy and Harry at breakfast in their hotel and offered them, subject to some changes in the show, a week's engagement at the Shepherd's Bush Empire. This booking, however, depended upon their success in a preliminary appearance at the Ardwick Empire, Manchester.

Although he had already had a bad experience with English audiences Jimmy was keen to grab the opportunity. He was firmly of the opinion that they would stagnate if they confined themselves to Irish audiences. He said:

Blood and tears is the only way an artist can get confidence—playing to audiences of every description. And there aren't enough different types of audiences in Ireland. Take the school of old-timers like Joe Gorman, Shaun Glenville, Willie John Ashcroft—they were all Anglo-Irish. If they'd confined themselves to Irish audiences they'd have got into a rut—and stayed there.

So, after a short Irish tour the company arrived at the Olympia Theatre, Dublin, in April 1930 prior to their departure for England. One of the Dublin critics wrote: "Some of the scenes, however, are so exaggerated that one doubts the wisdom of putting them on in London where the programme announces the revue will be produced next."

Within three days of its first appearance in England at the Ardwick Empire the show was booked for the entire Stoll circuit. A Manchester critic noted:

Jimmy O'Dea has a bird-like manner on the stage, which matches well his provocative attacks on men much bigger than himself. His bright eye follows, when it does not anticipate; the inquiring belligerent twist of the head which signifies that there is to be some trouble of an Irish sort and that whoever gets hit will not, in the end be Jimmy O'Dea. This feminine talent for a hit-and-run battle is particularly endearing when he becomes Mother for the purpose of "Marrying Mary." In this awkward situation Mother is the government and everyone else is in opposition. Here, there is plenty of humour; enough to catch a reflection of the Ireland which illuminates Mr O'Casey."

The revue was comprised of sixteen scenes, in the first of which, in the village of Belgooley, Jimmy and his fellow "smiles" leave prison with the express purpose of murdering "the talkies" and the last scene sees them return claiming to have carried out their purpose. Noel Purcell took over Harry's musical numbers with Eileen Marmion, and that was the beginning of a double act that was to last a lifetime: Noel and Eileen were married in 1941.

Early in June the company opened at the Shepherd's Bush Empire, where to their dismay, they discovered that the management had dressed the theatre attendants as broths of boys in knee breeches and caubeens complete with clay pipes; the programme sellers were dressed as dainty colleens in the idealised stage acceptation of such costumes. Jimmy and Harry protested and warned of the possibility of an irate backlash from the Gaelic League and other Irish nationalist bodies. They went right to the top and argued their case with Sir Oswald Stoll, who was, it is said, sympathetic to Irish expectations, and he ordered that the charade at the Shepherd's Bush Empire should be cancelled. The show was a resounding success and *The Era*, a stage paper, reported:

Jimmy O'Dea whose reputation is very well-known in Ireland adds to his laurels by his visit to this country, and to judge by his reception at Monday night's performance will be fully satisfied with his success.

The brunt of the work falls upon his shoulders and be it said that he is never at a loss whatever the situation. With his quaint mannerisms and his Irish brogue he keeps the audience in roars of laughter.

And *The Stage* was to say:

Most important of all, however, is the first appearance in London of the well-known Irish comedian, Jimmy O'Dea. Mr O'Dea is a comedian who should be well worth keeping in England. He has an unobtrusive comical style that causes any amount of laughter and he knows the value of a rich Irish accent among English audiences.

All of the critics were to comment on Jimmy's accent which to them, of course, had an undeniably Irish ring. But it was an accent that wasn't so easy for the Irish themselves to place. True, it was a Dublin accent but no one could pin-point it as belonging to any particular part of Dublin. It certainly didn't come from the Liberties where he was born, so it would seem to have been a peculiar sort of Dublinese that he invented himself and may best be described as being a refined Dublin accent with the characteristic nasal drawl and typical inflections and intonations superimposed upon it. Noel Purcell was to say that outside Olivier there was never English spoken like Jimmy spoke it, and it was true that each word was given its full value in enunciation and clarity. "Jimmy had quite extraordinarily clear diction," wrote John Jordan.

Off-stage his accent was certainly Dublin, but just as certainly it had been vamped as are vamped the accents of all actors. On-stage even when he aimed at the broadest kind of Dublin accent, he retained to superb effect, some of the actor's voice intonations. The result was a heady blend of the hilarious and the immutably dignified. I think it was partly due to this retention of at least an echo of polite actor's speech that not one of Jimmy's personations ever became truly ridiculous. The fortunes of the Widow Mulligan were generally in decline. but miraculously the throwing of an extra bit of vocal refinement convinced us that these near disasters were mere briars in the path of an indestructible *grande dame*.

Amongst the many favourable reviews that Jimmy received from the British press the most complimentary description he received was from the *Daily Mail* which called him "The Irish Dan Leno" and this bears some examination as Leno is revered by the British as their greatest comedian ever, one who was described as "the funniest man in the world" on a visit to New York.

Dan Leno was born George Galvin in St Pancras in 1860. His father and mother toured the halls as Mr & Mrs "Irish" Johnny Wilde. When his father died his mother married a performer whose stage name was Leno. Dan made his first solo appearance as Dan Patrick Leno, "Descriptive and Irish Character vocalist'" but he was to make his mark as a Cockney comedian. At Christmas 1886 he was engaged to play the Baroness in *Babes In The Wood* at Drury Lane's Theatre Royal, and he was so successful that he played panto there for fifteen consecutive years. His other London house was the London Pavilion, then a music-hall venue.

Christmas for many meant Dan Leno at the Theatre Royal, just as Christmas in Dublin came to mean Jimmy at the Gaiety Theatre. Their particular art seemed to be derived from the same sources and from a similar view of life, but above all both men were great character actors. Charles Chaplin in his autobiography wrote: "Dan Leno, I suppose, was the greatest English comedian since the legendary Grimaldi. Although I never saw him in his prime to me he was more of a character actor than a comedian." Dr Cyril Cusack who was a lifelong admirer of O'Dea has written similarly about his qualities as a character actor. Neville Cardus writing in *Full Score* said: "If the comedian or music hall performer of any kind did not have true powers of the actor he was soon herded among the 'middle of the bill' mediocrities."

Writing of Leno's portrayal of women, one of his script writers, Hickory Wood, might have been writing about Jimmy:

> He was homely, discursive and confidential not to say occasionally aggressive. His own personality was, of course, ever present but when I saw him playing this kind of part the impression he left on my mind was not so much a picture of Dan Leno playing the part of a woman in a particular walk of life as the picture of what Dan would have been if he had been that particular woman. In his studies of women in a humble walk of life Dan Leno's gait, manner and expression altered.

Leno always appeared solo (except for panto) and is credited with the introduction of patter material to accompany a comic song. Music halls were at that time forbidden by law to present sketches and dramatic items on the bill, these being the prerogative of the legitimate theatres with a patent under the Theatres Act of 1847. Still, according to his great champion, Max Beerbohm, Dan could miraculously fill the stage with the imaginary persons with whom he conversed. He never stepped outside himself, never imitated their voices; he merely repeated a few words of what they were supposed to have said before making his reply. Jimmy O'Dea worked in reverse to this—he was usually surrounded by a company of first-rate performers. Yet the only one one really saw was Jimmy. One was conscious of a great intelligence at work which drew one almost magnetically on to the stage with him. He was utterly unlike anyone you had ever seen or heard. He compelled attention and yet by some means he never revealed the method by which he conjured up laughter and invited everyone to share in the joke. Every member of the audience felt that he spoke directly to them and they were honoured to be the recipient of his quips and confidences. Gabriel Fallon described the experience as follows:

Whenever I see Jimmy before the footlights, he is for me all the stage all the time. Whenever he is not there the lights dim and passing events seem of little moment. Extravagant you will say. No doubt, but that's how it is. For me—and I don't care who knows it—Jimmy O'Dea is the greatest comic genius Ireland has produced in our time. Jimmy can press into one glance three minutes of legitimate acting to say nothing of ten lines of dialogue. But without personality, techniques and artistry go for nothing and Jimmy's personality possesses the indefinable quality of being sympathetic. See him in one sketch alone, "We Travel The Road," in which he is partnered by one of the finest actors we have in the Irish theatre—Denis Brennan. Yet, there is only one person on the stage—Jimmy. Watch him. Look at the infinite pathos he can get into the smoking of a "butt" as he portrays in the Irish mode all the mild, poor unfortunate little men that ever Charlie Chaplin shrugged his shoulders for. If it isn't genius, then I don't know what genius is.

Leno and O'Dea dealt with the comedy and pathos of ordinary people of no importance or consequence, seen from within. But that is not to say that they were without power. They had the inherited right of generations to challenge authority and bureaucracy and be content with exposing their injustice and stupidity with the only weapons at their disposal, contempt and ridicule. The recurring themes were "the two pair back"; "the pawnshop"; "the mother-in-law"; "the pub"; "the police"; "the lodger"; "disagreement over the marriage of a relative," and to use Montague's phrase "other such accessories to the life of the all-but-submerged" with such a compelling life-giving force that it was not repellent vulgarity but art.

Irish Smiles was such a success at Shepherd's Bush that the O'D company were booked to appear in excerpts from the show at the Stoll flagship, The Coliseum, in September. Here, as part of a variety bill, Jimmy shared top billing with José Collins, who made her reputation in *The Maid Of The Mountains,* Phyllis Neilson-Terry who appeared in a dramatic piece and Billy Bennett who was billed as "almost a gentleman" and delivered surrealist monologues. In the week before they played the Coliseum the O'D company were booked in a theatre in St Helens, Lancashire, and when they were packing up on Saturday night the stage manager asked them where they were playing on the following week. The Coliseum, they told him. He reminded them that there were lots of Coliseums and asked which one they meant. The London Coliseum, he was told. "Ee by gum!" said the Lancastrian "don't you wish you were."

Sir Oswald Stoll himself supervised the management of the Coliseum. He would prowl the promenades and corridors and pounce on any miscreant who might drop his cigar end on the carpet, enquiring fiercely if the vile offender would do likewise in his own home. Dressed in old-fashioned frock coat and top hat and wearing gold pince-nez, Stoll was an austere figure who neither drank or smoked. He was a pillar of respectability and sought to reflect this in his music halls. No drinks were sold in the Coliseum and notices in the dressing rooms warned against the use of strong language—coarseness and vulgarity were not allowed. He sought to inject a measure of culture into his halls and introduced classical singers and musicians; in 1912 he presented the Irish Players from the Abbey Theatre in JM Synge's *In The Shadow Of The Glen* as part of a variety bill. He was not a popular figure and his control of a large circuit gave him a stranglehold on the profession. He was able to exclude Marie Lloyd, the leading entertainer of her era, from the bill of the first Royal Command performance in July 1912 on the pretext that her material would be offensive to the ears of King George V and Queen Mary. His parsimony was legendary and it resulted in a fund of stories at his expense. The following told by Stanley Holloway was typical: Stoll lived at Putney and as he strolled home one evening he was accosted by a poor man selling matches and shoelaces.

"Buy a box of matches guv."

"Why?" said Stoll.

"Well, I've only taken tenpence all day."

"Really" said Stoll. "Tell me how does that compare with the same period last year?"

The O'D company excerpt from *Irish Smiles* was a sketch called "Mickey Breaks Into America" in which Jimmy as Michael Hegarty (a character who was to turn up in other sketches which suggest that Harry had early ideas of making him part of the O'Dea persona) gets in a fight as he leaves old Ireland and again on his landing at Ellis Island—the sketch was also known as "Mickey at Ellis Island."

Mr Wilson Disher described Jimmy as: "A little fiery fellow who has an expressive face and an intensity which lends itself to the caricaturing of melodramatic situations." The critic in *The Stage* reported: "Mr O'Dea, who has been called the Irish Dan Leno, has some claims to the title in point of view of style." A reporter from *Dublin Opinion* also saw the show and wrote: "What a splendid reception they got for their Ellis Island revelations." He went on to single out Tom Dunne for special mention in his role as an Italian immigrant.

They were rebooked for an early return to the Coliseum in November, when they presented a two-part sketch called "Mickey Tries Matrimony." In the first scene Mickey proposes to Connie Ryan, and in the second subtitled "The Legal Separation" the couple find married life trying. Between the two scenes Noel Purcell and Eileen Marmion performed one of their song and dance routines. Little Eileen was one of the hits of *Irish Smiles*, being described as a "captivating little artist who acts, sings and dances with charming ingenuousness," and Stoll, to his credit, saw to her comfort by ensuring that she had a dressing room complete with a large armchair to herself so that she could study her school subjects, as was required by law, in privacy.

They were exciting times in London theatreland in those days. Gracie Fields was topping the bill at what was then the number two hall, the Palladium, Charles

B. Cochran had three shows running including the first production of Noel Coward's *Bitter Sweet* with Sean O'Casey's wife, Eileen Carey, in the cast. Charlot's *Masquerade* with Beatrice Lillie was at the Cambridge; Sophie Tucker was at the Winter Garden, Pavlova was dancing at Streatham Hill, and Tallulah Bankhead was at the Lyric. In local music-halls all over London the old stalwarts were still holding their own—Nellie Wallace, Talbot O'Farrell, GH Elliott, Gertie Gitana, Ella Shields. There were some new faces too like Max Miller and an American act called George Burns and Gracie Allen.

The O'D tour of the Stoll circuit continued into the thirties and included most of the London halls and the principal provincial venues. At the end of September 1931 they made their first broadcast from the BBC. This was live from the stage of the Argyle, Birkenhead, which was unusual at that time because theatre managers generally were as wary of radio as they were of the cinema. DJ Clarke, however, realised the potential of radio as a form of advertising and the Argyle became one of the first music-halls to broadcast in the regions and even direct to the USA.

Dublin was not, of course, omitted from the company's itinerary and they made several trips home each year to present new revues and a Christmas pantomime at the Olympia before moving on to Cork, Limerick, Belfast and other Irish dates. Whenever Jimmy played a date outside his native Dublin he always cleverly associated himself with audiences in the venue. There were plenty of local references and he was always in sympathy with local characters, very often to the detriment of Dublin, which as the capital was good humouredly resented in say Cork or Belfast. In Belfast, naturally, the entire south could become the butt of his jokes. He used this technique, also, wherever he played English dates as is illustrated by a review in the *Waterford Newsletter:*

> Jimmy O'Dea is a very able comedian, with a distinct personality. He is small but very agile, and has a mirth

provoking face. A number of allusions to Waterford woven skilfully into his lines, give the show a very humorous local colour.

There seems little doubt that Jimmy preferred Irish audiences. Speaking to Joseph Holloway in Nassau Street in 1931 Jimmy told him:

The English only want women on the stage. The Irish audiences are really intelligent by comparison. It is a pleasure to play to them. One wants to know what they want and one soon finds out that they are the best judges in the end. When you come on stage you instinctively know what the audience in front expects, and if you give it to them they are delighted. An audience plays a big part in the success of a player; if you feel you haven't them with you, you can't give of your best. The player should never forget that he is the servant of the public.

Around this time he gave an interview to the *Daily Express* which reveals a business-like approach to his chosen profession. He told the reporter:

I'm a business man first, last and foremost. And I hate all this stuff about the art of revue and the art of the clown—it's all a bunch of junk! First learn the art of the box office and then you can afford to raise the eyebrows and talk about the art of it all. The Irish public enjoy revue, good revue with a bite in it. They like those stinging topical songs Harry turns out. They never get tired of them. There's plenty more revue needed here, and if I could get four other companies to alternate with mine we could run revue here (the Olympia) at a profit every week. In fact, it's my ambition to establish a permanent Irish revue in this theatre and with money, brains and equipment behind it there's no reason why it shouldn't be artistic as well. Oh, yes, I'm quite able to appreciate the art of the revue as well as anybody else, but you've got to

study your public first, gather your material, put a
kick into it, and get it across quickly with colour,
movement and pep. Never let an audience sit back
and think. You're there to amuse them, and you've
got to be definite about it. There's no time to be
vague in revue, or you'll be knocked down and killed
by scene-shifters.

As the reporter was leaving the stage door it was raining
hard and far down the lane queues of patient people
were waiting for the second house. "The art of the box
office?" said Mr O'Dea, looking forth into the night.
Luckily, as it happened, Jimmy didn't dissipate his
energies by dispersing them over too many projects. The
idea of having four other revue companies playing at the
Olympia would probably have been disastrous for the
simple reason that they wouldn't have had four other
Jimmy O'Deas to star in them.

He was at the height of his creative comic powers in
the thirties and was such a part of Dublin society
through his shows and records that he was a household
name—and his name was used in an ironic way. "You're
as funny as Jimmy O'Dea," was a popular rebuff; or the
Government or the Corporation, for instance, "was as
funny as Jimmy O'Dea."

When in 1936 Carreras tobacco issued cigarette cards
depicting Popular Personalities it was decided that the
first ten in the British series which dealt with the Royal
family would not be suitable for Ireland. They
substituted ten dealing with Irish sporting, political and
theatrical personalities. Number one in the English
series was King George V, and number one in the Irish
series was Jimmy O'Dea who was the king of Irish
comedy. Jimmy himself was humble and somewhat
surprised about his success and wasn't always too sure
about his ability to raise laughter. Even when he was
well established he confessed: "I wasn't aware that I was
funny until someone came up and said that I was. (This
must have been a recollection of Councillor Woods).

I think it was a help that I didn't know I was funny. In fact, I often think—am I funny myself?"

In June 1933 when the company was playing the Leicester Square Theatre with Cecil B de Mille's niece, Agnes de Mille (later a famous choreographer) on the same bill, it was announced that their agent was negotiating a deal for Jimmy to star in a new talkie in which he would be supported by members of the O'D company. It was probable that they couldn't start shooting until the end of the year as they were fully booked-up in variety. In fact, the film which was produced by Baxter and Barter wasn't released until 1935. John Baxter, who directed the the film, was a Christian Scientist non-drinker and non-smoker. He had been a theatrical touring manager and his continuing interest in the theatre and music-hall prompted him to film a number of show business stories featuring such famous variety acts as George Robey, Will Fyffe, Ella Shields and Bransby Williams at Sound City, Shepperton. He formed a partnership with John Barter and they worked at Cricklewood where Jimmy's film was made, with exteriors shot in Ireland. The film called *Jimmy Boy* was written by Con West and Harry O'Donovan and featured Guy Middleton, Enid Stamp-Taylor, Harry O'Donovan, Noel Purcell and Kathleen Drago. It was described by a trade paper as a film that attempted to do something with the comic talents of tiny O'Dea and is an account of the adventures in London of an undersized "boots" from Bantry Bay—first as a super in a film studio and later was a lift boy in a hotel. He becomes involved in a plot to keep a group of foreign spies from completing their plans to blow up London, a theme that Alfred Hitchcock was to use in his 1937 thriller *Sabotage*. The less ambitious *Jimmy Boy* which had its first Irish showing in January 1936 at the Corinthian was not a resounding success.

Chapter Six

Throughout the thirties Jimmy and Harry continued to present pantomime at the Olympia. Their show in 1930 was *Babes In The Woods* with Noel Purcell and Tom Dunne as the Robbers, Eileen Marmion and Vera Troy as the Babes and Jimmy as Nurse Dumpling. He was Idle Jack in *Dick Whittington* in the following year with Noel Purcell as Dame and former associate Ray Zack as principal boy. In 1932 the operatic singer, Flintoff Moore appeared in their revue, *Now Laugh,* and he was retained to appear in that year's pantomime *Cinderella* in which Jimmy appeared as Agnes, one of the Ugly Sisters. He played the title role in *Mother Goose* in the following year. Dick Forbes joined the company in 1934 in *Red Riding Hood* with Jimmy as Dame Mulligan. In the following year Noel Purcell was Dame Donegan in *Jack and the Beanstalk* and the fairy guarding the gate to the giant's castle was Maureen Potter, making her first appearance with the O'Dea company. Eire O'Reilly was the principal boy in their last Olympia panto in 1936 with Noel Purcell as Abdulla in *Ali Baba And The Forty Thieves,* Jimmy was Maggie Murphy and the cast also included JC Browner. The show was given a pre-Christmas premiere in Belfast which included a matinee and evening show on Christmas Day. The result was that the company had the unusual experience of having Christmas dinner between performances.

All of these shows had strong supporting casts drawn from the regular O'D company, including Charles

O'Reilly (formerly Charles L Keogh), Jimmy Wildman, Noel Allen, Lionel Day, Mollie Douglas and two troupes of dancers—the Odee Girls and the Odee Juveniles.

In addition to the pantomimes there were usually two or three revues each year and in April 1930 it is probable that Jimmy made his first stage appearance as Biddy Mulligan in a show called *Alive, Alive O!* The sketch was called "Mrs Mulligan In Court," subtitled "Widows are Wonderful," and it was recorded in the following June. The sketch seems to have been adapted from one called "Filling The Breach" in Harry's 1927 show *Dublin Pie* in which Joan Burke played Mrs McCarthy who was to become Mrs Mulligan.

The new management at the Gaiety Theatre headed by Louis Elliman was not unaware of the success of the O'D company, which could be relied upon to present a well-balanced and well-constructed show with scripts especially written to suit the talents of its star performer who know every nuance of the Irish character. So in 1937 Elliman offered the O'D company residency at the Gaiety to present a summer show during Horse Show week and the pantomime at Christmas. This appears with hindsight to have been a very astute move as the Second World War was not very far off and with it the availability of cross-channel performers was reduced to nil. Louis Elliman was the greatest impresario Ireland ever produced. Born in 1906, he was a member of a Dublin-Jewish family that had been associated with cinema and theatre since the beginning of the century. His father was Maurice Elliman, who had arrived in Dublin with very little money as a refugee from the Tsarist persecutions in Russia. Initially he ran various small ventures on his own, before establishing a cinema-seating business in Camden Street where his near neighbour, Noel Purcell's mother, took messages for him during his absences on business. He soon realised the potential of the early cinema and it was a short step from supplying seating to owning his own picture-house, the Theatre De Luxe which he opened in Camden Street. Louis graduated from the National

University and his father apprenticed him to a chemist in South Richmond Street where he worked for a number of years. Louis didn't particularly like his job and it was certain that he wouldn't make his fortune in it, so he went to London and became the agent for First National Films. His career in show business was under way. The Elliman family eventually controlled cinemas all over Ireland; Louis became managing director of Odeon (Ireland) Ltd and was chairman of various other groups. And it was he with a few others who brought to fruition the idea of an Irish film industry when Ardmore Studios, Bray were founded. Its subsequent chequered history is another story.

The Theatre Royal, Dublin, was rebuilt and opened on 23 September 1935. A richly lavish Moorish architectural scheme based on authentic details from the Alhambra at Granada in Spain had been adopted for the decoration of the auditorium. There were some concessions to sentiment and the new building incorporated some of the features of the old Royal which had opened in 1897. The new theatre employed John Compton, head of the great firm of organ builders, to build a magnificent Compton organ, and the orchestra pit was built on a special electric lift so that it could ascend to stage level at the touch of a button. When the Ellimans took over the Theatre Royal, one of the biggest and most advanced theatres in Europe, Louis made it comparable to the Palace Theatre, New York or the London Palladium; he engaged every world-class act visiting these islands and they often played the Royal before reaching the Palladium. Famous names like Tom Mix, Jimmy Durante, Gene Autry, George Formby, Danny Kaye, Judy Garland, Gracie Fields, Maurice Chevalier, Jeannette MacDonald, Betty Hutton, Bob Hope, James Cagney and many more graced the canopy of the Theatre Royal. In addition there were International Celebrity Concerts featuring the leading classical artists, musicians and orchestras. But "Mr Louis," as he was known to his colleagues and employees really came into his own when during the war years he kept both the Royal and Gaiety doors open with exclusively native talent.

The Theatre Royal shows which Elliman produced under the name TR Royle were really lavish productions worthy of any West End theatre. The shows were written by the clever Cork scriptwriter Dick Forbes who had to write a fresh script for each week. Forbes wrote what was possibly the best pantomime script ever seen in Dublin; this was *Mother Goose* which broke records at the Theatre Royal and was broadcast from Radio Éireann by the Radio Éireann Repertory Company years later after Forbes's death. His most popular creation was the weekly "Nedser and Nuala" sketches with Noel Purcell in the dame role of Nuala, a belligerent Dublin housewife, and Eddie Byrne as her scheming husband whose entrance through the doorway, each week, was a joy to behold— the movement was reminiscent of a snake curling itself around a tree. Their daughter Fionula was played by Pauline Forbes. Noel and Eddie were the resident stars at the Royal for the duration of the war and as in the case of Jimmy O'Dea their names were billed above the title of the show. The scripts had to be memorised each week—there might be several sketches, and Noel and Eddie would each have a solo spot in addition to appearing in scenes and ensembles. When the strain became too much Noel used to write his cues and responses on a blackboard which he placed strategically on top of the piano in the pit. The resident company supporting Noel and Eddie included singers Sean Mooney, a wonderful baritone in the Peter Dawson style, and Frankie Blowers, known as "Ireland's Bing Crosby." Robert Hennessy was a frequent performer, as were Michael Ripper and Norman Barrs. Seamus Forde stood in for Noel if the latter was occasionally indisposed. Other comedians were brought in on a regular basis to add to the fun, and audiences delighted in the parodies of "The Parody King," Cecil Sheridan; Harry Bailey and Jack Cruise were frequent visitors and Albert Sharpe appeared in the early shows before he went to New York. It was not unusual for May Devitt—a lovely soprano who at one stage in her early career did a double act with Peggy Dell—to appear in top hat and tails singing "Burlington Bertie from Bow," having spent the previous week in the Gaiety with the Dublin Grand Opera Society singing the lead in *Madam Butterfly*, but the music-hall songs were an aberration and her usual contribution at the Royal was in partnership with Joseph McLaughlin, with whom she sang popular duets. "Mr Louis" had an unerring sense for talent and, like many of his fellow artists at the Royal, Joseph McLaughlin was to find greater fame beyond Irish shores (using the stage name Josef Locke).

There were two troupes of dancers. The first, known as the Royalettes, had their routines choreographed by Alice Dalgarno and costumes designed by Babs de Monte. Alice and Babs devised a dance *scena* each week illustrating themes that might range from Dickens characters to a visualisation of songs like "Bantry Bay." They were very professional routines and greatly appreciated. The second troupe, the Royal Rockettes, were choreographed by Ivy Bourke, wife of Rick Bourke, who was then stage manager at the Queen's. The Rockettes did individual or ensemble routines but when the two troupes joined forces and spread across the stage in a high-kicking tap number it could be compared very favourably with Radio City music-hall in New York. Each troupe consisted of twelve attractive girls.

On occasion the resident company would be aug-mented by performers like Jack Doyle and Movita, or Jimmy O'Dea might be brought over from the Gaiety to join Noel Purcell in some of their early sketches like "Mine's A Pint" or "Seeing Him Off." Peggy Dell, another regular performer, suggested to "Mr Louis" that the format of a quiz show that she had seen in a film short in the Queen's, which ran short films between the first and second performances, might suit Eddie Byrne's talents as a compère, and so "Double or Nothing" (which had been called "Take it or Leave it" in the film version) was conceived. The rules of the quiz were simple—one's cash winnings were doubled as one progressively answered questions correctly but an incorrect answer meant that all was lost. When Eddie left the Royal with Noel to make films in Pinewood his role of compère was taken over by Eamonn Andrews. The famous musical director was the stylish Jimmy Campbell who was also an accomplished whistler—a fact that Jimmy O'Dea did not overlook when he did an impersonation of Campbell in a Gaiety show and arranged for earpiercing whistles to emanate from the stage as the apparent result of his own efforts. The huge Compton organ was used to provide a recital of popular music and to accompany community singing with the words flashed on the screen by means of glass slides; the organ was presided over in turn by Alban Chambers, A Gordon Spicer, Norman Metcalfe and George Rothwell, who was also musical director for a spell during a two year absence by Jimmy Campbell before he was replaced by Roy Fox. In addition to all this stage activity patrons were offered a good quality first-run film and the inclusive admission charge was a shilling (5p) in the afternoon, rising to 10p if one arrived after five o'clock. Noel Purcell claimed that on a cold winter's day it was cheaper to go to the Royal in the afternoon than light a fire. Patrons booked permanent seats for Sunday nights, and it was known for some to bequeath their seats to favoured relatives after their death.

"Mr Louis" set equally high standards for the Gaiety, which had been the cultural hub of Dublin society since it was opened by the Gunn brothers in November 1871. There was a very high standard of presentation at the Gaiety before the war, featuring the number one touring companies with original London stars and casts. Then Elliman, seeing that the Hilton Edwards and Micheál MacLiammóir Gate Theatre company were presenting plays which stood comparison with the best that had been staged in the Gaiety in the past, arranged that the Gate should give two seasons each year at the Gaiety. The Dublin Grand Opera Society (founded 1941) set a new high standard with entirely Irish casts and the best of Irish voices in the leading roles. The Rathmines and

Rathgar Musical Society (founded 1912) presented first class seasons of Gilbert and Sullivan, and two new amateur societies, the Dublin Musical Society and the Old Belvedere Musical and Dramatic Society, reached professional standards with productions of popular musical comedies.

Sometimes wearing his TR Royle hat, Louis Elliman produced shows in the Gaiety like *Showboat* which were lavish professional productions. *Showboat* starred May Devitt and Joseph McLaughlin (Josef Locke), and Eire O'Reilly stopped the show each night with her rendering of "Bill." "Mr Louis'" reputation of having an ear for talent was justified when he had a difficulty in casting the role of "Joe" and he discovered that one of his commissionaires in the Theatre Royal, Morgan Hayes, had a marvellous bass voice and gave a wonderful interpretation of "Old Man River."

A master at devising publicity campaigns for his stage productions, Louis Elliman was personally a very private and reserved man: he disliked giving interviews and being photographed. Many of his associates didn't even know that he played golf when on holidays and Jimmy's manager, Vernon Hayden, got a shock on a golf course one afternoon when "Mr Louis" emerged from a bush where he had landed himself in the rough. He died less than a year after Jimmy, on November 15, 1965 and hundreds of people from Irish and British show business attended his funeral. Although they were closely identified with the Jewish community the Elliman family were every bit as Dublinish as Dubliners themselves. Louis' showmanship was occasionally a little misplaced; on one occasion he stood with his lieutenants in evening dress in the foyer of the Royal waiting to receive the Archbishop of Dublin who was attending a performance of "The Messiah" and he turned to the manager of the Royal, the sharp-tongued Jimmy Sheil, to enquire if his bow tie, which unusually for that time was red, looked all right. Sheil informed him that he looked like the fuckin' crooner and Louis immediately hastened away to change to the conventional black bow.

O'D Productions' first venture at their new home was *Gaiety Revels*, so named because it was felt that it would attach them, in a personal way, to the theatre. Harry was to write:

Jimmy O'Dea's page in the history of the Gaiety came at a time when there was a break in that long continuity of famous people whose names had made this grand old building a tradition with the theatre-goer of Dublin. There were those that even scorned the suggestion that he should have a place in that hallowed book. But, if Dublin audiences
are somewhat conservative at time, and a little jealous of a tradition which their patronage has helped to build, they are too genuine as theatre-goers to hold on very long to a prejudice. So the regular patrons began to trickle back.

Revue had by this time abandoned all pretence to a storyline or theme; this meant, unlike the pattern in a variety show, that the star performer and his supporting cast worked right through the show in various sketches, song scenes and ensembles like "The Charladies' Ball" which ended the first half of *Gaiety Revels*. A popular sketch in the show was "Cinderella Three Ways" with Jimmy as Prince Charming; the three ways were illustrated as, Old Fashioned Way, The American Way and The Abbey Theatre Way. The show ran twice nightly and the supporting cast included Noel Purcell, Tom Dunne, Ray Zack, Peggy Stamula, May Tipple and Jimmy Wildman, with dances arranged by Connie and Michael Ryan. The show was produced as usual by Jimmy. In an article headed "Theatrical Record" the *Evening Herald* of 21 August 1937 reported:

Next week at the Gaiety Theatre Jimmy O'Dea and Harry O'Donovan will add a modern chapter to this house, so rich already in theatrical history, by being the first company to play one show for 48 consecutive performances in Dublin. This is a record for any

Dublin theatre, not only to have played for four weeks but to have done so successfully. The fact that 48,000 patrons paid to see "Gaiety Revels" in three weeks is the proof, amplified by the fact that forward booking plainly showed that a fourth week was indicated.

In the same month of August over at the Olympia, John MacDonagh revived one of his early shows, *Next Stop Dublin,* but this time he didn't have an O'Dea to play the avaricious landlady in the sketch "Our Visitors" and the show seems to have been notable only for the first appearance as musical director of Robert (Bobby) Bolton who was to be a popular figure for many years at the Olympia. Down in Pearse Street in Dublin's oldest theatre—built in 1829—of which Dr Cyril Cusack has written, "The Queen's...ah, sure the father and mother of a theatre," Cecil Sheridan, who had been first prize winner in a talent contest at the Whitehall Carnival, was given his first professional engagement as part of his prize. Cecil had a unique style that helped him to put over his clever parodies. Dressed in an old fashioned hearseman's overcoat and a flat cap, with hands concealed up the sleeves of his overcoat, he declaimed the marital horrors of a henpecked husband in a woebegone whine to hilarious effect. The following example of one of one of his parodies is to the air of "The Fleet's In:"

> She pawned the blanket, got the dough and drank it,
> Now the sheets in, the sheets in,
> The next she'll go for is the armchair and the sofa,
> Then the suites in.
> When she gets a couple of bob off to the Palais she'll
>   go,
> She calls it dancin'—I'd call it prancin', and oh, I've
>   seen her
> jitterbuggin.
> The kids are starvin', we haven't got a farthin' to get
>   meat in,
> She's always jazzin around the town,

We've got a family, and not countin' me, there's
    twenty three
walkin' around,
When we go on an outin' you'll hear people shoutin'
The Fleet's In Town!

Cecil broadened his horizons and developed a dame
character called Martha Mary Anne McGee who was
even broader then Cecil's horizons. But the character
was enormously successful when Sheridan became a top-
liner as resident comedian in Lorcan Bourke's variety
shows and pantomimes at the Olympia after the war and
he had to compete with cross-channel acts like Arthur
Askey, Ronald Frankau, Wilson, Keppel and Betty, Tessie
O'Shea and George Formby. Cecil had a caustic wit in
private life and never suffered fools gladly (one character
informed him airily that he lived on his wits, to which
Cecil replied it was no wonder he looked half dead) but
he was essentially a kind and caring man. He had a great
affection for a little hunchback called Mickser Reid and
he ensured the Mickser worked regularly in his shows by
writing special roles for him into the scripts.

Jimmy had a great respect for Cecil's work and at one
stage held the view that apart from himself, Cecil was
the only real professional in Dublin, by which he meant
a performer who knew the secret of projecting a comic
persona and had an inbuilt sense of timing. When there
were Sunday night charity shows in the Gaiety Jimmy
always invited Cecil to share number one dressing room
with him, an unusual honour for Jimmy to bestow, and
if he was not on the bill himself he left word with the
stage manager that Cecil was to be given the key to
number one.

1937 was an eventful year for Jimmy and Harry:
earlier in the year O'D Productions had embarked on
the production of their own film which was to be called
Blarney and turned out to be one of Jimmy's most
successful ventures into the film world. They were up
with the lark every morning and away to Dundalk by fast
car. There they spent the day filming before speeding

back to Dublin in the evening to be in time for the opening scene of *Gaiety Revels*. The film was written jointly by Harry and Jimmy and directed by Harry O'Donovan. The shooting title of the film was *Border Blarney*. It was shot on location around Carlingford, Ravensdale and Greenore and interiors were filmed in a concert hall in Dundalk which had been converted into a studio. The company was on location for about ten weeks and gave a useful boost to the local economy. The actual filming wasn't without its lighter moments— Harry was directing a couple walking through a field one morning when a very bad-tempered looking bull came charging into shot and heading straight for the camera; the entire crew fled in panic, leaving the camera running.

When the rushes were examined they were rewarded by some very strange scenic stuff—first, a charging bull, then vast expanses of sky followed by the tops of trees and bushes, and finally uninteresting clumps of grass. Harry was optimistic about this exclusively Irish undertaking: "I think the making of this film," he said, "is going to mark the beginning of a genuine producing unit in Ireland. From every viewpoint I see plenty of potentialities in our country for the creation of a successful film industry." How many times has that been said before—and since?

Blarney, which was titled *Ireland's Border Line* in the USA told the story of an itinerant salesman (Jimmy O'Dea) who inadvertently takes a suitcase full of stolen jewels in exchange for his own case of cough-cure samples. After his decision to take a job at an inn, the barmaid (Myrette Morven) throws the case into the dairy where it remains until the last few moments of the film. The police on both sides of the border become involved in the persons of an RUC Sergeant (Rodney Malcolmson) and the Civic Guard Sergeant (Noel Purcell) both of whom compete for the hand of the daughter (Hazel Hughes) of the local publican. The cast also included Tom Dunne and Jimmy Wildman in cameo roles as customers in the pub. The film opened in Dublin's leading first-run cinema, the Savoy, on 7 January 1938 and ran for a very successful three weeks until 20 January. The press was enthusiastic, and according to the *Saturday Evening Herald:*

> *Blarney* is an amiable comedy, and is one of the best produced films made in Ireland. The story is good and the photography perfect. It is a brilliant production.

The *Irish Press* reported:

> This is definitely a film that can compete with the farcing type for humour and plot. Great finale. Jimmy knocks down the border barrier at the end in effect to kiss the girl who gave him a job, a loft to sleep in and a loan of pyjamas. This film gives the industry in Ireland a better status than ever before.

The *Evening Mail* described Jimmy as: "...a pathetic little figure with a bowler hat reminiscent of Chaplin."

The *Irish Press* echoed this with: "His humour is of the Chaplin kind, helplessly wistful, yet cannily clever."

The *Monthly Film Bulletin* (of the British Film Institute) said:

> The local police are mere caricatures; the innkeeper's daughter is not a typical Irish beauty, the only attempt at real acting is made by Jimmy O'Dea and Myrette Morven. Julie Suedo and Ken Warrington make excellent crooks but have little to do. The scenery, country dancing, and Border explanations would have been better left to a purely documentary film.

It is possible that some of this advice may have been heeded because when the film was reissued in 1949, 25 minutes were cut from the running time.

It is said that in order to achieve success in films a basic requirement is that "the camera must like you."

Jimmy had no problems in that respect. As Billy Brannigan in *Blarney* Jimmy was a handsome figure and his goods looks were highlighted in the close-ups. He was, to use that much abused cliché, photogenic, and at times he bore a resemblance to his friend Micheál MacLiammóir, a fact that Jimmy exploited when he impersonated Micheál in Gaiety revues.

Harry's obsession with the border and partition, which one critic claimed was a blessing to the comedians of the North and the South, as any reference to it or the complications which arise from it is sure to fetch laughs from an Irish audience, paid off for O'D Productions, film-makers.

Meanwhile, at the Gaiety, following a tour of Ireland and England, the partners presented their first Gaiety pantomime, *Mother Goose,* based by Harry on the Hickory Wood version. Jimmy played Mother Goose—poor but contented. Albert Sharpe, who was to work with Jimmy years later in Hollywood, joined the company for the production. The following year continued what was to become an established pattern, broken only on rare occasions: a revue in Horse Show Week (*Gaiety Revels of 1938* in which Jimmy introduced Biddy Mulligan's daughter "Sweet Daffodil Mulligan" in song for the first time), and the panto at Christmas (*Cinderella* with Jimmy as Buttons and Ouida MacDermott as Prince Charming). More significantly the stage and film impresario Basil Dean, then head of Associated Talking Pictures, had seen Jimmy's work in *Blarney* and signed him to a contract to make films for ATP.

The first of these films was *Penny Paradise,* made in 1938 and directed by the young Carol Reed. It starred Jimmy O'Dea, Edmund Gwenn and Betty Driver, who later became a star in the TV soap opera *Coronation Street* as Betty, the soft-hearted barmaid. Harry O'Donovan's contribution to the film was to write the lyrics to the music of Harry Parr Davies. The film was based on a story suggested by producer Basil Dean who wanted a film set in his native Liverpool. Joe Higgins

(Edmund Gwenn) captain of a tugboat has one daughter, Betty (Betty Driver) and two ambitions—to become skipper of the *Mersey Queen,* the newest tug on the river, and to win the football pools. When he checks the results one Saturday night and he believes that he has achieved his second ambition he throws a hilarious party at the local pub and in the midst of the excitement caused by the turmoil between Higgins and Widow Clegg (Maire O'Neill) whom he is courting, and Betty's involvement with a young man who is after her for her money, recently acquired, Pat, Joe's mate, (Jimmy O'Dea) confesses that he forgot to post the coupon. All is not lost, however, for the resourceful Betty contrives that Joe's employers shall give Joe the coveted command of the *Mersey Queen,* worth more to him than money. The film was well received and the *Monthly Film Bulletin* reported:

> Good character-drawing, unaffected and telling dialogue, and many clever directorial touches help to make up the total excellent effect. The acting is good. Edmund Gwenn is quite at home in the part of Joe, and puts over a thoroughly sound and sympathetic performance. Jimmy O'Dea gives a neat and promising little character study as Pat.

Rachel Low, in her book *Film Making in 1930's Britain* writes:

> At the same time Carol Reed came back (to ATP) to direct an excellent small film about a Liverpool tugboat captain who mistakenly thinks he has won the football pools, *Penny Paradise.* Surprisingly realistic in its atmosphere and with the usual good acting, it starred north-country girl Betty Driver, a milder version of Gracie Fields, and an attractive little Irish comedian called Jimmy O'Dea.

The film was re-issued in 1948.

Harry wrote an original show for the Christmas

season 1939/40 called *Jimmy and the Leprechaun* and
since there was a large cast it was necessary to augment
the company, so they went to see a special performance
of the Jim Jonson Pantomime Company in Kilkenny.
The Jonson company toured Ireland all year round with
a full company of players including two dance troupes,
presenting pantomime each night, winter and summer,
which was an unusual but popular arrangement. The
company included Vernon Hayden, a young light
comedian who had been born in Somerset and first came
to Ireland with his mother's company "The Hayden
Family of Entertainers." Jimmy O'Dea and Harry made
Vernon and Jim Jonson and his wife Josie Day an offer
to join the O'D company in Dublin, which they
accepted. Jonson was to take over the role of Mick
Mulligan from Tom Dunne who, unfortunately, had had
a nervous breakdown. Tom was a dedicated performer
who overlooked no small detail in his comedy portrayals;
the larger details were rather more obvious, like the big
buckled leather belt he wore as Mulligan. On one
occasion he went to Jimmy to complain tearfully that the
wardrobe mistress Mollie Douglas had washed the
disreputable old shirt that he wore as Mick Mulligan,
and he couldn't somehow feel in character wearing a
clean shirt.

Vernon's position in the company was as a straight
man which, was, according to himself, a very hazardous
occupation: "Your timing had to be absolutely needle
sharp: you had to time the laughter from the audience
and let Jimmy go off script and ad lib when he wanted
to and then slowly bring him back; of course, Jimmy
O'Dea's timing was absolute perfection." O'Dea was
tyrannical with his cast on the subject of timing, which
was something that must have come instinctively to him.
"You must learn how to time a laugh," he would rage at
his accomplices. "A laugh rises and there's a big wave of
laughter but you don't wait for that wave to die: you
come in again as it is dying."

In the late forties Jimmy asked Vernon if he would

take over the management of the company for a fortnight. There had been several company managers including Walter Aubrey, DB Murphy and JC Browner. Vernon took over from Walter Ranken, not for two weeks, but nearly twenty years! *Jimmy and the Leprechaun* was to see the return of Maureen Potter, billed with her partner Maureen Flanagan as the "Two Maureens." The inevitable junior newcomer in the role of a fairy was, that year, little-eight-year old Ursula Doyle, who was destined to play another, but much bigger and more intimate role in Jimmy's life later on.

In the same year, ATP, which was now known as Ealing Studios, released two more O'Dea films, *Cheer, Boys, Cheer* and *Let's Be Famous,* both produced by Michael Balcon and directed by Walter Forde. *Cheer, Boys, Cheer* tells the story of rival breweries, Ironside's and Greenleaf's locked in a life-and-death struggle for monopoly. Matters become complicated when Greenleaf's daughter falls in love with Ironside's son, which results in the joining of the two breweries in partnership. The cast included Nova Pilbeam, Edmund Gwenn, Alexander Knox. It also featured Moore Marriott and Graham Moffatt who are best remembered for their films with Will Hay. *The Monthly Film Bulletin* of the British Film Institute said that:

> The best performance is given by Jimmy O'Dea as the Irish brewer at Greenleaf's who turns prohibitionist whenever he becomes drunk.

Rachael Low said that *Cheer, Boys ,Cheer* foreshadowed the ingenious and gently ironic post-war Ealing comedies. Expanding on this theme Charles Barr in his book *Ealing Studios* wrote:

> Asked to invent a typical Ealing comedy plot, one might produce something like this: a big brewery tries to absorb a small competitor, a family firm which

is celebrating its 150th anniversary. The offer is gallantly refused, whereupon the boss's son goes incognito from the big firm to infiltrate the small one and sabotage its fortunes. Gradually, he is charmed by the family brewery and by the daughter of the house, saves the company from ruin, and marries into it. Officials and workers unite at the wedding banquet to drink the couple's health in a specially created brew. To make this really Ealing, lay on the contrasts. The brewery names: Ironsides against Greenleaf. Grim offices and black limousines against country lanes, ivy covered cottages, horses, bicycles. Autocratic rule against the benevolent paternalism of a grey-haired old man who collects Toby Jugs. The beer itself: quantity against quality, machines against craftsmanship. The people and their manners: very harsh, very gentle. Small is beautiful. This, it will be guessed, is no invention. The film is called *Cheer, Boys, Cheer*, and Balcon produced it at Ealing in 1939. Whether we should call it an Ealing comedy is a nice academic point. It is a comedy made at Ealing, scripted by Roger MacDougal who, a decade later, would write the much more celebrated *The Man In The White Suit*; it may be less confusing to reserve the actual Ealing comedy label for the set of post-war comedies, that one included, to which historically it has been applied. But *Cheer, Boys, Cheer* is certainly a startling fore-runner, a reminder that those later films were not a sudden inspiration but had roots and precedents.

If *Cheer, Boys, Cheer* was the forerunner of a new genre of Ealing films, *Let's Be Famous* must have been one of the last of the old-style British comedies made popular by Gracie Fields and George Formby. It is significant that when Formby's contract with Ealing ran out in 1941 it was not renewed and he signed with Columbia whilst Ealing concentrated mainly on films with a war background.

Let's Be Famous opens in Ireland, and lest there be any doubt about this the opening shot comprises thatched cottages around which the art director liberally sprinkled jaunting cars and celtic crosses. Jimmy Houlihan, (no relation to Kathleen) played by Jimmy O'Dea, is the local general merchant and postmaster; he also fancies himself as a singer, and when he is recommended for a spelling-bee contest by a passing BBC official, a letter is wrongly drafted and he sets off for London under the impression that he is booked for a celebrity concert. On his train journey he meets Betty (Betty Driver) who has won a singing competition in a Northern theatre, a fact that she is trying to conceal from her father. Following Jimmy's disillusionment at Broadcasting House he meets an agent called Finch (Sonnie Hale) who contrives that Jimmy should appear on a sponsored programme on a Continental station. Unfortunately, they both get tight and lock themselves in the control room while the station is on air, and provide some tipsy hilarity using every possible sound effect available to give their impression of a shipyard working at full steam. As a result they are hired as comics by the advertiser who happens to be Betty's father. The songs (apart from Jimmy's rendering of "The Minstrel Boy") were by Noel Gay, and *The Monthly Film Bulletin* felt that:

> ...the actors were enjoying it even more than the audience...this unpretentious film provides laughs from beginning to end. Jimmy O'Dea and Sonnie Hale make a good team.

The late Leslie Halliwell in his book on comedians *Double Take And Fade Away* listed *Let's Be Famous* and *Darby O'Gill And The Little People* as Jimmy's best films.

Noel Purcell's last show with the O'Dea company at the Gaiety was *Gaiety Revels of 1940*. There had been an unresolved issue about salary and Noel just left quietly but he held no animosity against his old bosses and towards the end of his own life he spoke glowingly of

Jimmy: "He was very funny then," he said recalling their early days.

> To see the two of us together—me being six foot
> four and him five foot four was like looking at
> Goliath and Lester Piggot [trust Noel to make the
> racing simile]. I suppose we were all very funny then
> because we were young and were new in business.
> He was certainly a breath of fresh air to the people
> in England; they never saw the likes of this little
> fellow. He was a good companion in many ways, but
> he was a lonely little fellow and I liked him. He was
> certainly very good to me and we never had a row,
> although I should have had a row with him a couple
> of times.

At a Variety Club luncheon in Jimmy's honour in April 1964, Noel, with his snow-white beard hiding the microphone, said: "Through that famous man—and my old friend and best man at my wedding, Harry O'Donovan—I am successful." Noel went on to speak about the day in 1929 when they gave him his first break—and £8 per week. "Oh boys and girls, that was a great day for me; that time £8 was a lot of coconuts. I was in the gold mining business and for that I thank Harry and Jimmy." Chris Markey joined the company around this time and acted mainly as stooge to Jimmy. An inoffensive man, Chris got fed up after several years of being thumped by Jimmy. He never intended to hurt but it was said that his hands were so hard that a simple slap from him was almost the equivalent of a punch from a boxer. So Chris left giving as his opinion that "O'Dea was worse than Hitler!"

In October, Jimmy appeared in Shakespeare (the unfulfilled dream of Dan Leno). Hilton Edwards and Micheál MacLiammóir offered him the role of Bottom the weaver in their Gaiety production of *A Midsummer Night's Dream*. Jimmy accepted and his performance was acclaimed unanimously as a success. *The Irish Times* critic on Tuesday, October 29, 1940 wrote:

The choice of Jimmy O'Dea for the part of Bottom was, however, the producer's major stroke, not so much of good luck, perhaps, as of genius. For it seemed the most natural thing in the world to see our popular comedian playing it. Have we not seen him and loved him so often already in his own productions, as the little man who is always ready to undertake anything and everything as a matter of course, conceited, serious and fantastical? It seems almost too little to say that he was excellent. A modern dress effect, perhaps, on Shakespeare, but we can conceive of Shakespeare being hard put to it to find as good a local comedian for the part in his own day.

There was, of course, a dissenting note. Joseph Holloway writing in his diaries noted:

The only jarring note to me at all events was Jimmy O'Dea's Dublin accent, laid on thick for Bottom the weaver. (I usually see red when I hear Shakespeare spoken with a marked accent.) Only I had no breath to hiss with effect, I would have done so after his first scene in the piece. He otherwise played the role with drollery, with a too great abundance of exaggeration in performance. I refer particularly to the over-repetition of the same phrase. The audience liked O'Dea and the company and Hilton Edwards made much of him. The latter in an after-play speech said: "O'Dea is the greatest comedian that Ireland has given to the stage of our time, and a fine legitimate actor as well." And O'Dea took the special call at the end of the play also. He certainly was put on a pedestal by the company.

Holloway must have conveyed his displeasure about Jimmy's Dublin accent to Jimmy himself because on Friday, 1 November he received the following tongue-in-cheek reply:

Gaiety Theatre,
Dublin.
31 October, 1940

Dear Mr Holloway,
   Thanks ever so much for your kind letter received yesterday, and it is very pleasant for me to note that you took a deep interest in my efforts at Shakespeare. I will try to clean up my accent for my next attempt at straight plays. Thanking you again for your welcome letter.

Yours very sincerely,
JIMMY O'DEA

The memory of Jimmy's delivery of Bottom's speech when he awakes from the dream remained with one young member of the Gate company, Dermot Tuohy, for the rest of his life:

BOTTOM: I have had a most rare vision. I have had a dream, past the wit of man to say what dream it was: man is but an ass, if he goes about to expound this dream ...

Jimmy gave the speech with a great sense of wonderment and as Dermot said: "... it was absolutely spellbinding—and I was on the stage with him!"

   Gabriel Fallon, writing on Vaudeville technique, said:

The technique of acting in a revue to a vaudeville audience is of a harder and generally a finer kind than is needed for acting in a theatre. Jimmy possesses this technique in full measure. His early experience as an actor has been widened and deepened and made much more susceptible to the necessity for economy in the player's art, with the result that when he returned to the legitimate stage to play Bottom for Edwards and MacLiammóir, he practically laid waste *A Midsummer Night's Dream,* playing a bevy of first rate actors clean off the stage.

In view of Jimmy's success with the Gate company it seems, in retrospect, a pity that the Rathmines and Rathgar Musical Society did not invite him to play Jack Point in *The Yeomen Of The Guard*. In later years he joined the Gate company once more as guest star in the cameo role of Banjo, a Hollywood comedian, in a revival at the Gaiety of *The Man Who Came to Dinner* with Hilton Edwards as Sheridan Whiteside (based on the American journalist and wit Alexander Woolcott) and Micheál MacLiammóir as Beverley Carlton (a portrait of Noel Coward).

O'D Productions made a big break with established custom during the panto season 1940/41 when they abandoned the basis on which their success had been established, "twice nightly," and took what was at the time the dangerous theatrical risk of going "once nightly." The change of policy was an immediate success and the pantomime *Babes In The Wood* was more profitable than any pantomime for forty years. The babes were played by Maureen Potter and Maureen Flanagan, the principal dancer was Mary Poswolsky and Jimmy was Nurse Mayo. Any doubts that may have lingered about the new policy were dispelled when the new Horse Show Week revue, *So What* (reputedly, according to its cast, the most satisfying and best balanced show ever devised by O'D Productions), was most reluctantly taken off after nine weeks due to other commitments.

In the same year, 1941, Jimmy's mother, Martha died, aged 73.

Chapter Seven

In 1941 the British Broadcasting Corporation considered the idea of broadcasting an Irish review-of-events type of programme which would be of interest to Irishmen serving in His Majesty's forces and the thousands of Irish workers employed all over Britain. This format was abandoned and instead it was decided to invite Jimmy O'Dea and John Count McCormack to star in a light entertainment programme called *Irish Half Hour*. The first in the series was broadcast on Saturday, 15 November, 1941 with O'Dea and McCormack being featured on alternate weeks.

From the beginning, there was resistance to this programme from the Northern Ireland government. In July, their representative in Britain, EP Northwood, wrote to BE Nicholls, Controller of Programmes:

Dear Mr Nicholls,
    In thanking you for your letter of the 15th instant, I am directed to emphasise that our sole anxiety is that Northern Ireland, (which is in the United Kingdom and at War), should not be associated with Eire, (a neutral sovereign country), in the forthcoming Irish broadcast. If the BBC wishes to arrange broadcasts relating to Eire, it is, of course, no business of ours but I am sure you will agree that, especially perhaps in present circumstances, we should have cause for resentment if Northern Ireland were detached from the United Kingdom and linked in any shape or form with such broadcasts.

In September, John M. Andrews wrote from Stormont Castle to G L Marshall OBE, Director of BBC Northern Ireland:

> My dear Marshall,
>
> With reference to the two questions which you put to me this morning, I feel that I must answer them very frankly.
>
> In the first place, I cannot understand what is the underlying aim to be achieved by broadcasts on the lines suggested and particularly by including in them greetings in Erse which is a language expressive of separatism. I have no hesitation in saying that there would be considerable resentment in Northern Ireland if Erse were spoken during the broadcasts. It occurs to me also to mention that, as I understand these programmes are intended for loyal Irishmen in the British Forces, I cannot see why greetings should be given in a language which is so little understood.
>
> My view is that the Ministry of Information's aim should be to endeavour to produce a public feeling in Eire in favour of the Allied cause as opposed to the present anti-British attitude. I feel that the policy which the Ministry now seems to be adopting will be taken as weakness and to mean that Britain recognises that Eire is justified in maintaining her policy of independence and of opposition to the British Empire.
>
> I hope that the Ministry will reconsider the whole position.

Despite all this sniping the programmes went ahead as planned and were broadcast live (at first) from Bangor in Wales where the BBC had centred many of its programmes, including the famous Tommy Handley show *ITMA,* in order to escape the blitz on London. In Bangor Jimmy made a pretence of playing golf but rarely got out of the clubhouse. One of his drinking pals was Arthur Lucan who was also doing a live series from Bangor. It was Lucan's custom to put on the full dress and make-up of Old Mother Riley for the benefit of the live audience attending the broadcast of his show, but one evening he refused point blank to do this, having been filled with enough spirit in Jimmy's company to stand up to his bullying wife and stage partner, Kitty McShane. She was furious and accused him of drinking with "that other pouf" Jimmy O'Dea at the golf course. This was an ironic description of Jimmy who for a great part of his life was said, in Dublin to be the father of various imaginary small boys—always boys—who were invariably unbelievably witty and the spitting image of him. Jimmy wasn't the only prominent figure to be the victim of this sort of gossip in Dublin, and there is reason to believe that it was generally spread by jealous rivals or by those who just didn't like the victim. Jimmy never had any family but he did have one natural child— not a boy as the gossips maintained—but a girl.

Irish Half Hour was a success from the start with everyone but the authorities in Northern Ireland. The show was presented by Pat Hillyard and Francis Worsley and featured the BBC Variety Orchestra conducted by Charles Shadwell. The scripts were by Harry O'Donovan with occasional collaborators like Ted Kavanagh (who had written *ITMA*), Dick Forbes (resident script-writer at the Theatre Royal), Jack White and Robert MacDermot. The following extract by O'Donovan and Kavanagh was transmitted on Friday 15 May 1942 from 8.30-9.00 p.m. and featured Cavan O'Connor, Harry O'Donovan, Joe Linnane and Peggy Dell with Maye Tipple, Horace Percival, and Sydney Keith.

After the signature tune, "Rory O'Moore" Joe Linnane introduced the programme and listed the cast.

JOE: ... And they're all waiting to meet you in the thriving Irish metropolis of Ballygobackwards where we may even find Jimmy waiting to welcome us on the railway platform with a yard of red carpet. It's just a short journey so take your seats please; all aboard and we're off to Ballygobackwards and our Irish Half Hour. (Train effects; music)

VOICES OF
PASSENGERS: Porter, where's the station-master? (Etc. etc.)

HORACE: I say, you there. Unlock this carriage, will you?

JOE: I've nothing to do with your old train.

PEGGY DELL: Then who *is* in charge of this station?

JOE: Jimmy O'Dea, of course.

CAVAN: (Away) Jimmy O'Dea.

SYDNEY: (Away) Jimmy O'Dea.

HORACE: (Away) Jimmy O'Dea.
(Applause)

PEGGY: What kept you, Station-master?

JIMMY: I couldn't get a platform ticket. I put me money in the wrong slot and all I got out was a card saying I weighed seven stone nine and I had to be careful of a dark woman that was fond of children.

JOE: You should be on the platform to meet the train, Jimmy. What would happen if the train didn't stop?

JIMMY: The same as always happens. We lose a lot of trains that way. Come on—out yeh get, the whole lot o' ye. You can't be turning the train into a waitin' room.

HORACE: I say, Station-master, this train is half an hour early.

JIMMY: Yer wrong—it's eleven and a half hours late.

HORACE: I'm going by English summer time.

JIMMY: Well, it isn't summer yet, and this isn't England.

HORACE: But don't you put your clocks on?

JIMMY: I'll turn your clock back if you don't stop arguin' and it's more than your ticket I'll punch.

HORACE: That's a nice way to talk to a stranger.

JIMMY: Oh, it'll be worse when I know you better.

PEGGY: Can you recommend us a good hotel?

JIMMY: Sure I can. The O'Hooey Arms.

PEGGY: Is that the best place?

JIMMY:	It's the only place. It's all hooey—and no arms.
HORACE:	Damn good. I say, is there much fish around here?
JIMMY:	Fish is it? There's enough oul' cods in Ballygobackwards to stock the North Sea. Sure, yeh can't bate our fish.
HORACE:	What kind of bait do you use?
JIMMY:	One rod, pole or perch. Any more questions?
PEGGY:	How do I get to the hotel?
JIMMY:	To the Hole-In-The-Wall?
PEGGY:	No—the O'Hooey Arms.
JIMMY:	It's the same place. There's a taxi outside with no petrol. It's got a balloon on top, but that doesn't go up either. I'll tell you what I'll do, miss. I'll take your luggage—leave it to me. It'll be delivered by COD. Glory be by OD.
SYDNEY:	Say, Station-master, is there anyone living here named Murphy?
JIMMY:	Moify? Yeh mean Murphy?
SYDNEY:	I'm from the States, and I've come to look for my ancestors named Murphy.
JIMMY:	There's a hundred and forty-six Murphys in Ballygobackwards sir. It's a quare thing if you can't find an ancestor among them. Are you an American?
SYDNEY:	Yeh. Silas J. Murphy.
JIMMY:	Murphy. That's a real American name. Is there some money coming to them?
SYDNEY:	There is.
JIMMY:	Then there'll be *two* hundred and forty-six Murphys or I'm no judge. By the way—I'm a Murphy myself.
SYDNEY:	But your name's O'Dea
JIMMY:	I'm a cousin twice removed—once by the landlord and once by the police.
SYDNEY:	Say, I must look up your family tree.
JIMMY:	If you look high enough you'll find some of me ancestors hangin on it.

SYDNEY:	The more the better. Be seein' yeh, son. So long.
JOE(AS PAT):	Eh...Jemmy
JIMMY:	Ssh! Don't be callin' me Jemmy in front of all the swell passengers. Can't you see I have me scap on?
JOE:	Then put on your porter's cap me son. I have four goats in a first class compartment, for Doherty of the Cross.
JIMMY:	What d'ye mean, puttin' them animals in there? I'm tired tellin' you—goats have to travel *second* class.
JOE:	There's two cases of whiskey for Cork.
JIMMY:	Is there any bottles missing?
JOE:	No.
JIMMY:	Then take a couple out—don't be givin' them a bad habit.
MAYE:	Oh, Station-master, is this the up-platform now?
JIMMY:	Sufferin' Duck! Where are you goin'?
MAYE:	To Dublin.
JIMMY:	All right then. The down-train from Cork comes in on the up-platform so if you're goin' up to Dublin you go down on the up...ah don't be annoyin' me.
MAYE:	Is the local going to Tipperary today?
JIMMY:	If we have a few lumps of coal to start it, it might go, and then...it might not. There it is over there and if it ever starts it'll ruin me rhubarb.
MAYE:	Can I put my two prize bulls on it?
JIMMY:	Prize bulls on it? Woman dear, we had to take two Pekineezy pups off it last week before it would take the hill into Thurles. Eh, Larry boy. How is the Flyer today?
HARRY:	She's taken a turn for the worse, sir. She'll only go backwards now—and her back is facin' the wrong way for Tipperary.
MAYE:	I say! There are two trains coming together. Up and down.

JIMMY:	Put 'em on the turntable—
	(Effects: Train in distance)
	Holy smokes! Larry, get the Flyer off that line at once.
HARRY:	There's not enough coal in the box.
JIMMY:	Throw in a few chairs out of the Ladies' Waiting Room.
HARRY:	I used them for the Cattle Dealers' Annual Outing last Sunday.
JIMMY:	Sweet luck. What'll we do?
MAYE:	Haven't you a red flag in the office?
JIMMY:	I have but it's a green one. If I used a red flag I'd be insultin' the bulls.
	(Sudden wheezing and squealing and popping etc. as the Flyer starts)
JOE:	Larry, has the Flyer started?
JIMMY:	Good boy, Larry.
	(Crash)
MAYE:	You can't do that. My Aunt Fanny is in that train and she's going to Tipperary.
JIMMY:	Yer wrong Ma'am. She's goin' backwards to Killarney.
	(Two trains rush through; the Flyer squeals out)

This is the first segment of the show which is slightly reminiscent of *A Minute's Wait* (which Jimmy filmed years later) and an early gramophone record called "The Next Train" (Dominion Records). The next scene was set in the General Store, Peggy Dell and Cavan O'Connor each contributed a song and the Half Hour ended with Jimmy O'Dea in a bar scene as one of his Dame characters, Carmel Cassidy.

In March 1942, following the first broadcasts of the series, it was the opinion of the Dominions Office and of the Ministry of Information, that *Irish Half Hour* had a high propaganda value and should be resumed as quickly as possible. The programme appealed not only to 100,000 citizens of Eire who were members of HM Forces but also to Irish workers in England who numbered over 50,000 permanently employed there and about 9,000 migratory labourers. It was agreed that the programme might contain more Gaelic items but the suggestion that it should be called *Eire Half Hour* was rejected. The idea behind *Eire Half Hour* arose out of the objections in Northern Ireland to references to Eire as Ireland. Eire, it was claimed was the official name for the twenty-six counties, and as the programme was intended for loyalists in the British Forces whose homes were in Eire and not Northern Ireland, it should be given the correct title. (The use of the term "loyalists" was a bit strong, and no one seems to have realised that most of the men joined up for economic rather than political reasons.) The Northern authorities also objected to the use of "The Minstrel Boy" as a signature tune as it was not universally approved in Northern Ireland, several comments having been made "that the boy had not gone to war!" BE Nicholls, in a memo dated 12 January 1942, wrote:

> This was considered at Control Board on Friday and it was agreed that we could continue to use the adjective "Irish," but must drop the word "Ireland" and substitute "Eire." I imagine, therefore, that you will drop such references altogether, as Eire is scarcely a romantic word and does not bring tears to the eyes like the mention of "Ould Ireland." Of course, you need not edit songs about shamrocks and little bits of heaven, which may have the word Ireland somewhere in them. I do suggest your keeping Barbara Mullen if possible, whether Irish listeners consider her "phoney" or not. She certainly has the promise of being a first-class radio personality.

The problem at home was that half of the potential listenership, unaware of all the hair-splitting elsewhere, could not receive the programme at all. In the days before rural electrification radio enthusiasts depended upon battery-powered receivers for which very often they could not obtain batteries. This was highlighted in a letter to BE Nicholls from the British Ministry of Information, Mount Street, Dublin. It was written by the poet John Betjeman who liked music-hall and performers like Jimmy O'Dea, but his particular favourite was Max Miller.

> Dear Nicholls,
>   I am sorry to hear that the *Irish Half Hour* will be shut down during February and March. There has certainly been a lot of comment about it, some adverse from extreme nationalists who expect Irish folk songs à la Delia Murphy with plenty of Gaelic interspersed, and others more commendatory from people who enjoyed particularly Jimmy O'Dea and McCormack. The fact that there has been a good deal of comment shows that people have begun to listen, and I think there is no doubt that the programme has begun to have its effect. But when we are reduced over here to only half the normal listeners owing to a shortage of zinc for dry batteries (my letter to Doctor Mansergh of January 16th of which you have a copy) it halves the usefulness of what you are doing.

This letter was defaced by Betjeman in three places with the boldly written slogan: Get More Zinc For Eire! The general policy of fostering goodwill between the people of Eire and of the United Kingdom by wireless programmes had the full support both of the Ministry of Information in London and of the Dominions Office.

Jimmy was heard on radio in *Henry Hall's Guest Night* in November 1942, a programme that drew a rocket from the Director of Variety to the Programme Director in Birmingham:

> It was reported that the last five minutes of this was a blatant advertisement for drink and pubs, and considerable objection was taken to this. I did not hear the programme, so could not comment.
>   WK Stanton.

The spirit of Lord Reith was still, apparently, stalking the corridors of the BBC but less effectively than heretofore to judge from the reply to the above memo:

> I do not think the criticism of *Irish Half Hour* is justified, as the famous character—Carmel Cassidy—which Jimmy O'Dea plays is a barmaid and certain side-references to drink are inevitable. None of the Carmel sketches could be termed advertisements for drink—rather the reverse if one goes deeply into the matter. One of the characters in this sketch is a typical Dublin bar-scrounger who is always trying to beg a drink and never gets one—what could be more moral?
>
> John Watt.

The series continued into 1943 with the introduction of Mrs Mulligan. In May of that year the show was called *Monday at Mulligan's* but when the broadcasting schedule was altered in November, it became *Friday at Mulligan's*. In addition Jimmy was making separate appearances in programmes like *Round the Halls*, *Workers Playtime* and *Music-Hall*. Despite the difficulty of finding the time to do so, a new series called *Over To Mulligan's* was recorded in Belfast in 1944. To quote Harry: "We go on tour after the Panto, as there is loads of money for us just now in the country."

Pat Hillyard, Assistant Director of Variety, wrote to Jimmy in October, 1944:

> As no doubt you know, the series is now being re-broadcast on the General Forces Programme and on shortwave, and as well as this it was carried by the AEFP broadcast to the forces in Western Europe— in fact, I don't think there's a corner of the globe in which the dulcet tones of J O'Dea are not being heard.

However, relations between Harry and Jimmy were not good. Harry wrote to Pat Hillyard just after Christmas in 1944:

My Dear Pat,

I wrote to you some time ago re Jimmy when I told you I had given him notice of termination of partnership. Since then he has had a bad attack of the usual complaint [liver]. It happened on the first day of rehearsal and put me in a bad spot. However, I had anticipated something of the kind and had an understudy standing by. He is a chap called Wilfred Brambell and has made quite a hit. The panto is launched and business doing as good as usual and advance booking splendid. Jimmy will be able to go into the show in about three weeks or so, which will give it a good fillip for the latter half of the season. He *must* now go off "The Hard Tack" and we hope has got a lesson. I don't know exactly how bad the damage is, but he had a lot of bleeding and was in a serious condition for a week.

Regarding another Half Hour. I mentioned that, in any circumstances relating to our association, we could still do a series. If we are parted we could be engaged separately. We have dropped the question of parting for the moment but I am really a bit tired of being pushed about and given all kinds of unnecessary worries and I feel I am going to make the break. Perhaps you would drop a line and let me know what you think about it.

Pat Hillyard in his reply did not mention the pending breakup, but broached the subject of a new series to be recorded in either London or Belfast, as if nothing had happened between the partners.

By mid-January, Jimmy was back in the Gaiety, taking over the role of Buttons in *Cinderella* from Wilfred Brambell, who would later achieve fame as the old rag and bone man in *Steptoe and Son*. Harry wrote to Pat Hillyard again to say that he had cancelled his notice to end the partnership. and that the new series would have to be recorded in Belfast as Jimmy's doctor had advised that he must not chance sea journeys or put himself in the way of shocks for at least a year. *Over To Mulligan's* ran for two seasons in 1944/45 and were produced by James R Mageean in Belfast. The old stalwart of the show, Joe Linnane, played Mick Mulligan; Joe was a firm favourite on Radio Éireann during the war years and few listeners neglected to tune in to his quiz show *Question Time* every Sunday night. He was also a well respected Abbey actor remembered for his performance as The Covey in *The Plough and the Stars*.

The *Irish Half Hour* series under its various subtitles was universally popular. Stanley Jackson writing in *London Opinion* said:

> Jimmy is a great favourite with radio audiences and it's not difficult to understand why. (The same cannot be said for certain other comedians who imagine that an Irish brogue and a cracked baritone are a sufficient passport to the undying affection of listeners.) Jimmy O'Dea would still be a great music-hall and radio star if he were Yankee or Yid. His native Irish brand of comedy just happens to suit all his other gifts. His technique is first-class. Endowed with the gusto of Leonard Henry, the verbosity of Tommy Handley and a line of pleasing blarney that is all his own, his appeal is direct and complete. His vitality belongs to the music-hall of yesterday—and that is meant as a tribute. Jimmy doesn't need technicolour, Etonian comperes, diamond-studded mikes, a dance orchestra and a bevy of undressed young ladies to put his turn across. Take his act to bits and you will see that what makes it tick is real versatile talent, garnished with natural charm. Like all good comedians his timing of repartee is excellent. "Have you started sharing a bath with your neighbour?" he is asked. [A reference to war-time restrictions.] "Yes," says James, "But he talks politics and the water gets cold." There is art in his rapid changes of mood. One moment he is full of blarney. Do you recall the occasion when he referred to Miss Patricia Burke as "that smashing bit of skirt." The lovely Pat ticks him off with mock hauteur. "I was

only expressing my admiration in me own rough way," says Jimmy in a voice that would turn the Gestapo sentimental. But in a second his voice is angry and vibrates with rich indignation. "I've heard that actors are barmy," he says, "but you're definitely obtuse." Yet when you've taken into account his cracks, his gusto and his brogue you've still missed the essence of O'Dea. He is a fine actor and an ace of burlesque. He knocks off characterisations like Mrs Mulligan or Carmel Cassidy with ridiculous ease.

Jimmy remained as popular as ever at his home base in the Gaiety, where he continued to do the August show and the panto at Christmas. He was Carmel Cassidy in *Hansel and Gretel* in 1941 with May Devitt as principal boy, a role she repeated in the following year in *The Ace Of Queens* with Jimmy again as dame. The O'D company continued to attract the most talented supporting casts and their excellence extended also to the technical side of the productions. The decor for the August 1943 revue, *Laughter at Eight,* was by Louis Le Brocquy who also designed the special costumes for *Robinson Crusoe* the panto that year, with Jimmy as Maggie Crusoe. Unfortunately, nothing survives of Le Brocquy's work for O'D Productions.

Jimmy joined the cast of *Cinderella* as Buttons half-way through the run in 1944 and in the following year he was Jimmy the Wanderer in *Goody Two Shoes*—a plumber turned bullfighter with a bull called Banjax. Maisie Weldon, daughter of the old-time comedian Harry Weldon, star of the Fred Kerno company, was principal boy. Jimmy's material always included some topical impersonation: Veronica Lake was a popular film star of the period with a famous hairstyle and Jimmy transformed her into "Veronica Cassidy," complete with cascade of blond hair covering one eye.

Three more series of *Irish Half Hour* were recorded between 1946 and 1948 at the Aeolian Hall, Bond Street, London with the sub-titles *At the Mulligan Inn* (1946), *Merry Ireland* (1947) and *The Mulligan Menage*

(1948). The cast list had by this time included Maureen Potter, Vernon Hayden, George Arnett (who was appearing with the others in the Gaiety shows) and singers May Devitt, Stephen Black and Maurice Keary. Cyril Cusack had also appeared in some of the earlier Belfast recordings. Immediately after the war O'D Productions resumed touring in the UK and broke with Gaiety Theatre tradition by appearing in pantomime at the Empire Theatre Liverpool in 1946. It was a Tom Arnold production of *Queen of Hearts* and starred Jimmy in the title role with Evelyn Laye as principal boy and the Irish singer Jack Daly as the King; the cast also included Vernon Hayden, Frank Lawton and Maureen Potter. The scenery and costumes were really lavish and the show was produced by Robert Nesbitt. The reason for this unusual change of venue is not immediately apparent—the O'D company had been touring for Tom Arnold and when he offered them the Liverpool pantomime date it is possible that Jimmy and Harry in consultation with Louis Elliman decided that after the unbroken spell of wartime appearances at the Gaiety it might be a good idea to give their Dublin audiences a change of faces. After the Liverpool show there followed a tour of England which lasted from April to November. The revue which included in the cast Ted Ray and Peter and Mary Honri began as *Beauty and Blarney* but such was the advertising power of radio that it was found profitable to mention the name of Mulligan so the show was re-titled *Mrs Mulligan's Blarney* and later *Mrs Mulligan's Party*.

Touring has always been a rootless way of living, visiting a different town or city and a different theatre (not to mention a different type of audience) every week. There is a story that Harry Bailey, who was playing some English town in the 50s, was misinformed about the death of Jimmy O'Dea. He sent a telegram to the Gaiety management to the effect that he was saddened by the news of O'Dea's death. This was the cause of much merriment in the Gaiety Circle bar that evening, which culminated in a telegram from Jimmy to

Harry Bailey which read: "The only place that O'Dea ever died was in Barnsley."

Travelling was done on Sundays and no matter what the final destination might be there always seemed to be a change at Crewe. There every Sunday theatrical companies from all over England met on the station platform and old friends exchanged the latest news and gossip. Asked on one occasion for his impressions of these Sunday gatherings on Crewe station, Ted Ray said that his overall impression was one of "actors and fish." Each company was given its own carriage in the train and had the special concession of travelling at reduced fare. The name of their production was displayed on a sticker on the carriage window and in addition a goods wagon was allocated to carry the scenery, costumes and props in the ratio of one wagon to every twenty members of a company. The carriages were of the old style design and the seating was extremely comfortable while the steam-driven engines had no difficulty in heating the carriages in cold weather. Arriving at their destination at some time on Sunday evening the company would set about finding digs; this was no problem if the performers had played the date on a previous occasion but for the uninitiated there were recommended addresses in a booklet provided by the Actors Church Union which was a great help in finding suitable lodgings. Generally, Jimmy liked to share digs with some members of his company whom he referred to as "my people."

Artists usually have stories, humorous and horrendous, about theatrical landladies and Jimmy was no exception. In one English city which they happened to be playing during Holy Week, Jimmy reminded the landlady that the coming Wednesday was Ash Wednesday and assumed that the good lady would be aware that for Catholics this would be associated with a fish lunch and two collations. Imagine the surprise when on Wednesday there emanated from the kitchen the most glorious aroma of meat which the landlady placed before them in the form of a delicious stew with beautiful pieces of steak in a mouth-watering sauce. "But we can't eat this," said Jimmy weakly, "I told you this is Ash Wednesday."

"Yes I know dear," replied the lady "And that's what I've cooked for you—my savoury 'ash!"

On Monday mornings there was a band-call at the theatre attended by the entire company when all the music and lighting cues were sorted out. The company manager usually met with the local rail official to arrange for special concession tickets for the journey to the next engagement on the following Sunday. With luck the show would run smoothly for the week once the hurdle of first-house Monday had been overcome; the audience at this first show usually sat on their hands and was composed of the local theatrical landladies and small shopkeepers who were given passes for displaying publicity material in their windows. On occasion there could be embarrassing mishaps during the run, such as the time the O'D company were performing the sketch "Marrying Mary" in which Vernon Hayden played Mr Smyth who loses favour with Mrs Brady (Jimmy O'Dea) as a suitor for her daughter's hand. Mr Smyth is ejected rather forcefully and there is the off-stage sound effect known as a glass crash. This was achieved simply by transferring a bucket full of broken glass into another empty bucket, thus achieving a loud and seemingly painful effect. The company performed this sketch one evening complete with glass crash and later on in the show a well-known American pianist was half-way through performing his act when to everyone's horror at a particularly hushed and intense moment in the music there was the awful sound of the glass crash off-stage. A hasty investigation revealed that one of the stage-hands was responsible who explained that "he was putting the glass back into the first bucket in readiness for the next performance."

Golfing appears to have been the main form of relaxation for the male members of the theatrical fraternity since they had mornings and afternoons free and there was always the solace of the nineteenth hole. Jimmy was elected a member of the Variety Golfers'

Society in December 1947. Among other famous members of this society was the comedian Jimmy Edwards.

The highest honour that Variety artists can bestow upon each other is membership of the Grand Order of Water Rats, which was founded in 1889. Clarkson Rose in, *Red Plush and Greasepaint,* has this to say about the order:

> Most of the stars, past and present, have been and are members of the Order—and not only stars of our own country but many others. However, it isn't easy to become a Water Rat, and membership is a hallmark of the esteem in which one is held by one's fellows, and demands first-class qualities of character.
>
> The objects of the order are good comradeship, tolerance, justice and above all, generosity; and the members' benevolence extends not only to their own brothers in the order who are in need but to countless other charities that have called upon them from time to time.

Jimmy was initiated into the Order on 23 May 1949. His proposer was Harry Pringle and his seconder was Harry Seltzer. The King Rat in 1949 was Ted Ray but as he was absent at Jimmy's initiation, the King Rat pro tem was Will Hay and the preceptor of the day was "Uncle Fred" Russell. Jimmy was enormously proud of the honour, and his Water Rat necktie may be seen on display in the Irish Theatre Archives, City Hall, Dublin. He was also a member of the Savage Club, Whitehall Place, London from 1945.

Vernon Hayden and Jimmy O'Dea in *Buying a Turkey*.

Backstage at the Gaiety, 1937. *Left to right:* Harry O'Donovan,
Tom Dunne, Jimmy O'Dea and Noel Purcell.

Jimmy O'Dea with Maureen Potter, Gaiety, 1956.

Danny Cummins and Jimmy O'Dea.

Jimmy O'Dea as Stalin at a charity football match at Tolka
Park.

Jimmy O'Dea and Maureen Potter in *Dick Whittington* at the
Gaiety, 1957.

Vernon Hayden and Jimmy O'Dea in *Home James* at the Gaiety, 1958.

Hilton Edwards, Genevieve Lyons and Jimmy O'Dea in *The Man Who Came to Dinner* at the Gaiety, 1959.

Jimmy O'Dea and Maureen Potter at the Gaiety.

Maureen Potter.

Jimmy O'Dea relaxing in his dressing-room.

Jimmy O'Dea and Maureen Potter in *The Merrier We Will Be*
at the Gaiety, 1962.

Jimmy O'Dea and Danny Cummins in *The Merrier We Will Be*.

Jimmy O'Dea and Maureen Potter in *Finian's Rainbow* at the
Gaiety, 1964.

Jimmy O'Dea and Maureen Potter in the Gaiety.

Jimmy Campbell, musical director at the Theatre Royal and later at the Gaiety.

Chapter Eight

The O'D company hadn't played the Gaiety, Dublin since the panto season of 1945/46. The August show in 1946 was ...*And Pastures New,* a revue presented by Edwards/MacLiammóir with Noel Purcell in the cast. Noel also appeared as dame in the panto that year while Jimmy was in Liverpool. But the O'D company were back in the Gaiety in 1947/48 for the Christmas panto, *Hansel and Gretel,* in which George Arnett played Dame and Jimmy was Jimmy the Spiv—in which role he made his first entrance being wheeled on in a wheelbarrow. Although he was accustomed to topping the bill in Variety at important venues like the Metropolitan, Edgeware Road or the Chelsea Palace, Jimmy was obviously happy to be back in his beloved Gaiety.

The final *Irish Half Hour* series called *The Great Gilhooley* wasn't a great success and it looked as though the formula had run its natural span. There also seemed to have been trouble brewing between Harry O'Donovan and Jimmy again as Harry wrote to Tom Ronald in March, 1949:

Dear Tom,
    Since writing you last, James and I have kind of patched it up, although I think it is rather hopeless. We are going on, anyhow, to do the August show here. However, if any more broadcasts come up, I still think it would be better for Jimmy to settle

them and treat the scripts separately, so that he could, if he wants to, have the writing done in a different system. Such as someone else being in charge and me helping.

There is no further evidence regarding the progress of this latest disagreement but there can be no doubt that it was settled amicably. Jimmy made his first television appearance on June 28, 1948 in a variety show called *Mrs Mulligan's Private Hotel* which was produced by Richard Afton at Alexandra Palace. Jimmy was mistress of ceremonies and introduced his regular company in various sketches, The "residents" also included Frank O'Donovan, Rex Ramer, Brian Duffy and the Society Four.

In England, theatrical taste was changing rapidly, a movement spearheaded by the *Goon Show*, the inspiration of Spike Milligan. The variety bills were being topped by pop singers for as long as they managed to stay in the record charts. Pantomime, in order to survive, featured male pop stars in the role of principal boy, for long the property of generously proportioned thigh-slapping ladies. Panto must have gone out of favour altogether in Dublin because the O'D company abandoned it after the 1948/49 season. For six years, with the exception of 1951 when they gave traditional pantomime another try, they kept to their new style Christmas revue. In 1949/50 the Christmas show called *Alive Alive-O*, (which had very little hint of the Festive Season in it) celebrated the coming of age of O'D Productions. Maureen Potter's comic talent was recognised in the 1950 Christmas revue *As Happy As Can Be* when she partnered Jimmy in a sketch involving two Dublin girls, Dolores and Rose, who were to become firm favourites in subsequent shows. Maureen, as Dolores with the "fur hur from Furview" was the young impetuous and ingenuous one, while as a rather faded Rose, Jimmy was overblown, pretentious, all knowing, and bemused by her younger friend.

(Excerpt from "Dolores and Rose in France")

DOLORES: I wish we hadda stayined at home. I don't like Frenchmen they're very mastiline.

ROSE: Very what?

DOLORES: Mastiline Rose. You wouldn't understand.

ROSE: No. I don't understand.

DOLORES: Didn't that trumpet player out of the orchestra see you home last night?

ROSE: Dolores, please. Don't mention that trumpet player. When he was kissing me goodnight he absent-mindedly blew a top C and I had the wind up all night.

DOLORES: Well, the fella that I was with was tres been.

ROSE: He was what?

DOLORES: Tres been

ROSE: How on earth did he get that way. Oh, you mean *très bien*, which means game ball.

DOLORES: Rose, I mean the lad what was beside me at the dinner. Hey, why were you glarin' at me all through the dinner.

ROSE: I should think I was. When the waiter asked you if you'd like snipe you held out your glass for it.

DOLORES: Well?

ROSE: Well! You didn't know it was fish.

DOLORES: You know I'll never learn the language— when I asked the waiter for something in French he laughed at me.

ROSE: Why shouldn't he laugh at you, didn't you ask him for a slice of the manager?.

DOLORES: Ah, d'ye know, I think I'll stick to the English lads, but not the fella I met last night. Put the wind up me when he told me he was an archologist' I thought it might be an infection.

ROSE: Do you know what an archologist is?

DOLORES: Well, eh, no.

ROSE: You don't. Well it's a fellow that mucks about with old ruins.

DOLORES: Well the nerve of him pickin' on me!

Maureen Potter was born in Fairview on Dublin's North side. As a child she trained as an Irish dancer and attained championship standard. She was still very young when she toured Britain and mainland Europe with the Jack Hylton Orchestra and on her return she played various minor roles with the O'D company. After the war she did a season at the Capitol Theatre where her song and dance act had all the energy and ebullience of a Betty Hutton. Later, her roles with the O'D company grew in importance until eventually she was given one and sometimes two spots on her own in the shows.

In 1951 Jimmy expressed an interest in doing another radio series for the BBC. The Corporation was not unappreciative of the work that Jimmy had done for them, as the following internal memo dated 27 December 1951 from Tom Ronald to the Assistant Head of Variety illustrates:

> Jimmy O'Dea has appeared twice this year, once in a *Festival Parade* and once in a *Christmas Parade*. He has made a great success each time and is very anxious to do a series again on the BBC
>
> I think that this should be seriously considered as he gave up a great deal of his time during the war to the service of the BBC when there was no need for him to do so and he could have stayed in the security of a neutral country. Jimmy O'Dea will be working in Ireland until the spring, but if there is any hope of him getting a series a certain amount of preliminary work on scripts will have to be done fairly soon.

The reply to this from on high was as follows:

> I would like to hear a trial with Jimmy O'Dea supported by an English cast which would include someone like Tony Hancock. Do you agree?

The idea was discussed further but there is no record of the outcome, except that the series never materialised, which leaves unanswered the fascinating question as to what comic masterpiece might have evolved from the combined genius of O'Dea and Hancock, who was yet to develop his manic-depressive character from Railway Cuttings, East Cheam. In the 1951 August show, *Diversion,* Jimmy appeared as Joe Stalin (he had impersonated Winston Churchill in *Happy Holiday* in 1948), and returned briefly to pantomime that Christmas in *Cinderella* with himself and Maureen Potter as the Ugly Sisters, Rosy and Dolores. This was the last panto until 1955, when Jimmy appeared as the Baroness Baloney in *Puss In Boots.* Apart from Maureen Potter, Danny Cummins, Derry O'Donovan and the rest of the regular O'D company the cast also included Mike Nolan, a longtime favourite Dublin comedian, best remembered for his resident season at the Capitol Theatre where he was supported by Roy Croft and Freddie Doyle. In the same year of 1955 the Gaiety closed for three months for alterations and refurbishment, so the O'D company took their 1954 Christmas show to the Shakespeare Theatre, Liverpool. Called *Date With Laughter,* it was notable for the fact that the musical director was Bobbie Bolton, late of the Olympia, and the scenery and costumes were designed by Michael O'Herlihy who would later find another artistic outlet as a director of Hollywood films.

On St Patrick's Day 1952 Jimmy made his second television appearance in a variety show from St George's Hall, Liverpool but it would be another three years before he made another appearance in front of the TV cameras. Again it was on St Patrick's Day and as the programme was broadcast from the Nuffield Centre it was called *The Centre Show.* Jimmy presented one of his most celebrated sketches, "The Lost Railway," which should not be confused with another sketch with a railway theme, "The Next Train," which he recorded in 1929 and was ineffective on record because the script depended upon too many visual elements more suited to stage production. Briefly, it concerns the usual irate US visitor seeking information at a small branch line about the departure of the next train. When Jimmy, as the station porter, proves useless, the traveller demands to see various other officials; they all turn out to be Jimmy who manifests his variety of positions merely by changing his hat to suit each job. When, finally, the presence of the managing director is demanded, Jimmy dons a top hat and introduces himself as that personage. "The Lost Railway," which was never recorded but is preserved in the sound archives of RTE, was first presented in the revue *Stop Press* in 1949 and was destined to become one of Jimmy's best loved sketches. Harry O'Donovan was, of course, aware that Jimmy could draw the tears as well as the laughter, and recalled:

> One day I sat down and wrote a sketch called 'The Lost Railway.' It was just the story of an old Irish station master on a small branch line somewhere in the back of beyant. The station and the line and all that belonged to it were the pride of his life. His father and his grandfather before him had been station masters, and then came nationalisation, and the branch line and the station had become redundant and with them, of course, the station-master. It was quite a simple little sketch but it was different for as I wrote it there was a sudden switch near the end from rich broad comedy to pathos and yet it was a pathos that could be played as comedy. Which is what Jimmy did—at first.

And Jimmy admitted:

> I know I was obstinate about playing it for laughs but I just couldn't see myself doing the sob stuff. Then one night just for divilment, I started playing it as Harry had written it. If there had been a pin dropped in the house you could have heard it. I just couldn't believe it—I was terror struck. Then it suddenly began to dawn on me that the audience were with me."

(Extract from "The Lost Railway")

The scene is the terminus for the Ballygobackwards, Mayo, Moyvale and Greenvalley lines. A government official enters and is amazed to learn that the line is still in operation. His amazement turns to bureaucratic horror as the station master reveals how the line was being run. For example, money for the staff wages came out of the takings and if they happened to run short of cash the problem was solved by running an excursion. The sketch ends as follows:

OFFICIAL: Well, I'll tell you what I have to do now. I have to close down this line.

STATION
MASTER: Close down the Ballygobackwards...?

OFFICIAL: I have to close it down now. That train out there on the platform is the last train that will ever leave this station.

STATION
MASTER: You couldn't do a thing like that. What would I do, where would I go?

OFFICIAL: We'll pension you off.

STATION
MASTER: They don't pension off Ballygobackwards station-masters. We just drop dead. I've been on this job, man and boy, for the last forty years, and my father before me, and his father. My father was ninety when he died and finished up doing the job in a bathchair. And his father was a hundred—what they call a centurion.

OFFICIAL: Well, I'm very sorry, but I'll have to clear everything out of your office, your stuff and your furniture on to that train, and that's the end of your little railway.

STATION
MASTER: Couldn't we do something sir. Couldn't we send a deputation to the Minister: he was very decent to us last year when we wanted

boots for the staff—sent us four pair. Of course, we only needed three pair but we flogged the other pair.

OFFICIAL: Now listen mister, I'm afraid that when it comes to schemes like governments taking over railways that the little people just don't matter.

STATION
MASTER: The little people don't matter.

OFFICIAL: No, you see the day of the little branch line is over and I'm greatly afraid that your day is over too. Too bad but that's how it is. Goodbye. (Two porters strip the office. The station-master protests mildly).

STATION
MASTER: Ah, Packy. What are you doing Packy. Packy I knew you before you were born. (He stands in the empty room. The telephone rings) Hello... Hello, this is the Bally... this is the Ballygobackwards terminus for the Ballygobackwards, Mayo, Moyvale and Greenvalley lines. I'm the... I'm the station-master, or at least... I think I was. What? The next train; there'll be no next train sir. Oh, the last train. The last train has just gone sir. No sir, not the last train for tonight—the last train for always. (He moves off dejectedly) The little people don't matter!

This sparsely written little sketch manages in five or six minutes to encapsulate the anguish of sudden rejection and the destruction of a way of life for a man with a proud tradition. In 1949 it was timely for it anticipated the sorrow and loss of many real life "little people" in the years to come. A small minority of people regarded it as bathos and self-pitying but in all of Jimmy's subsequent tours of Britain, Australia, New Zealand and Canada it was always warmly received. *The Irish Times* review of its first production highlighted Jimmy's performance: "...in which he fights the cause of a small man drowning in a bureaucratic flood, with humour and pathos."

In August 1956 there appears to have been a new arrangement governing the production of the O'D Gaiety shows. Henceforth, the shows were presented by TR Royle (Louis Elliman) with the exception of a short period in 1960 when the shows again went on under the old O'D Productions banner. Fergus Linehan, writing in the *Irish Times* said:

> The story, as I heard it was that he [Jimmy] had lost his money, investing it in films, and had to be bailed out by the late Louis Elliman. Instead of producing his own shows, as in the past, he was now receiving a salary for doing them.

Had Jimmy been another victim of the ill-fated Ardmore Studios?

The August 1956 show co-starred Jimmy and Micheál MacLiammóir, who also designed the sets and costumes. The show was produced by Hilton Edwards and titled *Gateway to Gaiety*, a punning title inspired by Cecil Sheridan who, with Harry O'Donovan and MacLiammóir, wrote the sketches. All of which was evidence of "Mr Louis" touch. Although Jimmy appeared as many of his old familiar characters the show was inhibited somewhat by the rather "arty" contribution from the Gate Theatre partnership. Their material was inspired by their justly famous Christmas revues at the Gate, and indeed one scene, "A Cask of Amontillado," dramatised by Hilton Edwards from Edgar Allan Poe's tale which described how Montressor, (MacLiammóir) bricked up an enemy alive in a niche in the Catacombs, had been presented years earlier in a Gate revue called *Masquerade*. It didn't merit a second production: although it was perfectly presented and acted it just had no place in an O'Dea Gaiety revue.

Legends do eventually fade but nothing can dim the living memory of their greatness in their prime. This could be applied to Jimmy as far as his older admirers were concerned. He continued to attract new admirers with the passing years who could not understand the claims of more mature theatre goers in the late 50s that Jimmy was past his best. People like Billy Bourke, of the famous Dublin theatrical family, amazed younger listeners when he claimed that Jimmy was but a shadow of the riotously funny O'Dea of the 30s and 40s. Connie Ryan, who ran a well-known dancing school in Dublin and who had been one of the original members of the O'Dea company, appearing in sketches, and featuring on Jimmy's records, and who with her brother Michael devised the choreography for the early shows, was of the opinion that Jimmy was at his peak in the late thirties. Maureen Potter thought that the script material from Harry was past his best. The truth was that Jimmy and Harry were getting old; they had been around for a long time, but so too had their audiences. They had witnessed Jimmy as every conceivable sort of character extricate himself from every comedy situation imaginable that Harry could invent for him.

There was a policy that every new show include what was called "one out of the bag"—an old favourite sketch familiar to regular audiences. It was inevitable that this material—a sketch such as "The Baby Elephant"—would have lost its freshness and delightful innovation for seasoned theatre goers. Yet Jimmy could still produce the inspired flashes of comic genius for these older audiences: the big eyes still rolled wickedly and with his superb timing he could still make a familiar line sound uproariously funny. But this was no more than they had come to expect; the true magic was still there to be discovered by the younger newcomer if he could be persuaded to forsake television—still a novelty—and spend an evening in the Gaiety in the presence of a real live extraordinary personality, who from the beginning of the show, seemed to assure one in a marvellously unusual Dublin accent, that if you trusted him you would enjoy the experience.

It cannot be denied that some performers grow tired and stale and careless. Some have even been known to commit suicide when they lost the favour of the public; the character played by Charles Chaplin in his film *Limelight* is said to be based on a real-life star comedian who was, in the end, reduced to busking on the streets. In John Osborne's play *The Entertainer,* set in 1957 when Variety was dying, the central character, Archie Rice, a one-time star comedian tells his daughter, Jean:

> Oh, you think I'm just a tatty old music-hall actor who should be told the truth, like old Billy, that people don't wear sovereign cases and patent leather shoes any more. You know when you're up there you think you love all those people around you out there, but you don't. You don't love them, you're not going to stand up and make a beautiful fuss. If you learn it properly you'll get yourself a technique. You can smile, darn you, smile, and look the friendliest jolliest thing in the world, but you'll be just as dead and smug and used up, and sitting on your hands just like everybody else. You see this face, you see this face, this face can split open with warmth and humanity. It can sing, and tell the worst, funniest stories in the world to a great mob of dead, drab erks and it doesn't matter, it doesn't matter. It doesn't matter because— look at my eyes. I'm dead behind these eyes. I'm dead, just like the whole inert, shoddy lot out there. It doesn't matter because I don't feel a thing, and neither do they, We're just as dead as each other.

Archie is, of course, finished. Dead behind the eyes and with nothing of himself to give, technique alone is not, in the end, enough to draw an audience happily like a magnet.

At no point in his career could Jimmy be compared to the tired and empty Archie Rice. His entrance to his dressing-room each evening signalled the meticulous preparation for a new audience: Jimmy always found the audience to be completely different each night. When he changed into a costume the change was detailed and accurate and complete, even down to the appropriate shoes and socks. Then he relaxed and slowly allowed his mind to assume the character of the next role he was to play. Outside in the corridor members of the company took care to walk quietly past Mr O'Dea's door so as not to disturb his concentration. Jimmy's dictum was:

> You cannot make up comedy. You must live it. It must be real. It must be based on real people and real situations—a slice of life. And to find the funny side you must examine the sad side too. That's why Biddy Mulligan was a success with audiences. Everybody could identify himself with her. She might have been outrageous at times but she was always real. I often think I am Biddy and see things her way. And you know it's not baloney to say that the bond between you and your audience must be very strong, very close. The only way you can really get your audience is to make that bond close. You haven't an earthly unless you do that, unless you make friends with them in the first five minutes. You can—this may sound vulgar but I don't mean it like that—"smell" your audience and it might take you 15 minutes to get them but once you get them you have them for the night. I can never wait until I am back in the darkened theatre sizing up the crowd and waiting for the triumph of the moment when somebody chuckles. Then you know you have them and can play them like a piano. But it can be hard work because laughter for a comic is a serious business indeed.

These remarks, hardly the words of a man past his best, were made by Jimmy, in the sixties, towards the end of his career. Other artists who performed with Jimmy were never surprised if he suddenly increased the tempo of a sketch. He was always acutely aware of the audience and the reason for the sudden speeding up might be the fact that he sensed a certain lethargy in the audience at a given point or it might be that out of the corner of his eye he spotted a man in the front stalls lighting up a cigarette who couldn't have been giving his undivided attention to the stage. He kept his cast on their toes also and Maureen Potter recalls that in her early days with the company as a juvenile, Jimmy had her costumed in the distinctive dress of the old friend whom he very much admired, Alfie Byrne, the Lord Mayor of Dublin, who was so notorious for shaking hands in the streets with the citizenry that Jimmy called him "Alfie, the shaker." Maureen, complete with waxed moustache, fell asleep in the wings one evening only to be discovered by Jimmy who grabbed her by the collar and dragged her on to the stage exclaiming loudly, "Nobody sleeps while I'm on!"

In August 1955 Jimmy celebrated his 50th appearance at the Theatre Royal with his show *Royal Gaytime*. The Royal was the largest theatre in Europe with nearly 4,000 seats and 50 appearances was a respectable achievement. Still, there were the detractors, not least of whom was the reviewer who cast serious doubts on Jimmy's professionalism. This critic attached to one of the Sunday newspapers stated in his review of an O'D show that Jimmy's timing "was as reliable as the Ballast Office clock" which, as every Dubliner knew, was the most unreliable timepiece in the city. This piece of idiocy was not taken seriously by O'Dea who tended to ignore the press and was genuinely embarrassed if some critic praised him too highly—it made him self-conscious. Louis Elliman took a different view of the matter and demanded and got an apology. The newspaper sent their most experienced senior critic to review the show a second time. On the other hand eminent columnists like Desmond Rushe, the *Irish Independent* drama critic, could write as follows:

In the delicate and difficult art of comedy, Jimmy O'Dea had no peer. This was because his talent went considerably beyond the strict definition of a comedian; he was a comic genius first it is true, but away from that classic, vividly real figure of fun, Biddy Mulligan, he was capable of characterisation of impressive depth and pathos. It is, however, as the comedian that he will be remembered with the most enduring and pleasant memories. While others might arouse a storm of merriment of higher decibel level, he invariably reached those laughter-producing recesses of the heart with a more acute, unerring instinct. Whatever the circumstances, he seemed to be able to gauge the needs of his audience and give it precisely what it wanted. At improvisation he was probably the greatest master the Irish stage has seen. With the slow uprising of a brow from a large expressive eye he could speak more than any scriptwriter could write. Without the aid of lines, unwritten or forgotten, he could keep an audience convulsed for minutes on end. There were those to whom his type of humour did not particularly appeal, but for the great majority to whom it did, Jimmy O'Dea provided an enrichment without parallel.

Gabriel Fallon, too, was to comment on those, as Desmond Rushe put it, "to whom his type of humour did not particularly appeal." Writing on Jimmy's medium of Variety, Fallon said:

Of course it was vulgar. There was coarseness in it and crudity; the coarseness and the crudity that is to be found in Chaucer, Shakespeare and Cervantes. But it was based on a frank, joyous acceptance of life. For this reason he [Jimmy] has incurred the displeasures of the "Refained" the "Respectable" and indeed, the "Really Naice" people. One of his glories has been to show us that the all-but submerged are anything but submerged, indeed they rejoice in a vitality which is sadly lacking in the "Naice" people. The words of CE Montague might have been applied to the legions of Jimmy's admirers: "The root of all judgement is obstinate fidelity to your own personal relish and disrelish—to give yourself to the enjoyment of a thing because you do enjoy it and not because someone whom you think much of ènjoys it. What matters in criticism is not so much truth as reality, not so much your views being sound as being yours.

And John Jordan on the subject of vulgarity:

And, of course, there must be no "vulgarity." Not even the enunciation of any word vaguely sounding like a mildly indecent one. When Biddy Mulligan catches herself or anyone else about to say, for example, "Bottom," there is all the sorrow of the Fall of Man in those liquid eyes. And here we have a most subtle kind of satire. The extremeness of the reactions is itself a send-up of the mealy-mouthed and hyper-refined... Jimmy as Little Willie in a take-off of *East Lynne* : "Your end is at hand"—such vulgarity!

In December 1956, following on their partnership in *Gateway to Gaiety* Jimmy again starred with Micheál MacLiammóir in what must have been Jimmy's favourite panto *Cinderella*. (He appeared in six different productions of it during his career.) MacLiammóir and Milo O'Shea were cast as the Ugly Sisters, Marigold and Myrtle respectively. The press remarked that "Michael's comedy was sharp, rapier-like with eloquence in two or three languages; indeed it was rather wordy and would improve by curtailment." Michael seems to have padded-out his dame roles and one wonders how he was greeted at children's matinees. Jimmy was memorable as Buttons, particularly in the kitchen scene with Cinders to whom he sang "Getting to know you"—it might well have been the 1923 Queen's Theatre production all over again, in which Jimmy's appearance in the ballroom scene singing "Bridget Donohoe" is still remembered.

The pantomime was presented by TR Royle in association with Howard and Wyndham, a large English organisation which hired out complete pantos, including very high quality scenery, orchestrations and costumes; they even supplied the book of the show which could be adapted to suit different locations. The comedy roles were usually rewritten to suit the talents of those playing them and to include local topicalities. This task was undertaken by Harry O'Donovan (and Micheál MacLiammóir when he was involved). According to Vernon Hayden, Howard and Wyndham Ltd received 50% of the gross takings dropping to 10% in the final week for supplying this service, and the arrangement continued for many years.

Chapter Nine

In May 1957 a new Irish film produced by Michael Killanin was previewed at the Metropole Cinema, Dublin. This was *The Rising Of The Moon*, (which is also known as *Three Leaves In A Shamrock)*; made by Four Provinces Films and directed by John Ford. It was composed of three separate stories. The first was *The Majesty of the Law* which starred Cyril Cusack and Noel Purcell and was adapted from a short story by Frank O'Connor; the second was *A Minute's Wait* from an early Abbey Theatre one-act play by Michael J McHugh which starred Jimmy O'Dea as the railway porter—the cast also included Maureen Potter and two old colleagues from Jimmy's early days, May Craig and Paul Farrell; and the third segment was "1921" from Lady Gregory's play *The Rising Of The Moon* and featured many players from the Abbey Theatre. Jimmy's brother Joseph also had a role.

The story of *A Minute's Wait* is really a series of delaying incidents at Dunfaill Station which necessitates a constant declaration from the station master that, "There will be one minute's wait." The delays are due to the late arrival of: a prize goat, the bishop's lobsters and the local hurling team. Two first-class passengers, an English colonel and his wife, are mislaid, while the other passengers and the train driver and stoker pass the time at an impromptu hooley in the refreshment buffet. Out on the platform the delay is long enough to confirm agreement on the terms of a hard-fought marriage bargain.

Maureen Potter recalled the filming of *A Minute's Wait*:

> We did it down in Clare, near Kilkee because they had the narrow gauge railway. [This was the line made famous by Percy French in the song "Are yeh right there, Michael?".] Jimmy played the porter and I played the barmaid; and John Ford, of course, was directing. John Ford was an extraordinary man, and he just liked Jimmy, and he liked me, and the first morning what happened was, he said, "You're the barmaid, honey, get in there and ad lib." I was lucky that I had worked with Jimmy O'Dea, otherwise I'd have been dead, because that's what you did with Jimmy O'Dea; you did it sometimes to keep things going.

The trilogy, in general, received a mixed reception from the Irish critics. There were complaints about stage-Irishism which were offset to some extent by the reasoning of M A T in the *Dublin Evening Mail*.

> ... a worthy successor to *The Quiet Man*! The people who objected to *The Quiet Man* as a travesty of Irish country life, a libellous enormity, a disgrace to the fair name of Erin, and so forth, will no doubt be equally indignant about *A Minute's Wait*...the only one of the three which is set on the farcical plane that was used for *The Quiet Man*. We who have some common-sense can afford to turn away disdainfully from the splenetic meanderings of the numbskulls who don't know the difference between farcical extravaganza and documentary intention.

Tom Hennigan in *The Sunday Press* said:

> ... *A Minute's Wait*... moves with the gaiety of a 16-hand reel. There is never a dull moment...

Michael Trubshawe and Anita Sharpe Bolster turn in performances which might easily cause howls across the channel about "Stage English..."

The Irish Independent reported that:

...there was a superb display of acting by a team of actors and actresses who were just as effective in the small parts as in the bigger ones."

And Kevin O'Kelly of *The Evening Press* wrote:

In the farce—*A Minute's Wait*—Jimmy O'Dea is the star. John Ford has given him every opportunity to show his prowess both for making us laugh and cry and Jimmy has seized the opportunity to the full.

The Monthly Film Bulletin remarked that:

...the dance performed by Jimmy O'Dea and Maureen Potter would not be out of place in Judge Priests's County!

A Minute's Wait was certainly one of Jimmy's most successful film appearances

In July 1957, TR Royle, instead of presenting the usual August revue, starred Jimmy as Finian McLonergan in the first Irish production of *Finian's Rainbow* with lyrics by E Y Harburg and music by Burton Lane. The show had had a long Broadway run and was filmed successfully in 1968 with Fred Astaire in Jimmy's role. The story concerns a whimsical Irish immigrant Finian McLonergan who lives in Rainbow Valley, somewhere near Fort Knox. He argues that America's riches have accumulated as a result of the country's gold buried underground at Fort Knox. He decides to reap the same reward by "planting" a crock of gold he had once stolen from Og, a leprechaun. Milo O'Shea replaced another performer and played Og towards the end of the run, and there was a strong supporting cast including Maureen Potter, Godfrey James and Vernon Hayden.

That Christmas Jimmy appeared as Dame Sarah in *Dick Whittington* with Micheál MacLiammóir once again sharing the top billing as King Rat. Down the cast list was the name Dermot Kelly. He had at one time been stage manager at the Abbey, but eventually achieved television fame as "Irish" a comic character in the Arthur Haynes Show in which he and MacLiammóir appeared as a couple of scroungers. The panto, which was written by Harry O'Donovan, was produced under the direction of Jim Fitzgerald. After the run of the show Jimmy flew to California to appear in what was to be his best film, Walt Disney's *Darby O'Gill and the Little People*. Filming seems to have run over schedule and Jimmy didn't make it back to Dublin in time for the opening of his 1958 August revue which was postponed until 15 September. The show was called, appropriately, *Home James* and in a programme note Louis Elliman wrote:

> The August show with O'Dea and O'Donovan has long been a Gaiety tradition. This year Hollywood claimed Jimmy O'Dea, but he was determined to appear—better late than never. I hope the long Gaiety-O'D association will continue, for as the company sing in the opening scene: "August Means Jimmy O'Dea" So—as our title says—"Home James, and don't spare the laughter."

From Mr Louis this could almost be described as emotional but there can be no doubt that the showman in him was fascinated by Hollywood which he visited himself as Irish representative of Republic Pictures. Louis wasn't the only one expressing concern over Jimmy's absence. *The Irish Times* critic, Seamus Kelly, published a piece called "Comedy's Uncrowned King" in his Quidnunc column:

> No show without Punch? No Horse Show without O'Dea. That's the way it had been for fifteen years past [sic] when the O'D show in the Gaiety was as essential a part of our Autumnal frolics as the Aga Khan Cup

competition. This year we were consoled for the maestro's absence by the charm and novelty of *The Heart's A Wonder* but there's no show without Punch, and now Punch is back, having abdicated his Disney Hollywood throne as King of the Leprechauns to return to the Republic where he is the uncrowned king of comedy.

It seems a bit wrong, somehow, to talk of Jimmy as the "uncrowned king" when most of the courtiers think of him as Biddy Mulligan or Carmel Cassidy or some other of those wonderful Dublin "wans" that he has brought to exuberant life over the years. Anyhow, king or queen he's back and his return has already been greeted with pleasure backstage. It remains for us out front to say "Welcome Home, James—and *we* won't spare the laughter!"

The cast included the regular members of the company with the addition of John Molloy, Godfrey James, Patrick Bedford and Albert Le Bas.

It wasn't long until panto time again and the subject that year was *Robinson Crusoe* with Jimmy as Mrs Crusoe. Hal Roach was Man Friday and the principal boy was Agnes Bernelle. Agnes was, and is, a remarkable performer. She first came to prominence at the Establishment Club, London, singing the German cabaret songs of the 1930s which she still records on LP albums today. In 1958 she travelled from England by boat on a very stormy night to take up her engagement at the Gaiety and arrived tottering and desperately sick in Dublin. Early in the morning the first person she was taken to meet, in Neary's pub, was Jimmy O'Dea. And sick as she was, she listened to Jimmy's strong recommendation, and allowed him to buy her five Irish coffees. "These settled me totally," she said, "I was fine after that; I had never heard of Irish coffee but Jimmy assured me that they would cure me, and they did."

Agnes thought that Jimmy was a marvellous person but like many others she did not escape his disconcerting sense of humour: for instance, during the rehearsals which were conducted in two of the theatre bars, Jimmy and his comedy team including Maureen, Danny Cummins and Hal Roach went through their scenes in one bar while the second bar was reserved for rehearsals of the "straight" characters. For weeks Jimmy pretended that he wasn't really aware of what was happening in the second bar and he expressed feigned surprise when he "discovered" that there were scenes with dialogue between Robinson Crusoe and his girl friend Polly Perkins and her father Captain Perkins. "What are they doing in the show?" he would enquire in puzzlement to the embarrassment of the performers involved, who were given the impression that it was Jimmy's considered opinion that there should only be comics in the show and no other people at all with the possible exception of a song or two. Agnes, in private life Lady Leslie, invited members of the cast down to Castle Leslie in Glaslough and in turn invited members of her staff in Co Monaghan to see the show, greatly to the delight of Jimmy who insisted upon pointing them out to the rest of the audience. When Agnes's housekeeper Bridget came to see the show Jimmy found out and regaled the audience with stories about her and the fact that Robinson Crusoe (Agnes) was terrified of her. The unfortunate Bridget who had scarcely ever been out of county Monaghan was mortified to find herself the centre of attention in the Gaiety Theatre. Jimmy's old friend, Myles na Gopaleen, (Flann O'Brien) the celebrated *Irish Times* columnist, was to say of these typical O'Dea ad libs.

Producers are usually alarmed when a player departs deliberately from the script but Jimmy's improvisations and spontaneous raillery gloriously transcended many a script. Often a good citizen who suspected he was himself a Big Shot and permitted himself a box was never quite certain of his status until he suddenly found himself mercilessly but amiably pilloried by the gabby Pride of the Coombe or some other spectral layabout. That is to say that usually Jimmy was not before his audience but with it, and that is a fusion rare in the theatre.

When the run of the pantomime had settled down Agnes sought revenge by trying to "corpse" (that is to try to make him laugh when he shouldn't) Jimmy; this invariably took place in the desert isle scene when Robinson Crusoe finds a chart. This was referred to as a "chawrt" by his girlfriend Polly Perkins, who was played by Paula Patina in a plummy Roedean accent, to the delight of Jimmy who repeated the word "chawrt" in the same accent. Gradually Agnes began to change the word *chart* and the rest of the cast waited in anticipation every night. Jimmy was presented with posh renderings of the word like, diagram, map, graph, ordnance survey, outline, and eventually more convoluted versions like sheet of authoritative directions. Agnes claims that he finally "corpsed" when he was presented with "sheet of tabulated diagrammatic information!"

In 1958 Jimmy and Harry celebrated 21 years at the Gaiety and the occasion was marked during the run of *Robinson Crusoe* when during the grand finale one evening Hilton Edwards and Micheál MacLiammóir walked on to make a presentation and speech.

The anniversary was be the theme of a special O'D show in February, 1959; called *Look Back In Laughter*, it featured the outstanding sketches of the previous 21 years. In July the summer revue was brought forward a month in order to facilitate the Dublin Theatre Festival. The show *Festival Of Fun* was directed by former Abbey Theatre producer, Frank Dermody, and the cast included Milo O'Shea who performed one of his mime acts, "A Day In The Life Of A Surgeon." When he came back from America Milo began to include mime in the acts that he did for revues and cabarets. He told Des Hickey:

It was difficult to make ends meet as a legitimate actor, so I concentrated on musicals, pantomimes and revues. I created an image in Dublin of a comedy artist which is completely at variance with my image abroad. I never wanted to become identified with any character. Jimmy O'Dea had been a tremendous influence but I did not want to be forced into the position in which Jimmy had found himself. He had begun as a straight actor playing Chekhov and Wilde until audiences discovered his comic genius. When he capitalised on this image he found that he could not escape from it. The public would not allow him to escape. Jimmy had also decided that Ireland was to be his home and he did not want to leave. He turned down Broadway and Hollywood offers and had to be forced into a film for Disney. I remember being told that Jimmy had said of me: "There is the next Jimmy O'Dea," but I did not want to be the next Jimmy, even a pale imitation of him. I wanted to be Milo O'Shea and I did not want to be forced into the same situation. I am a Dubliner and I enjoy living in Dublin but I want to be able to play in London, New York, Hollywood and Rome.

Here, Milo was obviously referring to the Jimmy O'Dea of nearly sixty; when Jimmy was Milo's age he went to work at whatever distance was demanded at the time, and besides it would not be long before Australia, New Zealand and Canada beckoned. It was also a fact that Jimmy could still work in the "legitimate" theatre. In September of 1959 he appeared in the Dublin Globe Theatre Company production of Bernard Shaw's *The Simpleton of the Unexpected Isles,* as part of the second Dublin International Theatre Festival. The play, which was presented at the Gaiety, starred Anew McMaster as Pra, Milo O'Shea as Iddy and Jimmy O'Dea as the Angel. The director was Godfrey Quigley.

Asked by a reporter if he regretted being more or less forced into comedy Jimmy replied:

Not then. Not then at all. I was very happy about it. And I am not like every comic who is supposed to want to play Hamlet. But now that I have got used to comedy, I'd like to be allowed do something more serious. Maybe it's just egotism and I want to prove that I can do it, because actually before I became a comic I played in Chekhov, in Ibsen and Shakespeare. It would be impossible for me to do that now. It's a question of supply and demand, you know, and the public don't want me in anything too serious. But in the second last Theatre Festival I played a small part in a Shaw play—mark you it was a comedy part—but it was Shavian humour: it was in *The Simpleton of the Unexpected Isles*. It is not a very well known play. The part I had occupied only about 15 minutes. I was the Recording Angel on the Last Day. And, of course, it was Shavian sarcastic wit. The public were great. But you see it was sophisticated, and I am afraid I am inclined to like sophistication.

The Shaw play marked a turning point in the career of Derry O'Donovan (daughter of Frank O'Donovan) who was a permanent member of the O'D company, and was referred to by Jimmy as Deirdre. The General Manager of the Globe Theatre Company, Bill Ryan, was desperate to find someone to design the costumes for the production and he talked a reluctant Derry into doing the complete show. She already had a reputation for designing special individual costumes for panto and revue. In any event it was to be the beginning of the now well established firm of Derry O'Donovan Theatrical Costumiers with premises in Mount Street.

Jimmy's work with Disney may have restored his fortunes sufficiently to present that year's pantomime, *Aladdin,* under the old banner of O'D Productions Ltd with Jimmy as the Widow Twankey, Maureen Potter as principal boy and Ursula Doyle as principal girl, and Jimmy also took on his old role as producer once again. It had been a busy year with five Gaiety productions, but there was in addition the world premier of *Darby O'Gill and the Little People* at the Theatre Royal on 24 June 1959 which was attended by Walt Disney and members of the cast, including Sean Connery, JG Devlin and Jimmy O'Dea.

The film was described by Leonard Maltin in *The Disney Films* as "not only one of Disney's best films, but certainly one of the best fantasies ever put on film, the key to its success being its convincingness with the theme of credibility being carried out to the last degree." The story concerns a roguish old storyteller, Darby O'Gill (played by Albert Sharpe), who works as a caretaker on an estate. He is told that he will be retired in favour of Michael McBride (Sean Connery), a handsome young man who soon makes an impression on Darby's daughter, Katie (Janet Munro). While chasing a runaway horse to the top of a haunted hill, Darby accidentally falls down a disused well and is captured by Brian, King of the Leprechauns (Jimmy O'Dea), but manages to outwit the little monarch in a drinking bout and holds him captive in a large sack until he is granted three wishes. His real wish is that Katie and Michael McBride be united in marriage. Unfortunately, Katie goes after a runaway horse to the top of the same haunted hill where she falls and hits her head against the rocks. Katie lies near death and Darby hears the cry of the banshee. Then, from the sky comes the dreaded death coach driven by a headless man. Darby, grief-stricken, tells King Brian that his third wish is to be taken away in Katie's place. Brian agrees and Katie begins to recover the moment her father enters the coach. Then, up in the flying coach the solitary Darby is suddenly joined by King Brian who tricks him into making a fourth wish. Everyone knows that a fourth wish always cancels out the first three and Darby is suddenly home again with his family and friends where all is well.

The film was written by Lawrence Edward Watkin from the *Darby O'Gill* stories by HT Kavanagh and the special effects combining humans with the Little People are brilliantly executed. The songs include "Pretty Irish Girl" and "The Wishing Song" sung by Darby and King Brian.

The *Monthly Film Bulletin* reported:

All attempts at Irish charm seen pretty synthetic, a notable exception being the playing of Jimmy O'Dea, who makes King Brian, five shamrocks high, the most likeable and beguiling leprechaun yet to appear on the screen.

The American showbusiness bible *Variety* wrote:

> Sharpe's performance is a gem. He benefits from the combination of being lovable, yet humanly frail and prone to greed and pride ... but embellishes the role with a refreshingly individual manner of expression that should endear him. Jimmy O'Dea is every bit his match as King Brian, striking the perfect blend of charm and deviousness that characterises the leprechauns in general.

There can be no doubt that Jimmy had, at last, got a strong performance on film. When he was offered the Disney role there were, at the same time, offers of two other film contracts and he found it a bit tantalising that the three offers should come at the same time. It is perhaps fortunate that Jimmy was persuaded to do *Darby O'Gill*. It is his most successful film in which one catches glimpses of his sparkling personality and his genuine theatrical persona. Film-acting is a completely different technique to acting in the theatre, and to contain Jimmy within the frame of a film was literally like presenting a negative image of his overpowering magnetism. But the script of the Disney film suited Jimmy and might almost have been tailor-made for him by Harry O'Donovan. The O'Dea guile and belligerence are there, and yet he is able to sustain a sense of wonderment as if he were playing to an audience of wide-eyed children at a matinee of the Gaiety pantomime. *Darby O'Gill*, together with *Blarney* and *A Minute's Wait*, a few selected pieces of TV video, and some of his early gramophone records are all that remain to give a slight clue to the art of Jimmy O'Dea.

The association between O'D Productions and Radio Éireann had been fairly constant since the 1940s. In 1947 the station, which at that time seemed to regard broadcasting by an artist as free publicity courtesy of Radio Éireann, offered the O'D company the ridiculous fee of £10 for the broadcast of an excerpt from their pantomime *Hansel and Gretel.* They had asked for £42 and been refused, but the broadcast had been announced and so it went ahead. By 1949 pre-recording on wire had been introduced and a 90-minute version of *Cinderella* starring Jimmy with script by Harry O'Donovan and production by John Stevenson was recorded before a live audience in the Phoenix Hall. In 1954 Larry Morrow produced a potted version of *The O'D Story* which was followed by a comedy series called *Meet The Mulligans.* It was during this period that Jimmy first met James Plunkett, author of the powerful novel *Strumpet City* who was later to become Assistant Head of Drama and Variety in the television section. Plunkett at first televised many of Jimmy's better known sketches in a series of variety programmes but their theatrical origin was obvious, and reflected a problem foreseen by Harry O'Donovan in 1958 when he wrote an article called: "O'Dea v TV!"

At a time when television is taking up more and more of people's attention the "live" show is fast becoming something of a novelty. Dublin once had three regular music-halls. Now, except for the Royal's cine-variety policy, we have none. Twice a year the O'D company move in with a revue to the Gaiety, so the question is being continually asked: Will T.V. eventually wipe out this type of show?

This is difficult to answer generally. In particular, speaking of Dublin, I can say that in my experience, Dubliners will always go to any entertainment that is the best of its kind; whether it be a boxing match, a revue or an opera. A revue must be built in one of two ways. With six or more top-notch performers, of equally high merit, such as *The Globe and Lyric Revue* and *Airs on a Shoestring*, or to have one star whose reputation is sufficiently high to not only entertain people but to bring them in. For many years now,

O'D Productions have worked on this scheme with Jimmy. Our show is often compared to the visiting English revue. We have even been told that we must present this type of show, which is clearly not possible. We should have to import a string of performers, in the course of which, we would lose a lot of the racy comedy that Dubliners like so much. The methods, as I have explained, are different.

Jimmy and I began to operate here thirty years ago, on the principle that we produce shows that could stand up to outside opposition, and not just attract on the ticket: "Local Boy Makes Good." We still present the same kind of show, although we have had changes to suit the times. We could and already have on a few occasions adapted ourselves to television. A performer of Jimmy's standard can be good in any entertainment medium but I shall just hate to see him caged within a twelve-inch square. I am certain he'll find some way to break out of it.

And break out of it he did, brilliantly! His friend James Plunkett had discussed with Maev Conway, Head of Children's Programmes, the possibility of getting Jimmy O'Dea to do a series for them, the main drawback being that they hadn't a lot of money to pay someone of O'Dea's stature. RTE had temporary offices in Clarendon Street at the time and on his way home one evening James Plunkett met Jimmy at Newell's on a corner of Grafton Street. They repaired to Neary's and James took the bull by the horns and asked Jimmy if he would be interested in doing a series of 10-12-minute children's programmes; he couldn't offer much money—£25 an episode, perhaps...? Yes. Jimmy was interested and not too worried about the money aspect so long as the shows were nice.

Plunkett engaged Padraig O'Neill to adapt the stories from familiar fairy tales and the first one was screened in September 1960. The series was an instant success with children and suddenly Jimmy had a whole new audience—the probability of which Jimmy did not overlook when he agreed to do the series. There are today countless Irish men and women who never saw Jimmy O'Dea in the flesh and to whom Biddy Mulligan is just a song, but they remember him from their childhood days when they switched on every week to see him as the old man who looked vaguely like Pinocchio's father with grey hair and a pair of wire-rimmed spectacles on the end of his nose. Jimmy's appearance and what little action there was—he lit a candle at the beginning of each episode and blew it out when he had finished his story—was pure television and would have lost most of its impact on radio. The series was called *Once Upon A Time* and Jimmy was in his element: he adored children and always enjoyed playing to children's matinees in the Gaiety pantos. As far back as 1937, Joseph Holloway had written in his diary:

> As Mother Goose Jimmy's most popular 10 minutes with children was when he got them singing "Daisy Bell" with all the enthusiasm of their little beings. The audience left the theatre delighted and the name of Jimmy O'Dea was on the lips of all as they passed into the street after the show.

Jimmy himself remarked: "It's such a pleasure to play pantomime particularly; it's hard physical work and mental as well but everything disappears when you get that wonderful laughter from the children." During the run of *Once Upon A Time* and its repeats, it wasn't unusual for youngsters to ring the bell of Jimmy's apartment in Pembroke Road and ask to be told a story by the "man who tells the fairy tales"; and it is to Jimmy's credit that he sometimes obliged his new young fans. One mother from Finglas wrote to an evening paper that she had taken her four children to visit Santa Claus when they happened to pass a TV shop and from the sets on display in the shop window the face of Jimmy O'Dea beamed at them. "Oh! Mammy, we've missed Jimmy," moaned her disappointed brood.

"But you wanted to see Santa," the mother replied guiltily.

"We could have seen him some other day," she was informed, "But Jimmy is always on Thursday."

On the bus home her youngest daughter, aged 4½ kept crying because her mother had been responsible for making her miss her weekly date with Jimmy. It was quite an achievement that his young audience should place him before Santa Claus!

In the same year O'D Productions presented two summer shows—*Flights of Fancy* in July, and *Vintage O'D* in August, for both of which Frank O'Donovan joined the company. Noel Doyle teamed up with his sister Ursula once more in the song-and-dance double act for which they were famous since they were children and which they had worked together for a run of over a year at the Victoria Palace, London. The Christmas pantomime was *Babes In The Wood* with Jimmy as the nanny. All of the shows were directed by Jimmy himself.

There was no summer show in 1961 due to Jimmy's indisposition in hospital but he was well enough to take the title role in Louis Elliman's production of *Mother Goose* at Christmas. With the imminent demolition of the Theatre Royal in 1962, "Mr Louis" took to using his own name. "TR Royle," a mysterious figure to most Dubliners, died with the theatre and became part of its history.

In the same year, Jimmy's last film, a British one called *Johnny Nobody* was released. It was directed by and starred Nigel Patrick with Aldo Ray, William Bendix, Yvonne Mitchell, Cyril Cusack, Noel Purcell, Eddie Byrne, and many other Irish actors. The story concerns a bestselling author, Mulcahy who, inflamed by drink, harangues the inhabitants of the Irish village of Monavullagh. Father Carey is called on to deal with him as he stands outside the church challenging God to strike him dead as a blasphemer. A stranger appears and shoots Mulcahy dead. A nationwide religious contro-versy begins, but the deed is found to have a mercenary motive. Leslie Halliwell called it: "A mysterious rigmarole which irritates more than it entertains."

The *Monthly Film Bulletin* was of the opinion:

> The more one thinks of it, the more one is amazed
> that anyone should have thought a plot and players as
> uniformly unlikely as these could have worked out
> satisfactorily. The performances are mainly monu-
> ments of unrewarding miscasting.

The film was made in 1960 and Jimmy's role required
him to cycle around the village as the postman, a role he
played competently enough within the confines of the
part.

It wasn't a good year for Jimmy, apart from his illness
and the poor reception of the film. *The Irish Times* was
critical of the pantomime, *Mother Goose,* remarking that
it lacked the old robust humour of Mrs Mulligan from
the Coombe days. The truth is that by this time Mrs
Mulligan was almost an anachronism. Much of the truth
and reality on which Jimmy based his most famous
character was no longer valid. The Mrs Mulligan of the
sixties no longer lived in the Coombe but in one of the
new suburban housing estates and although her
counterpart might still be found selling her fish and
apples and oranges from a stall in Dublin's Moore
Street, it was very likely a thriving little business, and the
shawl that used to be draped around the shoulders had
had its day, to be replaced by warm overcoats and fur
lined boots. Colourful headscarves had replaced the
little bonnet. Visits to pawnshops were not so much in
evidence and with the lack of business most of them
closed down. And Biddy no longer drank in the snug of
a public house but in one of the new beautifully
carpeted and upholstered lounge bars.

The cast of Jimmy's August show in 1962 included
the famous Theatre Royal dance troupe, The Royalettes,
who were now without a permanent home due to the
closure of the Royal. Louis Elliman maintained that the
Royal was making money when it closed, and he as
Managing Director was in a position to know. The

theatre columnist of the *Evening Herald*, John Finegan, has observed:

> Three of the factors which led the Rank organisation, owners of the Royal, to decide to close the theatre were the high fees demanded by visiting artists in the 1960s, high overheads and the coming of television. Another reason was a five-week strike (which also affected the Gaiety and Olympia) in May-June 1961, which was followed by a substantial pay demand. Louis Elliman told Ranks in London of the situation. Back came the message, "Close the joint." The third Theatre Royal vanished in dust after a brief 26 years.

The money tycoons in London who had no sentiment or sense of tradition decided that the theatre would be more profitable as a development site, and the result is the existing Hawkins House. Very soon afterwards the Capitol Theatre was sold and that site together with another city landmark controlled by Ranks, the Metropole complex of Cinema, Bars, Restaurants and Ballroom, became the British Home Stores.

Alice Dalgarno and Babs DeMonte as ever directed the Royalettes in *The Merrier We Will Be* and even helped out in the sketches with Jimmy. Another institution from the Royal, Jimmy Campbell, was musical director of the show and he maintained the habit of a lifetime in showbusiness of wearing a carnation every evening in the orchestra pit. Jimmy Campbell could be relied upon to play his part to perfection and with style. The Gaiety Theatre is comfortable and beautiful and it is an experience to sit in the parterre in the warm but subdued glow of the amber house lighting and sense the air of expectancy as Jimmy Campbell enters the orchestra pit immaculate in evening dress and carnation, a portly figure with a fashionably thin moustache and dark hair plastered down. He raises his baton and the overture begins. It is stirring and exciting, played by a full theatre orchestra with every chair occupied in the wind, brass, strings and percussion sections. When it is finished Campbell acknowledges the applause as he stands in a spotlight; suddenly the house lights dim and there is a greater concentration of bright lights on the stage curtain; the lights on the music stands are mere specks by comparison. On a signal from the conductor the band plays the opening chorus of the revue as the beautiful yellow and gold brocade front curtain sweeps upwards out of sight. The entire company is on stage singing what is inevitably a variation of the first O'D Productions opening chorus in 1928— recreated here by Terry O'Donovan:

> Look who's here, look who's here,
> Let's give him a lively cheer.
> He's the rage of the stage;
> Soon your cares will disappear.
> Come along, join the throng—you'll be happy for a
>   year;
> Chase those grey skies far away.
> You'll feel like a child at play.
> You can bet you're gonna be gay,
> 'Cos look who's here.

Here the principals stood aside and the dancing troupe executed a fast high-kicking routine at the end of which the principals repeat the chorus:

> Come along; join the throng—you'll be happy for a
>   year.
> Chase those grey skies far away;
> You'll feel like a child at play.
> You can bet you're gonna be gay,
> 'Cos look who's here.

The drummer is working overtime on his drums and cymbals; the company on stage stands in formation, each member with an arm extended towards a rostrum at the back of the stage and suddenly there stands a lone figure dressed in a neat single-breasted check suit and a bowler hat. It's Jimmy O'Dea. He comes quickly down the steps from the rostrum and stands at the footlights smiling broadly. Then a quip. "You'll excuse me if I don't take off my hat, I'm afraid I'll catch my death of cold. Did you hear what they're saying—as God is my judge—they're saying, did you see O'Dea—he's losin' his hair." As the spotlights pierce the gloom of the auditorium one feels that one could reach out and touch him.

Chapter Ten

The panto in 1962 was *Goody Two Shoes* with Jimmy as Dame Mulligan; Hazel Yeomens was principal boy and Milo O'Shea was Denis the Menace. Early in 1963 while the panto was still running James Plunkett again approached Jimmy one Saturday after a matinee in the Gaiety to ask him to do a completely new television series, designed this time for adult audiences during prime time on Sunday evenings. Jimmy agreed on certain conditions. The first of these was that he wanted Brian O'Nolan as scriptwriter. O'Nolan, who was an old Blackrock College boy, was one of Jimmy's regular drinking companions in Neary's, but more importantly he had an enviable reputation as a writer with the *Irish Times* because of his amusing column "Cruiskeen Lawn" which he wrote under the name Myles na Gopaleen, and as Flann O'Brien he was the author of one of the most extraordinary novels ever written *At Swim-Two-Birds*. Secondly, Jimmy stipulated that he would work only with the production team that had made *Once Upon A Time*. And so the extraordinary situation came about that Maev Conway, whom Jimmy liked, and whose exclusive concern was children's programmes found herself financing and taking some responsibility for an adult programme within her department.

James Plunkett, as producer of the series, approached O'Nolan and after some discussion it was decided that he would write monologues for Jimmy in the role of a railway signalman and that these would be humorous and pretentiously erudite with the comedy arising from the character and his verbal misconceptions. Each episode was to be set in a signal-box and it would last for fifteen minutes. O'Nolan submitted the scripts under the title *The Ideas of O'Dea* but James Plunkett altered this and the programme was televised as *O'Dea's Yer Man*. Plunkett had one episode filmed and showed it to Jimmy, who rejected it outright. He did not like the monologue format with the long speech and no action, and suggested that a second character, with whom he could set up a rapport and bounce ideas off should be written into the script. Jimmy had a particular actor in mind for the part and as it happened this notion had a touch of genius about it. David Kelly was a promising young actor who regarded Jimmy O'Dea as a colossus and was in awe of him ever since the days when as a child he was taken to see Jimmy in pantomime. Although both of them drank in Neary's they had never been introduced: the most that they ever exchanged was a nod. David was enjoying a drink in Neary's one morning when he became conscious of a figure standing in front of his table. "Could I have a word with you?" said the figure, "I'm Jimmy O'Dea."

Confused, young David replied, "Yes, I think I know that."

Jimmy suggested that they should discuss their business in relative privacy upstairs. He explained to David the trouble he experienced with the scripts of a new TV series and said that in his opinion there should be a second character. (Anne Clissmann in her book on Flann O'Brien states by way of explanation: "Jimmy O'Dea was ill and aging rapidly, and was not by then able to keep long speeches in his head.")

It should be explained that at that time TV studios did not have autocues and that programmes recorded on video tape could virtually be termed live shows. Once the taping had begun and a considerable part of the material had been filmed there was no going back if errors were made because suitable splicing machines did not then exist to excise offending material. Ms

Clissman's explanation is possible especially in view of Derry O'Donovan's experience in 1959 when Jimmy was appearing in *The Simpleton Of The Unexpected Isles.* Jimmy had some pretty lengthy speeches and since his position on stage was close to a well he asked Derry to conceal herself in the well each night and prompt him if it should be necessary.

David Kelly, in retrospect, has another explanation and one more artistically and theatrically satisfying. It was a well-known fact that Jimmy never hogged the spotlight unnecessarily and audiences left at the end of his shows with the uneasy feeling that they hadn't seen enough of him. While other comedians did solo gags and stand-up spots, Jimmy seemed to do less. Of course, he knocked himself out, withholding nothing while he was on, but he always left people wanting more. It would be typical of Jimmy to reason that a mildly argumentative duo viewed every Sunday night for 26 weeks would be more effective than just Jimmy himself delivering what amounted to a fifteen-minute mono-logue which could just as easily be done on radio. He offered David Kelly the second role which was, of course, accepted, and James Plunkett was duly informed. The pair of them sat in the signal-box and Jimmy carried on long and supposedly knowledgeable discussion with his lean assistant, Ignatius (David Kelly) who didn't appear to have any specific duties. He just sat in a chair and marvelled at Mr O's grasp and breath of vision of such subjects as "The Meaning of Malt;" "The Horse Show"; "Supermarkets"; "The Language Question"; "Is TV a Good Thing?" and any other subject that might be initiated by Ignatius, who was described by Brian O'Nolan (according to Ms Clissmann) as: "a stupid, vacant gawm who has little to say, that little being stupid and meaningless."

In fact O'Nolan was notably unsuccessful in rewriting the monologues as conversation between the two characters. Plunkett found that the scripts as duologues were failures because Ignatius was not a real character and his dialogue consisted merely of token exchanges.

He (and John O'Donovan according to Ms Clissmann) adapted the scripts to make them more credible. Nobody admitted to, much less took credit for, tampering with the work, and a vituperative explosion was expected weekly from O'Nolan. But it never came. It is possible that he attributed the alterations to his friend Jimmy O'Dea, who would have the comedian's instinctive knowledge of dialogue that would work. He knew that Jimmy altered new scripts to suit his own comic sense and furthermore, that he frequently went off the script altogether in performance if he thought he had accidentally hit upon a richer vein. In any event James Plunkett was paid by RTE to doctor O'Nolan's scripts and if the latter was ever really aware of it he must have trusted Plunkett's judgement.

Jimmy and David never rehearsed the show; they just went into Studio 3 and did it. The results had all the appearances of spontaneity. Sometimes Jimmy forgot his lines and they ad libbed until they managed to get back to the script; on occasions such as this neither Brian O'Nolan's original script nor James Plunkett's rewritten version was incorporated in the finished programme. Jimmy always signalled these lapses of memory to David with preliminary remarks such as: "Sure what am I talking about?"

On one occasion during one of the impending dries, David started humming to himself just to keep things going. Jimmy grasped this like a drowning man: "That's a beautiful singing voice you have Ignatius. There's a wonderful Slavonic quality in your voice!" David nearly broke up with the laughter and he was taken out of camera shot just in time. The set decoration of the signal box was notable for the presence, week after week, of an uncut prop loaf in the centre of the table at which the characters sat. The director James Plunkett began to receive correspondence of a sarcastic nature from viewers demanding to know when the loaf would be cut or replaced by a fresh one. What viewers didn't realise was that the undoubtedly stale loaf of bread actually housed the microphone. The series was not uproariously funny; it had a gentle humour which depended on the personalities of the performers and their handling of the dialogue, which had its share of malapropisms and puns. The following is a short extract which was recorded in February 1964.

(Extract from—"The Meaning of Malt")

JIMMY: What the doctor pumped into your brother's backside, Ignatius, is called, in medical terms, the anti-dote.

IGNATIUS: Whatever it was, it had the brother back on his feet in a few days.

JIMMY: It was probably Strychneen. Strychneen is a pisen, but it's a great man to fight another pisen if you give it in the right quantities. One pisen fights the other. That's why they call it the anti-dote. Do you folly me. Ignatius.

IGNATIUS: I think I do, Mr O. If you get pisened with wan thing, you pisen yourself with another thing—and in a few days you're sitting up and eating an egg. (*Thought strikes him*) Suppose you wouldn't have a glass of Strychneen in the medicine chest, Mr O?

JIMMY: I would not. And If I had I wouldn't give it to you. I know perfectly well that what you're sufferin' from Strychneen is not the right anti-dote. (*Emphatic*) You, Ignatius, are a classic case of an overdose of *Fusial Oil*

IGNATIUS: I told you, Mr O. it was whiskey I was drinking.

JIMMY: That's what you thought. Whiskey is a good drink. What am I saying! Whiskey is the king of drinks—if you get it right. It loosens the arteries, smooths the nairves and gives the party takin' it a lovely complexion. Because whiskey is made from the grain—like bread.

IGNATIUS: I never got a hangover like this from a feed of bread.

JIMMY:	(PATIENTLY) Let me explain Ignatius, There's another particular thing that arrives in the ferment-iation of the grain that isn't a health food or a body builder at all, at all. Our friend the enemy—Fusial Oil. And that's the boy that does the party drinkin' it no good at all. *Fusial Oil* is *Pisen*. And that's what you got in your cousin's whiskey.
IGNATIUS:	I'm a peaceable man, as you know, Mr O, but if puttin' that class of stuff into a man's ball of malt is that yella belly cousin of mine's joke, he's going to get a right belt on the jaw from me when I get home to him.
JIMMY:	Wait now, Ignatius, don't be flyin' off the handle. How was your cousin this morning?
IGNATIUS:	I don't know because I didn't see very much of him. The mother had a feed of bacon and eggs for him at breakfast but he just looked at it wanst and said "Excuse me. Oh, my God!" and off with him upstairs again. I couldn't get into the bathroom to shave myself. I think he must have fallen asleep in there.
JIMMY:	That was the Fusial Oil workin' on him too. The poor devil was dyin' like yourself. Fusial Oil could easily drive a man mad. I remember when I was in the first World War the Jairmins was very strong in our part of the front. They were stuck in front of us for weeks and no power on earth could dislodge them. At last the General came to me and "Sergeant O" says he "What the hell are we goin' to do about this impasse?"
IGNATIUS:	Impasse?
JIMMY:	It's a French word meaning being like the cockle picker when the tide comes in. "Mr," says I, "get me an issue of twenty gallons of whiskey and leave me a free hand with the Quartermaster Sergeant and we'll take them

positions to-morrow." "Right, Sergeant O," says he, "You have *carte blanc*."

IGNATIUS: What was the cart blonk for?

JIMMY: It meant I'd a free hand. I made certain arrangements with the QMS and we went over the top at dawn. The Lord preserve us but the slaughter was ferocious. We didn't only dislodge the Jairmins—we captured every man jack of them. The general came to me afterwards. "Sergeant O" says he, "how did you do it?"

IGNATIUS: It must have been the best of whiskey—not like the stuff the cousin brought up with him.

JIMMY: Wrong, Ignatius. It was exactly the kind of stuff your cousin had the misfortune to be stuck with by some blackguard of a publican. We went over the top that morning, a detachment of the Dublin Fusialiers, every manjack of us stuffed to the gills with whiskey that was ninety per cent Fusial Oil.

IGNATIUS: I suppose the general didn't tumble to the real reason for your enthusiasm under fire.

JIMMY: He tumbled to it all right. That night he invited me into his dugout and opened a bottle of Napoleon Brandy. "Drink up, Sergeant O," says he, "I'm going to call your detachment of the Dublin Fusialeers by a new name. I'm going to call them—the Dublin Fusial Oils."

The series ran for 26 episodes from September 1963 to March 1964 but in August 1963 before the programme went out on television Jimmy asked David Kelly to join him in his show at the Gaiety *We're Joking, Of Course* in which they did a stage version of *O'Dea's Yer Man* by permission of Telefís Éireann. Jimmy was obviously ill and on one occasion between the matinee and the evening performance he was taken by ambulance to receive medical attention. David watched Jimmy's great discomfort off stage, and with the conceit of the young would resolve to give Jimmy every possible support in their signal-box sketch, but as David himself admits, when O'Dea stepped on to the stage he was a completely different man. Despite the circumstances of his illness when you got on the stage with him, you had to fight for your life, or he'd practically stick you to the scenery, metaphorically speaking. Jimmy, in sickness or pain, showed enormous courage (acknowledged many times by his fellow-performers) and gave the audience everything that it was accustomed to expect of him.

That Christmas Jimmy played his last pantomime role, Bedelia (Queen of the Circus) in *Goldilocks And The Three Bears*. Bedelia was a name that Harry O'Donovan had often bestowed upon Mrs Mulligan on their gramophone recordings of the 1930s. The ambulance and hospital routine was repeated after a particular matinee performance and an anxious cast assembled to rearrange the casting for the evening show—Danny Cummins would take over Jimmy's part and so on. Then just before curtain-up in the evening Jimmy reappeared through the stage door demanding to know what the hell was wrong with everybody before going to his dressing room to change and carry on with the show as if nothing had happened.

In July 1964, Louis Elliman revived his 1957 production of *Finian's Rainbow;* Jimmy played his old role for Finian McLonergan, but he had aged and lost weight and it was obvious that he was extremely ill. Antoinette Fortune of *The Standard* wrote:

> I was at the last night of that show, and it is no exaggeration or imagination to say that a great shivering pall of sadness settled over the audience as he made his final speech from the stage... "We've seen the last of poor Jimmy," I said as we came out. "Yes, I'm afraid so...
>
> It was noticed by Derry O'Donovan that many members of the cast had tears in their eyes as they filed off the stage after the final curtain. In a sad and

uncanny mixture of reality and pure theatre Jimmy achieved his finest moment of tragedy and pathos and poignancy on stage in his career. In the final scene as Finian McLonergan, he bids farewell to everyone and in that moment reality and illusion were fused briefly as the great comedian was himself bidding a last farewell to his audience in his beloved Gaiety Theatre. It was an unbearably moving moment when Jimmy O'Dea spoke his last lines on any stage just before the curtain fell for the last time on *Finians's Rainbow* on 5 September 1964: "Farewell, my friends, I'll see you all one day in Gloccamorra."

There were tears in his eyes as he left the stage for the last time to thunderous applause and by the time he reached the wings they were streaming down his cheeks.

Four months later he was dead.

3

James A

THEATRE ROYAL

STAGE:

JIMMY O'DEA

IN

ROYAL RAINBOW

WITH

DANNY CUMMINS • JOY BRENNAN • VERNON HAYDEN

AND

WALTER JACKSON • JUMPING JAY

THE ROYALETTES

JIMMY CAMPBELL and the THEATRE ROYAL ORCHESTRA

TOMMY DANDO

SCREEN:

ELVIS PRESLEY

IN

LOVING YOU

WITH

LIZABETH SCOTT • WENDELL COREY

SEVEN SONG HITS WITH ELVIS

Technicolor and VistAvision!

Chapter Eleven

One afternoon in the early 1940s a voluble lady spotted
Jimmy O'Dea and Jim Jonson leaving the Gresham
Hotel where they had just had lunch. "Oh, looka!"
screamed the woman excitedly, "There's Jimmy." He
glanced at the woman coldly and said, "Mister O'Dea to
you madam!" He was never willing to accept the role of
the popular buffoon. The public had christened him
Jimmy O'Dea, and it was sensible to retain it as a stage
name in the interests of business. He had always been
known as Jim to his immediate family and his own
original choice of billing, James A O'Dea, would not be
likely to attract much business in Bolton or Wood
Green. But his self-image was that of a college-
educated, middle-class business man, who happened to
trade in the theatre because he was given to understand
that he had something to offer. He had made it his
business to learn his art inside out, an art he then
displayed under the trade name of Jimmy O'Dea. This
may seem to be cool and calculating on the part of the
private James A O'Dea but it was equally true that the
staid James A craved for an audience and satisfied the
desire through his *alter ego* Jimmy O'Dea who wielded
great power. It was always a comedian who led a
company and topped the bill, and if he was a great
comedian he had the power to reduce an audience to
tears as well as laughter. The ordinary little man became
an extraordinary one when he used his personality and
skill to manipulate an audience as he desired.

Most members of his company, who had worked with him for years and sensed this self-esteem and an aura of authority out of proportion to his size, never called him Jimmy. There may have been a few exceptions to this rule and some may have called him that in exceptional cases in his later years when he grew mellower in every respect, but generally, to most of his associates, all of whom confessed to a sense of awe in his presence, he was Mr O'Dea or Sir. With the passage of time the use of "Mr O" might be tolerated, and in Maureen Potter's case, "Guvvy" was permissible.

There is a line in one of his sketches, a burlesque on *East Lynne* in which Jimmy as Little Willie remonstrated with Chris Markey who was playing the First Angel: "Don't call me Jimmy. I'm Jimmy in Jammet's, but I'm the Guvnor in the Gaiety."—and never was a line so close to the truth. A newspaper reporter to whom he granted an interview in Bristol in 1930 wrote: "He was so unlike the usual type of comedian that I called him Mr O'Dea all the time we were talking."

All of the members of his various supporting companies agreed that he could be autocratic and temperamental, and in matters relating to the shows such as the timing of the gags he could be merciless. The nervous offender would be summoned to dressingroom number one, and Jimmy would give the unfortunate a really rough time. In spite of this most offenders were actually grateful for the opportunity to learn from a master of the art of comedy. Sloppiness and carelessness were anathema to him and he saw everything from the point of view of the patrons who paid to see the show. In the early years it was said of him that he would fire people at the drop of a hat—which is literally what happened to one of the dancers on one occasion: the girl's hat fell off during one of the dance routines and Jimmy would probably claim that it was the girl's responsibility to ensure that it was properly pinned on in the first place. The girl was fired and replaced shortly afterwards. Then there was the straight man who during the performance of a sketch was stupid enough to prompt Jimmy during a deliberate pause in the dialogue—timing again! He was replaced at the end of the week. If these dismissals grew fewer with the passage of time it was only because the O'D company had learned their craft well from "the Guvnor." Jimmy had an eye like a hawk and if he spotted anyone backstage whose make-up was not properly blended around the line of the neck the offender was sent back to the dressingroom to complete the job properly. It is not surprising, therefore, that the nickname by which he was best known, behind his back, was "The Little Napoleon." (This may also have been inspired by the fact that he played the role of Napoleon in several sketches written by Harry and he was also filmed in the part in one of his British movies.) But like Tony Hancock, while he was decidedly rough on those who worked with him, he was hardest on himself, and besides it was useful to be known as a bit of a bastard—it kept people on their toes. His leadership and direction were obvious to audiences over the years. He always had a strong and talented company and there was never any evidence that he employed lightweight support in order to highlight his own efforts.

Jimmy will never have a successor. As Micheál MacLiammóir wrote:

To us in Ireland Jimmy is irreplaceable, as all great loved ones are irreplaceable. Jimmy O'Dea was, in fact, a rainbow; shining at the oddest moments from the murk and mire of a humdrum world, and lighting the dullest places of everyday life with an exuberance of absurdity unequalled in his time.

But it is just possible that he may have had an equally popular Dublin predecessor, long ago in the nineteenth century. His name was Pat Kinsella and he was once described by the gentle-humoured Percy French as: "The bright particular luminary of all stage-gazers." His Dublin origin was unconcealable and he rapidly became the city's number one character comedian. He played comedy roles at the Queen's Royal Theatre, did solo singing and dancing at Dan Lowrey's Star of Erin, and was principal clown in the Christmas pantomimes at the Royal, at the Queen's and also at the premier theatre, the Gaiety. Pat's greatest creation was Conn in Boucicault's *The Shaughraun,* but he was also renowned for rollicking songs like "The Mud Island Fusiliers," "The Ballybough Brigade," and "Ballyhooley." Eugene Watters and Matthew Murtagh say of him in *Infinite Variety,* their fascinating book about Dan Lowrey's, that, "Pat Kinsella knew the temper of the Dublin street, quick, humorous, cynical." Pat saw the comic side of serious things and tumbled into burlesque. When the Shah of Persia paid a state-visit to England, "His Ever-Serene & Sublime Highness the Shah of Dublin, King Patroshki Kinsella" arrived in Dan's, where he kept the audience on the best of terms with themselves." (*Telegraph.*) In Horse Show Week came the "Eminent Jockey & Animal Surgeon Mr Patrick Kinsella." With war threatening, "Admiral Pat Kinsella" enacted the Defence of Dublin. "...has to be seen to be believed." said Percy French's comic journal *The Jarvey.* When Tom Costello came singing his robust "Died Like A True Irish Soldier," he was followed by "General Kinsella" singing "Died Like A True Irish Tailor."

His characterisations and material seem to have been broadly similar to those of Jimmy O'Dea but without the wide universal success of the latter. Pat had a hard life, no worldwide fame and no security. In 1882 Dan Lowrey presented a Christmas show called *The Magic Shamrock* with a cast of sixty, which was produced under the direction of Mr and Mrs Pat Kinsella, the heroes of the hour: "The production of *The Magic Shamrock* will long be remembered as one of the most successful enterprises in this city."(*The Irish Times.*) Pat became an institution. With eyes crinkling in a rubicund face this melodious clown of the Liffeyside halls was known to every child at the Christmas shows. He acquired the little Harp Theatre in Adam Court which he ran on "free-and-easy" lines, saying it was the one place left in

Dublin where a man could bring his pint into the auditorium and enjoy the show (which was the essence of the original music-halls). Pat kept the Harp until 1893 when, in a fit of depression following the sudden death of his son, he let the business lapse. Few would be aware of this great performer but for the valuable research of Messrs Watters and Murtagh. Kinsella's last recorded appearance was at the Empire Palace (late Dan Lowrey's) in Dame Street in 1899, which was, by coincidence, the year in which James Augustine O'Dea was born just down along the quays in Lower Bridge Street.

Unlike such people as Dan Leno or Charles Chaplin, to whom he has been compared, James A did not in his youth have to undergo a depressing, squalid, and often physically dangerous apprenticeship on the halls. Even his very funny and talented supporting comedian Danny Cummins spent a tough apprenticeship with the comedy ensemble of juveniles in *Casey's Court* before joining the Queen's Theatre Happy Gang. Here his song and dance routines particularly with the debonair Jimmy Harvey were guaranteed show-stoppers. From the start Jimmy O'Dea had a secure and reasonably privileged existence, and in contrast to the dirt and poverty which surrounded him in the streets around his birthplace he was pathologically clean and fastidious. He presented a dapper figure as he strolled down Grafton Street. His handmade shoes shone and although it wouldn't be immediately apparent his shirts were hand-tailored in Tyson's—not a very widespread method of ordering one's linen in those days. A tailored suit and overcoat were crowned by a jaunty trilby worn on the Kildare side in the manner of the London idols like Jack Buchanan or Noel Coward. When he acquired the habit of taking snuff he was careful to order coloured bandannas in order to conceal the snuff stains. He also expected the members of his company to be neat and clean and a credit to their profession, which he held in very high esteem.

Harry's son, Terry O'Donovan, when a very young man, was a frequent visitor backstage at the Gaiety, and like many other young men Terry was a little careless about his appearance at times and guilty of small lapses. These never escaped the eagle-eyed O'Dea, who would, if given the opportunity, declare loudly in the Circle bar after the show, "I cannot abide people who don't polish their shoes." And it would be painfully obvious to poor Terry as he surveyed his grubby footwear that the denunciation was for his benefit. It is apparent that there would be two forces at work here, especially early in Jimmy's career. First, he liked to establish his supremacy, (and how better to do this than by criticism?) and second, he had a wicked sense of humour which he unleashed gleefully to the discomfiture of his victims. It was a sort of straightfaced leg-pulling. It was said of him in some quarters of the BBC that he was difficult to work with but it is probable that his English colleagues did not understand his sense of humour which could admittedly be double edged; it could be taken as merely joking but in certain circumstances, if it suited him, he could turn it into a mode of vicious attack, thus displaying a certain deviousness in his character. For instance, on one occasion on the stage of the Gaiety during rehearsals he asked Vernon Hayden which members of the company were persistently late for rehearsals, to which Vernon replied that Maureen Potter was an occasional offender. Jimmy turned on his heel and walked towards the wings where he spotted Maureen with script in hand. Jimmy stopped in his tracks and turned back to Vernon shouting venomously: "How dare you say that members of my company are late for rehearsals!" Regardless of Vernon's feelings the whole performance was for Maureen's benefit, of course, but in such a devious way. Terry O'Donovan usually travelled with the O'D company as pianist when they toured the smaller Irish dates and even then his transgressions did not escape notice. One evening Jimmy sent for Terry who duly presented himself in "Napoleon's" dressing-room.

"How much do we pay you?" enquired O'Dea.

Terry mentioned the amount.

"And how much are your digs?"

Again Terry volunteered the information, half-hoping that an increase in salary might be on the cards.

"Well," said James A cleaning his finger-nails, "it would appear to me that there is a sufficient balance to enable you to afford a razor blade!" Even over the stage lighting he had noticed that Terry, who was playing at a distance from the stage, hadn't shaved himself on the previous evening. Jimmy was equally tough on his stage hands—he walked into the Gaiety one morning and told the stage staff in no uncertain terms that a proscenium border that they were hanging was crooked, and ordered them to hang it properly without delay. It was typical of him that when his wrath subsided and the job was completed to his satisfaction he took the entire crew over to Sinnott's, which in its South King Street site faced the stage door of the theatre; when the stage door was moved to the back of the building in Tangier Lane the favoured hostelry became Neary's of Chatham Street.

Jimmy had a great sympathy for ordinary working-class people and compassion for the poor of the city. It is probable that he was influenced by his father's charitable work, and he could not have been unaware from his childhood of the enormous problems of the less fortunate. He was an admirer of Jim Larkin the labour leader and approved of Larkin's efforts on behalf of the workers of Dublin. Jimmy performed in countless Sunday night charity concerts which were usually sponsored by Alfie Byrne whenever he was in office as Lord Mayor—which was most of the time. Jimmy and Alfie were great friends and Alfie would sometimes announce to his staff in the Mansion House: "I'm off to have lunch with Jimmy O'Dea and exchange scripts perhaps!" Jimmy played many working-class types in his sketches over the years: plumbers in particular but also road workers, waiters (and waitresses!); he also played soldiers and policemen but there was never anything derogatory in his interpretations. Each character was played without losing sight of his own personality, as if he himself was a particular tradesman and any shortcomings were his alone. He was a great favourite with the stallholders in Moore Street who referred to him as "Jemmy," a form of address which he deplored but which he accepted from them, aware perhaps, that he owed to them much of the success in the creation of Biddy Mulligan, and that their pronunciation of his name was peculiar to their mode of speech. He enjoyed a stroll down Moore Street and the exchange of banter.

He was also genuinely concerned about the level of employment in Ireland. As far back as 1937 when he was a guest at a luncheon given by Messrs Kelly & Shiel Ltd who were introducing the latest model of the Ekco radio receiver for which they were the agents, Jimmy in an after-dinner speech expressed the hope that the company might, some day, consider establishing a factory for the manufacture of the radio in the Free State.

When the magnificent Theatre Royal closed its doors for the last time Jimmy said: "Speaking from the stage of the Theatre Royal, I think most people in our profession regret very much the passing of a theatre, a live theatre; that is not to say that live entertainment will go—it never could go as long as people are alive." But he went on to voice his concern about the livelihood of the employees—the backstage staff, and the front-of-house people; there was nowhere comparable to the Royal to absorb them and he genuinely sympathised with them.

His concern for the underdog extended to the prisoners in Mountjoy Jail. He used to bring his company to the prison on a Sunday afternoon at Christmas each year and present excerpts from his current Gaiety panto for the benefit of the prisoners. After a number of years he noticed that the best seats close to the stage were being allocated to visitors to the prison, semi-official people who really had no business being there at all except that they may have been attracted by the drinks reception which the governor laid on for the cast afterwards. Jimmy made it plain to the prison authorities that he would cancel his annual visit unless the prisoners were seated close to the stage and the visitors, who could in any case visit the Gaiety at will, were seated at the back.

He was often a source of frustration to Vernon Hayden—in fact he was the bane of his life. Vernon claims that Jimmy had no regard for money. The evidence shows rather that he had an ambivalent attitude towards it. For instance, it often happened that Vernon would give Jimmy his weekly salary which would immediately be counted in Vernon's presence. On occasion it would be found to be short by a considerable amount and Vernon would explain the deficit by telling Jimmy that he had paid his bar bill in the Green Room. This would result in vague protests and end in a fit of sulks (if it was intended that Vernon should pay Jimmy's bar bills out of the company accounts he had never been instructed to do so, and in the absence of such a direction he never did). Again, there was the occasion when the O'D company gave a Sunday night performance in Valleymount for which they were paid a fee. Several weeks later Jimmy met Thelma Ramsey who was Musical Director at the time and asked her if Vernon had put extra into her pay-packet for the Valleymount Show. Thelma replied that she had received something only that week. "You're lucky," observed Jimmy, "I got nothing, so far." Here was the backbone of O'D Productions, uncertain as to when he would receive payment for a show and reluctant to ask about it. How does one describe such a man's attitude to money, especially in view of the fact that on other occasions he lost out completely on engagements by holding out for too much? After a session in Sinnott's or Neary's some out-of-work performer might meet Jimmy and relate his tale of woe with the not infrequent result that the jobless artiste would be told to report to Vernon who was then saddled with the job of fitting the unexpected newcomer in the new show, and have a fruitless argument later with Jimmy about the dire financial consequences of overspending on the budget. Apparently budgets were intangible concepts of finance (as opposed to hard cash) to Jimmy and were of no consequence.

Many of the cast of O'D Productions rarely had a Sunday night free when they were playing the Gaiety. Jimmy would take them off to some country hall to do a charity show in aid of some church or other which was urgently in need of a new roof or other repairs. On one occasion he did a concert for his stepsister May who was head of the Ursuline Convent in Sligo and he went through the scripts himself excising anything doubtful with all the enthusiasm of the narrow-minded book censors of the time, so as not to offend the unworldly ears of the sisters. He also issued an instruction that the girls' frocks should be worn well below the knee. His charity was legendary, and he was a frequent visitor to friends, old performers and acquaintances in hospital. Derry O'Donovan recalls a hospital visit from Jimmy when he brought her the biggest box of chocolates she had ever seen. These hospital visits were made by taxi and the meter was left running while Jimmy paid his respects. Actually, he had a regular hackney driver who normally picked him up at his home in the morning, and was waiting for him again in the Green Room after the show at night. One amused patient who delighted in a long visit from Jimmy expressed amazement, not at the fact that the taxi meter was left running, but that the visit took place during valuable drinking time. Father Cormac O'Daly OFM, once Chaplain to the Stage Guild, at one stage said: "Jimmy was a most charitable man and had a great affinity with artists. He was accustomed to visit old and sick artists and was very generous to them. Money would be found—sometimes a £5 note—on the table when he had gone. This was a characteristic which was little known about him." Asked once if it was true that all great comedians are sad, Jimmy replied: "Yes, I think so. I am a sad man. Everybody who looks around him and studies his fellow men must be a little sad. And, you know, as a comic you are very much alone."

The private O'Dea liked a quiet life and long solitary walks. When he was in Dublin the day began with a visit to his bookmaker in South Anne Street. He used all sorts of permutations from the straightforward each-way bet to elaborate up and down cross-trebles and Yankees. A friend who saw Jimmy on one of his late-night strolls around Ballsbridge, remarked to Mrs O'Dea that Jimmy had been deep in thought as he walked with hands deep in overcoat pockets, and wondered what he might have been thinking about, expecting to have confirmed her own preconceived notion that he was planning a new comic creation. "Probably planning his bets for next day," was the reply. After placing his commissions (like the lady-punter in "Sixpence Each Way") he might visit either the shop or the workshops in Dixon Hempenstall, the opticians of Grafton Street, for a chat, or else call on his sister Rita who was still managing James A O'Dea, Optician, by now situated in 10 Duke Street. He sold this business to Rita in 1943 in what was virtually a hand-over, because the arrangement was so favourable to her. There was some illogical arrangement whereby he lent Rita the money to buy his own business. He retained an academic interest in optics until the end of his life, and he himself made the old-fashioned wire-frame spectacles worn by the old storyteller in the children's TV series *Once Upon A Time*.

He took an inordinate interest in the eyesight of others and if he thought that a colleague's eyesight was suspect he would tell the victim: "I think you could be doing with glasses; go down and see Rita; she'll fix you up!" Sometimes he supervised the entire process himself and when the spectacles were ready he would present them as a gift, but some people, including Maureen Potter, claimed ever after that they ended up wearing glasses too soon. One cannot help remembering the newspaper headline when he played London for the first time—"Comedian-Optician makes people see jokes."

There was a corner seat in Neary's bar much favoured by Jimmy and if it was occupied by another customer it was immediately vacated when he appeared on the scene in recognition of his prior claim to it. It was a gesture that surprised him and in an increasingly selfish world lacking in respect he appreciated it. Nothing was said except perhaps: "Hello, Mr O'Dea." He would ensconce himself to partake of his favourite tipple which was Dimple Haig Scotch. He was not an alcoholic but except towards the end he drank to excess. This caused him at times to make serious misjudgements. Whenever he returned from a tour of Ireland or abroad the first place he made for, still with hand luggage, even before he went home, was Neary's. In the early 1960s he toured Australia and New Zealand with a company which included Josef Locke, Charles Lynch, Jack Barrett and his Ceili Band, Minnie Clancy and Vernon Hayden. Jimmy and Vernon had a further engagement in Canada but they decided first to take a short holiday in Hawaii. One afternoon Vernon was sitting on the veranda of their hotel gazing out at the magnificent vista of sandy beaches, palm trees, blue sea and sky, and the warm sun sparkling on the fountains, when Jimmy appeared looking very down in the mouth (one cannot be absolutely certain whether or not he was wearing his famous overcoat). "Isn't this an absolutely beautiful place," said Vernon happily.

Jimmy gazed mournfully at the million-dollar scenery. "Hum," he sniffed. "I'd give anything to be back in Neary's."

Neary's was his refuge from the world, in his favourite part of the city. There in his special corner he held quiet conversations with special friends who were mostly characters like himself like Brian O'Nolan or the painter, Sean O'Sullivan. And the story circulated in Dublin that their serious deliberations one morning resulted in their unanimous agreement that it was a great pity and loss that Dublin no longer had any characters. Jimmy liked a quiet life when he was away from the theatre and a quiet drink in agreeable company, and confessed that in the end he found it hard to dislike anybody or anything very much. If he wasn't attracted to someone for any reason he just ignored him. In all social circumstances he was inclined more to listen and observe rather than try to be the centre of attention, in contrast to other comedians who as a breed, with few exceptions, tend to allow their private lives to become extensions of their stage performances. That sort of behaviour was intellectually repugnant to James A O'Dea. He considered it cheap to feel compelled in normal life to keep the company entertained with jokes and gags; he never did even on the stage where his comedy was derived from character and situation. He circulated in company, of course, greeting old friends and acknowledging people, and enquiring, out of courtesy, about people whom he may not have seen for some time. This was a nightly ritual after the show in the dress circle bar of the Gaiety.

Jimmy didn't even have a party piece and his contribution was usually restricted to a brief piece of doggerel about Sweet Fanny Adams:

Sweet Fanny Adams, beautiful and gay,
Carved her name on the old apple tree
In the merry month of May.
But the woodpecker came in December,
And the woodpecker would peck away.
Now all that's left on the old apple tree,
Is Sweet F...A...!

In 1955 when the Gaiety closed for three months for renovation, Jimmy Sheil, a genuine Dublin character who saw humour in almost everything but was, nevertheless, always on the look out for business opportunities, and managed the Theatre Royal with a more serious-minded colleague, Charlie Wade, heard from Mr Louis that the Parterre bar, a magnificent old-fashioned construction in oak, marble and glass was to be disposed of or scrapped. Sheil suggested to O'Dea and O'Donovan that they should acquire this centre-piece with all its Gaiety connotations and install it in Sinnott's across the road which he advised them to buy as an investment. Unfortunately, perhaps, for both of them they were not keen on the idea, and it is possible that Jimmy's bank manager, whom he always consulted in such matters, advised against it. When Jimmy took an apartment in Pembroke Road he had an opportunity to buy the whole house but his bank manager advised him that his business was in the theatre and that he was not really suited to be a landlord.

Chapter Twelve

Jimmy and Harry were complete opposites. Harry was the quiet thoughtful pipe-smoker who liked a game of golf and was always a soft touch for midweek pocket money for the juvenile members of the cast who adored him. Jimmy was full of vitality and temperament when a new show went into production, and was ever-watchful when the run began. It was generally agreed that they appeared to suit each other very well and few if any seemed to have been aware of their serious private differences. In minor disagreements at rehearsals they might argue about the merits of a script or Jimmy might complain that he couldn't possibly get a laugh with a certain line. Harry would take the script to a quiet corner and rewrite the allegedly dull joke. But nobody else was permitted to criticise Harry's work. Rehearsing a script one morning a senior member of the company was heard to voice the opinion that the piece would be a flop as there wasn't one decent laugh in it. Jimmy lit on her with a vengeance and demanded that she go over at once to Harry and apologise. "And then," added Napoleon, "we shall have to consider your future with the company."

Jimmy and Harry had their disagreements over scenery, costumes and casting—and God knows what other problems that bedevil the production of an expensive show—but in a partnership spanning almost forty years it would be extraordinary if things were otherwise. The success of O'D Productions was due to both men's understanding of what made people laugh.

Although he rarely told jokes in the stand-up comic fashion Jimmy doubted if there was such a thing as a new joke: "I think it's the way you tell them," he said. When he was asked what he thought made people laugh he replied:

> Ah. That's funny. I went all over Australia and came back to Canada, and I was interviewed by many men. The first woman who interviewed me asked me that question. I think it's a difficult question to answer. It depends on the individual, on the way they take it, but I think you should give them something that's factual. I have never depended on anything manufactured to get a laugh. I believe in giving them an actual fact, something that's happened to yourself, something you've seen or heard.

The apparently quiet O'Dea, watchful and listening, in the poshest bars in Dublin or the most drab public house in some country town, was always on the lookout for something that might help to inspire Harry into writing another neat microcosm of life. A perfect example of this is their early sketch, "Crossing The Border." Jimmy was crossing the border with presents of a half a dozen bottles of whiskey after a show in Belfast. The customs officer on the Free State side stopped him and he declared one bottle—the other five were under the seat of the car. The fellow told Jimmy that he was allowed only a quarter of a pint, so Jimmy asked him what he should do and the customs man replied, "Well, I'm not a teetotaller." So they sat down on the side of the road and started on the bottle, then two more fellows came across from the Northern hut, and it wasn't long before there was a good dint made in the bottle. Harry turned this incident into one of their most successful sketches.

The evolution of the sketches into definitive versions was not as clear-cut as might be imagined. Harry wrote the scripts and Jimmy improvised on them on the stage. They were revised and altered every night for about three or four days until they were as finished as possible. Jimmy admitted that he did not like the critics to come on the first night to review the show (these were the days before previews) because he was still experimenting until by the Wednesday or Thursday of the first week he'd have found his feet, and then he'd experiment with the laughs because he knew where they came and try to improve and elaborate on them. Jimmy was himself surprised at some of the material that got laughs.

It's amazing how often something that you think is no good, no use at all, makes the house howl with laughter [which must say something for Harry's judgement]; you can have an ideal from experience of what will make people laugh but you can't be sure until you are in front of an audience. The audiences are the judges; they pay their money and they call the tune and rightly so, because they never get their money back even if they don't like the show. That's why I always have to play dames like Mrs Mulligan. A good percentage of my audience love her. Therefore I must like her. She's like Queen Anne. You know, you say—"as dead as Queen Anne," but then someone says she was never dead—there was some mystery about her. No, I don't dislike Mrs Mulligan because I known that she's a real person.

As he became an old hand at the game Jimmy gradually shook off the nerves and the butterflies in his stomach every time the curtain went up. It all became second nature to him according to himself. Nevertheless, most of his associates were aware of a tension in him while he waited to make an entrance but, of course, it disappeared the moment he set foot on the stage. Although he was the star of the shows, he was professionally generous and allowed everyone to get their fair share of laughs. He deplored people who tried to be selfish and take the centre of the stage at all time; he was equally annoyed by those who went in the opposite direction and had an inferiority complex about him. As a producer it could be said that he favoured ensemble playing but he always had the best role. Once the show settled into its run audiences expected and looked forward to the inevitable ad libbing and private sides on the stage. One classic example of this was in a Mrs Mulligan sketch with Danny Cummins as Mick her husband who was about to be made Lord Mayor of Dublin. Mrs Mulligan laments, "There goes my ambition of being First Lady." To which Danny Cummins replied, "Never mind, you will always be my first lady." Then one night he substituted, "You will always be My Fair Lady" (the show of which had just opened in London). And quick as a flash Jimmy responded with "Not bloody likely!"

Jimmy's professionalism was legendary and manifested itself in even the smallest ways. Terry O'Donovan expresses unreserved admiration for him because of an incident that occurred when Terry was accompanist on one of the Irish tours. One night after the show Jimmy took him aside and told him that he was making a bags of the music for his soldier act (one of his rare solo acts which he usually finished by singing "The Dublin Fusiliers") and demanded to see Terry at ten o'clock on the following morning. Jimmy turned up at the hall on time much to Terry's surprise and seeming to indicate that the complaint was grave. It seemed that at a certain point Terry was playing a wrong note which was very disconcerting and put Jimmy out of tune. Terry took out the piano copy and played it over and at the disputed spot Jimmy enquired what a certain chord was. Terry informed him that it was A major. "That's wrong," said Jimmy, "it should be A minor." Terry insisted that the arranger had written it as A major. Derry O'Donovan, Terry's cousin, happened to be backstage arranging the wardrobe for that evening's performance and Jimmy involved her in the argument. He asked her to fetch the full band-parts which, luckily, were in the skips for use in Cork and Limerick where a full orchestra would be used. On examination of these the disputed chord was found to be A minor, as Jimmy had claimed. However, Derry, who could read music, confirmed that Terry was correct and that the piano copy was incorrectly written with an A

Derry O'Donovan, Maureen Potter and Ursula Doyle (Mrs Jimmy O'Dea).

Left to right: Harry O'Donovan, William Boyd (Hopalong Cassidy), Jimmy O'Dea and Louis Elliman.

Left to right: Dudley Hare, Maureen Potter and Milo O'Shea.

Maureen Potter and Jimmy O'Dea in *A Minute's Wait*, 1957.

The King of Comedy.

Jimmy O'Dea and Ursula with friends on their wedding day,
October 1959.

Jimmy O'Dea as Biddy Mulligan.

Walt Disney, Jimmy O'Dea as King Brian and Albert Sharpe as Darby on the set of *Darby O'Gill and the Little People*.

Mr and Mrs Jimmy O'Dea.

Vernon Hayden and Jimmy O'Dea in a radio broadcast.

Jimmy O'Dea and his wife Ursula with Mickser Reid.

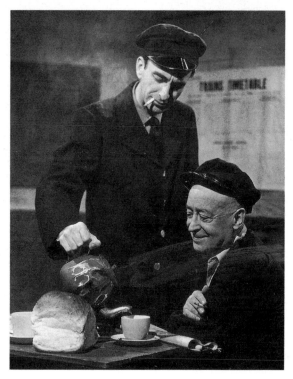

David Kelly and Jimmy O'Dea in *O'Dea's Yer Man* on RTE television.

Jimmy O'Dea in *O'Dea's Yer Man*.

Jimmy O'Dea as the storyteller in *Once Upon a Time*, RTE television.

Jimmy O'Dea's goodbye, "Farewell my friends, I'll see you all one day in Gloccamorra," *Finian's Rainbow* at the Gaiety, 1964.

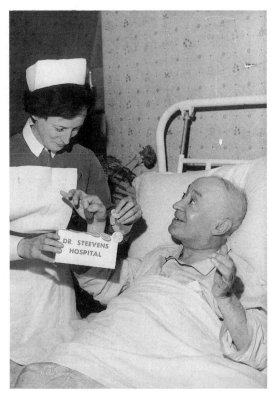

The impatient patient.

major. Jimmy admitted to being both right and wrong and the matter ended amicably over whiskeys in the nearest bar. Terry adds to this story: "It was a wonderful example of his professionalism. He wasn't a musician, but he knew straight away when something was wrong."

No matter what the circumstances, Jimmy rarely admitted to being wrong, a trait which Vernon Hayden attributed to an inferiority complex. When plans were announced for the Gaiety to close for renovation Vernon suggested to Jimmy that they should do the August show that year in the Olympia. He was agreeable so Vernon went ahead and made the necessary business arrangements with the lessees of the theatre, Stanley Illsley and Leo McCabe, who had a successful policy of presenting world theatre at the Olympia. At that time Catholic clergy were forbidden to attend theatres and it was Jimmy's policy to permit his friends in religion to view his shows from the wings backstage at the Gaiety. In addition he had various other friends whom he entertained in the Green Room but when he learned that visitors were not encouraged backstage at the Olympia he told Vernon to cancel any arrangements he had made for an appearance there. A few days later Jimmy met Illsley and McCabe in Grafton Street and told them enthusiastically that he was looking forward to playing their theatre once again in August. The partners informed him that Vernon had cancelled the date, at which Jimmy expressed complete surprise and commented darkly, "You'd never be up to that fellow."

He also seemed to find it necessary to establish his ascendancy over people with authority. At the time when *O'Dea's Yer Man* was on RTE the Director General was an American, Edward Roth, who was reputed to be a very devout Catholic. One morning at Montrose, Michael Barry, the Controller of Programmes, introduced Roth to Jimmy. The big American towered over Jimmy and shook hands. "How do you do," said Jimmy, "I believe you're a very religious man!" There was no answer to that.

Jimmy never publicly declared his political leanings, which was understandable for a man in his position as an entertainer and in consideration of the bitterness which existed between opposing factions from 1922 onwards. There is a generally held opinion that he had no politics except for his obvious moral support for the spirit of Larkinism. But there is some evidence to suggest otherwise. Why, for instance, did he keep a printed throwaway communiqué issued from the Four Courts in 1922?. This was printed on cheap paper, sepia in colour, and is, naturally, slightly tattered. Nevertheless, Jimmy had it handsomely framed, and it was hung on a wall in each of his four Dublin homes in turn. By all accounts he was very proud to be its possessor. The document reads:

STOP PRESS

POBLACHT NA h-ÉIREANN

Wednesday, June 28th, Seventh year of the Republic

COMMUNIQUE FROM THE FOUR COURTS

We have received the following message from Major General Rory O'Connor, I.R.A.

9 a.m. Wednesday, June 28th

At 3.40 a.m. this morning we received a note signed by Tom Ennis demanding on behalf of "The Government" our surrender at 4.a.m. when he would attack.

He opened attack at 4.07 in the name of his Government, with Rifle, Machine and Field Pieces.

THE BOYS ARE GLORIOUS, AND WILL FIGHT FOR THE REPUBLIC TO THE END. HOW LONG WILL OUR MISGUIDED FORMER COMRADES OUTSIDE ATTACK THOSE WHO STAND FOR IRELAND ALONE?

Three casualties so far, all slight. Father Albert and Father Dominic with us here.

Our love to all comrades outside, and the brave boys especially of the Dublin Brigade.

(Signed)   RORY O'CONNOR
                  Four Courts
                  Major General I.R.A.

At the bottom in smaller type the document continues in vituperative vein against Winston Churchill, England, and the traitors in our midst. It is a little difficult to understand why a man who never kept a single copy of his own press clippings or a programme of his many shows should proudly preserve this document. Granted it is of great and important historical interest; it is also evidence of a sad period in the history of Ireland. Did he simply agree with the sentiments expressed and implied?

He did, of course, make political jokes on stage and comment on the behaviour and statements of politicians of every class. Some were easy targets, like Oliver Flanagan, whose name raised a laugh at the mere mention of it, which is not surprising since Deputy Flanagan was credited with the statement that there was no sex in Ireland until the advent of television. During the war years lines like: "A bit of bread and a peaky cap, and they think they're Mussomolinis." was enough to rout the foe in any pantomime. Many of O'Dea's songs and sketches look forward to the day when the North and South of Ireland will be united politically, and in the final sequence of the film *Blarney* he actually knocks over the wooden structure which supposedly marks the border. After Jimmy's death Hilton Edwards remarked:

> Ireland does well to mourn: her 32 counties have suffered a great loss: one of the strongest links that bound her, the catalyst that united them in universal laughter. If genius is, as I believe it to be, accessible by degrees of uniqueness Jimmy O'Dea undoubtedly had more than his share.

One of his songs, "Orange and Green," in particular, describes a peculiar Irish hybrid, whose mother was from Dublin and father from Belfast, and the conflicting loyalties which this entails. But when he performed the song in Belfast dressed in an orange and green shirt he experienced difficulties on some evenings when it was not at all well-received. But Maureen Potter recalls a more bizarre incident:

I'll never forget the night that Costello [the then Taoiseach] decided to do what he did in Canada—declare Ireland a republic. We were opening a new pantomime that night or the night after, and Jimmy O'Dea was being wheeled on in a wheelbarrow as a spiv—and you know he cried. He went forward and made a political speech and said: "What have they done to my country?" People backstage were in a panic saying, "Get back to the pantomime...get back to the show," in loud stage whispers. And he was really so upset about De Valera's ideas being scotched or knocked on the head at the time.

It is, perhaps, no coincidence that Jimmy received a Christmas card from De Valera every year.

In 1963 the President of Ireland gave a garden party at Árus An Uachtaráin in the Phoenix Park for the American President, John F Kennedy, and Jimmy's old friend Sean Lemass ensured that his name was on the list of notables invited to meet JFK. Jimmy was understandably proud of the honour as he had a high regard for the American president. Jimmy accompanied by a fellow guest Sean O'Sullivan proceeded in good order *en route* to the Phoenix Park by taxi from Neary's. Their progress was punctuated by a visit to practically every pub on the way but they arrived in good time and still in good order to meet the great man.

There were occasions during Saturday matinees in the Gaiety when Jimmy would increase the tempo of the sketches, and it wouldn't be for any of his usually valid reasons. It meant simply that a rugby match was being broadcast and he wanted to get back to his dressing-room as quickly as possible. And if there was any change in the score while he was still on the stage the news was conveyed to him by means of chalked boards held up on the wings. He said of his interest in sport:

When I was a young fella, I played rugby and still get a kick out of seeing a rugby or even a soccer match. I'm not an advertisement for the GAA—I used to play golf too.

He liked to read autobiographies and listen to LPs of classical music—even operas as long as he didn't have to watch them. A favourite book was James Stephens' *The Crock Of Gold*, and he liked good films, continental ones in particular, although he could never remember the titles afterwards. As he grew older it became increasingly difficult to get him to visit the Abbey or the Gate Theatres, not because he disliked their attractions but because like all of the first-run cinemas they were situated on the north side of the city. "We'd have to cross the Liffey," he would inform his wife almost fearfully at the prospect of visiting a suddenly strange and hostile land, only to discover perhaps on his return that the Gaiety and Neary's had disappeared in his absence.

Touring England, too, began to lose its attractions. "Travel was very exciting," he recalled. "But now you fly quickly everywhere, and somehow it's not the same at all." Perhaps he was thinking too about the Mediterranean cruise which he took in 1933 on the SS *Homeric* in the company of his wife, Bernadette, Harry and Eileen O'Donovan, Noel Purcell (who won prizes for ballroom dancing and was, as the most extrovert member of the party also the most popular), Father Allen and Eddie and Kitty Twomey of Cork. Jimmy, as a performer, was acceptable in all areas of Britain—a fairly unusual achievement. Many top-ranking comedians from the London area would not venture north of Watford and North-country comics and their Scottish counterparts usually failed in London and the South. Scotland was almost out of bounds to English performers and the Glasgow Empire was known as the comedian's graveyard. News of Jimmy's death was received with much sorrow in Scotland and Jack Short, managing director of Jimmy Logan's Metropole Theatre, Glasgow wrote:

The passing of that lovable character, Jimmy, was a great shock to the theatrical profession in Scotland, especially here in Glasgow where he had lots of friends and was a great favourite with theatregoers. In the old Metropole he played many seasons and his fund of stories and native wit will long be remembered here. Jimmy was to Ireland what Harry Lauder was to Scotland—a symbol and ambassador of his native land."

Clarkson Rose wrote in 1964:

"And now let us leave Scotland and look over the sea to Ireland. Many Irish comedians have made good in the English music-halls. To give examples, there was Pat Rafferty in the nineties and the early part of this century, and today there is that fine all-round comic, Jimmy O'Dea, who, although he only makes fleeting visits to England nowadays, has long been a favourite on our halls, particularly in the North, but his native Dublin never seems to tire of him—and no wonder, because he embraces nearly every facet of the comedian's art."

Jimmy's appearances in Britain were growing fewer at that time. He did a four-week season in the Metropolitan music-hall, Edgeware Road, London in November 1959 in the old twice-nightly format. The show was presented by Phil Raymond and it must have been very nearly the last show at that historic and atmospheric old venue before it was closed and reduced to rubble due to a miscalculation on the part of the engineers entrusted with a road widening scheme. After the Metropolitan season Phil Raymond took the show on tour under the title *The Irish Are Here* to such dates as the Empire, Newcastle. The sketches included such old-time favourites as "Mrs Mulligan In Court"; "Marrying Mary"; "The Irish Way"—the three of which Jimmy had presented in England as early as 1930, and "The Lost Railway," the only one of the four which he hadn't also recorded. It was a Moss Empire's tour and it was a great compliment to Jimmy and Harry's material that they were still acceptable to Cissie Williams, the

Moss Empire Booking Controller, who was feared for her notorious single-mindedness in maintaining high standards. At that time Variety was dying fast and only acts with a reputation in some other medium could be guaranteed to fill the Variety theatres such as a current recording star usually seen on TV. At the Moss Empire in Newcastle, for instance, the acts which followed Jimmy's show in the following weeks were presented by Bernard Delfont and included Bernard Bresslaw, then famous for his appearances in the *Carry On* films, and Bruce Forsyth, compère of the popular *Sunday Night At The London Palladium*. The Christmas pantomime was to be *Cinderella* with Danny La Rue very far down the bill as one of the Ugly Sisters.

Jimmy O'Dea, himself, of course, was far from being a spent force, as his Disney film *Darby O'Gill and the Little People* was doing the rounds of the cinemas. There is strong evidence that Jimmy was always acutely aware of the importance of film, radio and television appearances to boost his live appearances in the theatre. But he missed some good opportunities around this period. Jack Hylton, who then controlled Associated-Rediffusion Television and had made a series starring Tony Hancock in 1956/57, made a pilot programme starring Jimmy, supported by his regular company. Hylton was very pleased with the result and was anxious to go ahead and make a series. This could have been a completely new departure for Jimmy, a new career in many respects, but when Vernon Hayden had completed all the business arrangements, and the Hylton organisation entertained the entire O'D company to dinner to celebrate the deal, Jimmy fouled it up by listening to others who claimed that he should ask for more money. Although Jimmy wasn't interested in money as such, he always refused to sell himself short, and took the view that since they were in the big league in London, he could hold out for more. Jack Hylton took a different view and the deal was cancelled.

Towards the end the touring was confined almost exclusively to Ireland. He loved the countryside and was always assured of his share of adulation in the different towns where he was greatly appreciated because for generations a large proportion of his audiences were made up of the older country folk whose visits to Dublin at Christmas time always included a visit to see Jimmy in pantomime. There were still periodic visits to England whenever some impresario could muster a strong bill, and it was during one of these visits to Manchester that Jimmy's spot on the bill followed the great old-timer, G H Elliott—"The Chocolate Coloured Coon"— famous for the song "I Used to Sigh for the Silvery Moon." Jimmy was doing his soldier spot and he noticed each evening that Elliott formed the habit of sitting on a chair at the side of the stage when he finished his act, and watched Jimmy perform his, and he was terribly touched that such a legendary figure as Elliott should be so interested in him. Jimmy basked in this glory until Robb Wilton told him the truth of the matter—G H Elliott was then so old and decrepit that after his exertions on the stage he couldn't make it up the stairs to his dressing-room until he had rested himself at the side of the stage after each performance. Jimmy enjoyed the joke even more than Robb Wilton and told it against himself on many occasions.

Typically, he would tell Vernon to arrange a tour of Ireland, change his mind and cancel it, and then change his mind once more. When television became a widely popular form of entertainment, available at the touch of a switch in peoples' homes, the tours rarely made money and were a drain on the company's resources. But it is probable that Jimmy regarded himself as a responsible employer, and made every effort to provide work for "my people" as he referred to the members of his company. He was only too well aware of Vernon's mania for golfing and if they hit a bum date in some town that left something to be desired, Jimmy's inevitable comment would be: "There must be a bloody marvellous golf course around here somewhere!"

Jimmy, of course, travelled by car to these dates, but sometimes, especially in the early days, the travel arrangements for the supporting cast were less than luxurious. They would travel in the truck transporting the costumes and scenery, and leave it just before they reached the town railway station and stroll into town as if they had just arrived by train, the girls carrying their make-up cases and looking a million dollars. Later, when digs had been arranged for the week, everyone would be expected to lend a hand in setting up the show for the first performance that night.

In the early days the company played D...n, where the dressing-room facilities in the town hall were very meagre. Jimmy took one room, leaving the other two rooms for the ladies of the company. This meant that the men had to dress in a sort of garage next door to which they had access through a door backstage. Complaints about these facilities reached Jimmy's ears so he investigated the situation in the garage. The performers were making up for the evening performance, but the first thing that struck Jimmy was the sight of a large red fire engine. It was an amazing sight: the fire engine was covered in jackets and trousers, shirts, socks and singlets, while the cast were making-up with the aid of small mirrors balanced on the bonnet. The captain of the fire brigade happened to be present and Jimmy said to him: "It would be a bit awkward if a fire was to break out in the town," to which the captain replied:

"Don't be worrying about a thing like that, sure we never have a fire here."

"But supposing," insisted Jimmy, "that there should be one...I wouldn't like to think..."

But the captain was dismissive, "What odds?" he said, "sure it wouldn't affect you at all."

Jimmy had a vision straight from a Mack Sennett movie. "Yes, but what about the fire engine here? Wouldn't it be a bit strange to see it dashing into action with the boys" shirts and trousers and underclothes festooned around it?"

The captain's tone was comforting as he assured Jimmy that they'd never get the fire-engine-out of the building anyhow. "You see the way it is," he explained, "four years ago we had a bit of a fire here in the fire-station itself and when they built the new doorway with the engine inside they built it so small that we could never get the engine out. The fire engine just sits here—it's the firemen that goes out!"

On another occasion in Galway there was a tenor on the stage singing "The West's Awake," dressed in patriotic garb and brandishing a sword. It was Saturday night and the stage staff opened a gate, level with and close to the back of the stage, in order to load the scenery on to a lorry, preparatory to making an early start for the next engagement. All that stood between the tenor and the open scenery gate were a few tricolours and other such emblems. He finished his song with dramatic verve and much waving of the sword, stepped back to frame himself in the flags expecting to feel the closed gate at his back, when he suddenly tumbled backwards out of sight of the audience and into the back of the lorry.

On one tour Vernon's smugness about his digs was very upsetting. He would come to the hall each evening and regale the company with descriptions of the culinary delights that his landlady had just provided for his dinner. The meals he described were unbelievable for the amount of money that Vernon was paying for his digs. There was hare soup and pheasant and grouse, not to mention salmon and trout. But his epicurean descriptions of his gourmet meals suddenly ceased when Vernon discovered that he was lodged in the home of a notorious local poacher.

Generally speaking the tours were happy events. The company played each town for a week and changed the show every night. The company was a happy family and following rehearsals in the morning the rest of the day was their own. Swimming was a favourite pastime, and golf, tennis and cycling were also popular. They had picnics which Jimmy occasionally joined, but more often than not he would be seen walking alone far out on a country road dressed in his Crombie overcoat and trilby hat with his hands behind his back, deep in thought.

Vernon, recalling this picture of Jimmy, described him as: "Really an ordinary but rather sad man, like the classical picture of a clown." Jimmy described his long solitary walks as going for a "waamas"; there can be no doubt that these letters stand for something witty in relation to going for a stroll, and their exact meaning may be found some time, perhaps, in the writings of his friend Myles na Gopaleen.

It did not go unnoticed that wherever the company might be Jimmy paid a visit to the local church almost every day. The very prominent heading to an article by Gabriel Fallon in the *Catholic Standard* after O'Dea's death was: JIMMY O'DEA WAS A DEEPLY RELIGIOUS MAN; and in it Fallon wrote of Jimmy:

Dublin was his butt and sea-mark and it was here in his well-loved city that he had his understanding with death. That rendezvous was marked by an indomitable courage and with a determination that the great flame in the little lantern should burn brightly to the very last. The secret of this amazing courage was due to the fact that known to few—perhaps only to God— Jimmy O'Dea was a deeply religious man. Outside the usual theatre stamping-grounds our ways seldom crossed. We encountered each other hardly more than five times on the streets of our native Dublin. On three of these occasions Jimmy was making an exit from Saint Teresa's, Clarendon Street. Let those sour pusses, true descendants of Oliver Cromwell, who used to write to me at the *Standard* complaining about the "morally subversive" nature of Jimmy's art reflect upon this fact. And when their own moment of truth comes let them beg—as I surely will—for something of that great courage which so ennobled his.

Jimmy, like all true Christians, was light years away from the "holier-than-thou" brigade, and had been known to become embroiled in unseemly arguments with ministers of the Church. There was the time, for instance, when he was playing a town in the south of Ireland and he arrived late for the last mass on Sunday morning. The local canon was at the back of the church castigating any late-comers and Jimmy did not escape his attention. "I am very surprised," said the Canon, "that a man in your position Mr O'Dea, who should be showing a good example, could not be on time for Mass." Only the flames of the votive lamps stirred as Jimmy's fellow miscreants at the back of the church strained their ears and awaited Mr O'Dea's reply with bated breath.

"I'm very sorry," said Jimmy, "but I was delayed down in the hall with my company fixing the running-order of the show to-night."

The Canon moved in for the kill and thundered, "That is no excuse, we can have shows at any time, Mr O'Dea, but when God asks us for a half hour of our time every Sunday, we are duty—bound to be on time." The silent listeners trembled for Mr O'Dea at the unassailable truth of this broadside.

Jimmy was, no doubt, aware of the attention that this argument between church and theatre was attracting and the likelihood of its subsequent retelling around the town, and replied: "Is that a fact now; well let me tell you that in order to earn a living I have to change my show every night of the week which is hard work and this is what I was arranging this morning. This of course, is in marked contrast to your good selves who have been running the same show for the past two thousand years!"

As he used to say: "You can't puzzle Jimmy."

In Elphin, the parish priest had a tendency which was difficult to pinpoint: in the name Elphin he either omitted the "l" altogether in pronunciation, or laid emphasis on the last syllable "phin," leaving the "l" almost silent. Jimmy attended this man's mass and visibly shook with laughter in his seat. The PP announced that the following Sunday was the annual graveyard Sunday when the usual cleaning and tidying would be done. He emphasised his point: "As you know the E(l)phin graveyard is in a terrible state, and next Sunday I want every E(l)phin man, woman and child out and we'll clean up the E(l)phin graveyard." The O'D company enjoyed playing the sticks, as they called the small towns, despite the obvious hardship, but they were glad to get into real theatres in Cork or Limerick or Belfast where they were always well received and there was no necessity to change the show every night. Jimmy was badly beaten up in Cork at some point in the 40s and he was missing from the show for several nights. The reason for the attack was strictly private and personal but when he reappeared in the show the Cork audiences gave him a standing ovation.

Chapter Thirteen

It was arranged with the Walt Disney organisation that Jimmy would fly to Hollywood after the run of his Gaiety pantomime *Dick Whittington* towards the end of March 1958. A few days prior to his departure he called Maureen Potter and Vernon Hayden into his dressingroom and assured them solemnly that there was no need to worry about him while he was away: "I will be alright," he added bravely. What prompted this complex yet simple man to make this declaration? Did he have a genuine need to believe that his close associates would be concerned about him? There was nothing to be concerned about but it seemed to be an expression of Jimmy's misgivings and apprehensions about working in Hollywood. Whatever about himself, he was determined that his company would be looked after at home and given their usual employment. He arranged with Vernon to book a tour to be known as The Jimmy O'Dea Company from the Gaiety Theatre, Dublin. It was like *Hamlet* without the Prince and a financial disaster.

Jimmy's preconceptions about Burbank, California were correct—he hated the place. He couldn't even go for a "waamas" in the evenings in peace. In a land where the automobile was king it was decidedly strange to see a small man with hands behind his back strolling thoughtfully along the sidewalks of Burbank—with the result that he was picked up on several occasions by patrolling police-cars. In all probability he was mistaken for a vagrant and the part of the ensuing proceedings at the station house that annoyed Jimmy most was the close examinations of his wallet and its private contents.

Work on the film itself was uncomfortable and Jimmy was to say later, "It was tough going particularly when I was working in a padded costume and heavy make-up under lighting that for trick photography was three times the normal intensity." One of the pleasures of working on the picture was the presence in the cast of Jack MacGowran, an O'Dea fan since his childhood, who was soon to become the world's leading interpreter of the works of Samuel Beckett. In his biography of MacGowran, *The Beckett Actor*, Jordan R Young writes:

> Jack would never forget his first visit to the theatre—the majestic Gaiety in South King Street—as long as he lived. A packed house buzzed with anticipation as the magnificent yellow and gold brocade curtain rose. Young Johnny sat spellbound in his plush red seat as Jimmy O'Dea, the five-foot-four clown prince of Ireland, entered to the accompaniment of his familiar theme. The audience roared with delight as their beloved Jimmy, adorned in dark wig and rusted skirt, replete with apron, shawl, and petticoat, became Biddy Mulligan of the caustic wit and razor-edged tongue. Jack would later remember him as "my earliest and most profound influence." Now Walt Disney had cast MacGowran's boyhood idol, as the 5,000-year-old king of the leprechauns—and Jack was signed to play his lieutenant, Phadrig Oge. The salary was more attractive than the role Jimmy O'Dea invested the film with great fun but he did not enjoy the job any more than MacGowran. He was getting on in years and the extra harsh light required to photograph them as miniatures made the film a gruelling chore.

> Socially, Jimmy had some nostalgic reunions with old friends like J M Kerrigan, of whom he asked, "Don't you ever feel homesick for Dublin?"
> "Homesick?" said Kerrigan, "I never left Dublin!"

Jimmy's letters home were surprisingly cheerful and gave no hint of his disillusionment with anything. They probably reveal more about Jimmy than they do of the USA. The following examples were written to his sister Rita from his address in Burbank, California—The Bel-Air Palms Motel.

26th May (1958)

Dear Rita,

I have written Ber (his wife, Bernadette), Harry and now yourself. You are certainly owed one as you were good enough to send me two. You will appreciate how home news and thoughts are so much welcomed when the recipient is 6,000 miles away. (Please check on that as I am not sure, the US forces you to be statistically minded.)

It was interesting news about Actors Equity, but I am afraid that apart from MacAnally [Ray] and the Secretary I just go there annually for a laugh.

This is quite a Catholic population right here, and I enclose one of our weekly bulletins which are handed to us after Mass. Tell Father Nolan I do wish him all the very best for his health, and that I thought of him last Sunday, particularly as our talk was on St Francis Xavier. (They don't preach here.)

Of course put me down for Toto Cogley and remember me to both her and Coralie.

My work here is slow as they were not at all ready for my shots, having had to build a million dollar special studio for them, which is only complete now.

Of course I am having a good time as it is sun all the time. I swim in our pool each day and meet celebrities. Have had dinner with Arthur Shields, Eithne Dunne, The O'Herlihys etc., My hosts are the most charming people, and are out of this world.

Will write again. Love, Jim.

The Coralie mentioned in this letter was probably Coralie Carmichael, who was for many years leading lady with Edwards and MacLiammóir at the Gate. The frequent religious references seem to verify Gabriel Fallon's headline in *The Standard*.

Sunday, 15th June (1958)

Hello Honey,

Glad to get your correspondence with all the noose [sic]. I am dating Nora O'Mahony and Mary Brady to-night for dinner at the Knickerbocker. Jest made it. You bet ye. Sorry about that, but it's what I've been hearing in the last few weeks and it's hard to escape the impact of the English language massacred by cromium [sic] plated savages.

Yes I'll meet Nora who is lonely and Mary whom I do not know, to-night for supper.

The picture is not leaping but progressing. It may be a classic, it may be a flop. As far as your brother is concerned I am not fully extended mentally or artistically, but physically more than.

Last night I was a guest of Ella Logan. What a supreme artiste. She knew my work intimately. She is, of course, a divorcee, but in her garden with swimming pool attached she has a shrine to the Little Flower and St Francis of Assisi with perpetual light. Her one request to me is for a Catholic Stage Guild prayer book. Perhaps you could arrange. She lost her only sister a month ago.

The address is (although she opens in New York next month and has invited me if free) 12812 Sunset Pacific, Pallisades, California. I am so glad that the Guild tea was a success, should I not have asked you before, would you find if my presidential emblem is with Ber. I left it in a special pocket in a suit to my tailor Lehane, and he may be keeping it for safety sake. Laurie Shields married to Arthur Shields (protestant) whom I have visited twice is president of the Holy Name Society and frequently twits me about my position. She of course is a militant RC There are no other kind.

I have not answered all your lovely and most acceptable news, but here goes till I hear from you next time. Love, Jim.

Writing Ber, Ken and M Joseph Veronica in that order. Nellie's child wants $ for the missions.

Jimmy was, of course, first president of the Catholic Stage Guild, and he appears to have taken his position very seriously. Most Reverend Dr G O Simms, Archbishop of Dublin, eulogised Jimmy in an address to The Actors' Church Union:

Those who serve society through the stage are a company, that at its best establishes a personal and friendly relationship with thousands that hear and see them, and benefit from what they have to give. Names stand out from time to time of special personalities, as leaders, as "stars" that shine more brightly. Such are often the first to recognise that only with others can they do their brilliant work, only as members of a company and community can they perform and achieve results.

One whom we specially remember in the Actors' Church Union at the close of life of brilliant gaiety and deep, human friendliness is he who is familiarly known by thousands as Jimmy O'Dea. When President of the Catholic Stage Guild, he went out of his way to establish good relations with the Actors' Church Union. He saw that both organisations had the similar aims of spiritual care and friendship for the lonely and the stranger. Through these societies service was extended to those who in the acting profession experienced lean days and from time to time sensed the depression which comes when redundancy, illness and even personal failures cloud a career. Jimmy, by his kindness and cheerfulness, seemed to interpret the purpose and place of the church in the stage world.

We think of what he did in the cause of unity. His perception of our aims and work in the Actors' Church Union made him show such friendliness that we have thanked God many times for his example. Anything approaching prejudice or exclusiveness was completely alien to him. His outlook was always positive. He saw good in people and places, because he was constructive and on the watch for what was best.

Then we thank God for his interpretation of life. Through his comedy he showed up hypocrisy, removed needless personal barriers, broke silences, and helped those who were estranged or who belong to very different circles to talk to each other. He took risks that often helped to improve the temper of a community. He made us see ourselves as others see us.

We recall, too, his capacity for fun. He impressed upon us the importance of leisure and relaxation. Many were able to forget their worries under the spell of our dear friend appearing in the nineteen and more different costumes of an evening's entertainment at Christmas time.

His friendship made him an unofficial ambassador and gave him access to circles usually closed. He brought opposites together and prevented them from taking themselves too seriously. In his show, many forgot themselves and their self-styled importance. Such even learnt to give more to others by way of service and sociability.

How the children would laugh and respond to the lead Jimmy gave and to the jokes he cracked. The children respected him, too. They sensed his dignity and his artistry; the professional skill might sometimes be concealed, but it was never absent. The voice could be Shakespearian, no less than of the Coombe; the jokes could drive home a truth more forcibly than could any sermon. The "magic" of Jimmy sent his audience home thinking afresh about something wanting in their attitude and outlook that should have been obvious beforehand. Only Jimmy seemed to be able to shame them or shock them into burying a grievance or throwing a prejudice out of the window…His faith was as infectious as his fun.

Contained in this eulogy is the *raison d'etre* for the Actors' Church Union and the Catholic Stage Guild despite the cynical opinion of Eamonn Andrews, whose idea of an amusing one-liner was: "I always felt a Catholic Stage Guild in Dublin was like forming a league of decency in a convent."

Two weeks later, another letter to Rita:

Sunday, June 29th [1958]

Dear Rita,

I am glad you contrived a holiday, and found yourself in convivial company, there have been so many publicity hounds after me out here that gallantry precludes me from mentioning that I appeared in silent pictures with Ria. I shall convey your message to Dan O'H.

I have met Nora O'Mahony a few times and we had food together. I shall give her Cathleen Delaney's message.

They have built a special stage [studio] for this picture alone, or for one sequence. I understand the lighting is of the greatest intensity yet in a picture. It blacked out the city of Burbank (80,000) last week. We can only shoot 3 minutes at most a time.

I hope to be home D.V. Aug. early, and if possible to fly to N.Y. and by sea to Cobh for the rest.

Jimmy O'Dea will get plenty publicity in England and Ireland but believe it or not, they are selling me over here as Brian Connors, King of the Leprechauns. So much for primitive mentality. It will all come out in the wash. They really believe in "The Little People."

My love to all, Yours, Jim.

Apart from the letters there were also postcards describing idyllic weekends swimming and sailing in the

Pacific, but when shooting on the film finally finished Jimmy lost no time in returning home. His Irish friends saw him off at Los Angeles airport and he thought they did so because they felt it brought them a little bit nearer home.

He had the same feeling a couple of years later in Australia when he said of Irish emigrants: "It was very touching the way they'd come to the plane to see us off, and touch our hands simply because we were going back to Ireland. It was good that they thought so much of their own country and that I was a link as it were." It was a humble assessment of the situation for he entirely discounted his own magnetic personality and the possibility that people came to say a last goodbye to Jimmy O'Dea.

He travelled from California with Jackie MacGowran. Jordan R Young wrote: "The happiest part of the experience for both of them was the long voyage home—when they discovered that the ship's cabins had been liberally stocked with vodka, courtesy of Disney Productions."

It must be said that Jimmy's partiality to vodka is doubtful. MacGowran admired a man like Jimmy O'Dea who never got drunk when important people were around. Jackie would down every drink put into his hand—O'Dea cleverly poured his into the potted plants.

Back in Dublin Jimmy was welcomed home with a party at the Moira Hotel, at which the principal dish was specially-garnished crubeens—a reminder, perhaps, that he was back in the world of Biddy Mulligan. Jimmy was certain that there would be offers after *Darby O'Gill* was shown, and although he was not a young man he would have liked to make a film a year for the next five years or so.

There was also the possibility of a lucrative sideline for Jimmy, arising from the fact that the Disney organisation issued King of the Leprechaun figurines, tea sets, and other small ornaments in which Jimmy would share in the profits.

Chapter Fourteen

Jimmy's wife Bernadette, who was a gracious and friendly lady, made a comfortable home for him at 10 Herbert Avenue, Merrion—their third home. They left their first home in Fitzwilliam Square and moved to Ely Place before settling in Merrion. Tragically, for the last fifteen years of her life Bernadette suffered from a brain tumour. It did not prevent her from leading a reasonably active life but the condition was obvious to the casual observer from her appearance. She was often the helpful mediator for those attempting to interest Jimmy in some idea which he might not otherwise have entertained. They used to dine together in the bar-grill in the Moira Hotel in the early evenings, and a scriptwriter, for instance, might try to interest Jimmy in his work. Jimmy's stock reply to such people was that Harry O'Donovan was his writer but Bernadette would cajole him into reading the aspiring writer's material. He would do this to please her but matters never progressed further than that. During the first weeks of the pantomime *Robinson Crusoe* in 1958/59, Jimmy was aware that Ber (as he called her) was terminally ill. Because there were matinées each day it was impossible for him to arrange for fittings for a mourning suit, so his tailor had to come to the theatre. Agnes Bernelle recalls that she visited Jimmy's dressing-room for some reason during this period and witnessed the slightly macabre scene of "Mrs Crusoe" being fitted by his tailor for a funeral suit. Mrs Bernadette O'Dea died in January 1959.

The cast of *Robinson Crusoe* included a young actress called Ursula Doyle who played the Fairy Queen. Ursula, who was born in 1931, had been on the stage since childhood as one of the Connie Ryan's Cuties. Later on she and her brother Noel developed a double act consisting of song and dance in a mixture of styles—"Mick McGilligan's Ball" was as important in their repertoire as the latest hit from Tin-pan-alley, and Noel and Ursula Doyle became well-known in every theatre and town hall in Ireland. Ursula had first been featured in an O'D show in 1939, when at the age of eight the role of a fairy was taken by "Little Ursula Doyle" in the Christmas show *Jimmy and the Leprechaun.* Just after the war she and her brother went to London where they stayed for four years and during which time they appeared with Lupino Lane in *Sweetheart Mine* (for which Noel Gay wrote the music) in a run of thirteen months at the Victoria Palace. After a period spent in Ireland, mainly in the Dublin theatres, Ursula and Noel went to Canada where they played the cabaret circuit billed as Peggy and Pat Doyle, names that were calculated to emphasise their Irish origin. Ursula returned to Ireland in October 1957, leaving Noel in Canada where, as part of the act, "Benny and Pat," he worked with another partner for a while before going into the technical side of television. Back in Dublin Ursula was looking forward to taking it easy for a spell after the hectic pace of her transatlantic experience when she was asked to play Fairy Queen in the O'D 1957 panto. It was marvellous to be back, with old girlfriends like Maureen Potter and Derry O'Donovan. They had grown up in the O'D company, and when they were children many years before they felt privileged to be acknowledged by the Boss, "Mr O'Dea" of whom they were in awe. Imagine Ursula's amazement when, one evening in 1959, Mr O'Dea informed her, out of the blue: "By the way, I have every intention of marrying you."

Jimmy's idea of ideal womanhood may best be described by the girl in the song, "The Girl That I

Marry" from the show *Annie Get Your Gun*. He liked
women to be ultra-feminine and Ursula certainly fitted
the bill in that respect. He couldn't warm to the tweedy
type of female and had on several occasions criticised his
sister Rita's country-type hats. Ursula was flabbergasted;
to her Mr O'Dea was an unapproachable genius who
stood high on a pedestal reserved only for those with
unique talent and impeccable professionalism.

The courtship began with boxes of chocolates to the
dressingroom, to the delight of the girls with whom
Ursula shared the room; then there were the gourmet
meals and Jimmy's insistence that she be driven home
each night after the show by his private driver. After
many years of addressing Jimmy as "Mr O'Dea," Ursula
scarcely knew what to call him and felt self-conscious in
this new fairytale situation until one day she saw him
signing a document, "James A O'Dea" and from then
on he became James A.

Ursula's father Edward James Doyle was, like his
father before him, an employee of the Dublin Gas Co
and lived with his wife, Josephine, in Tara Street. They
objected, initially, to the relationship between Jimmy
and their daughter—it could not be denied that he was
twice her age. But in typical O'Dea fashion it wasn't
long before they were won over and they grew to love
him dearly. Ursula recalls: "There was a great rapport
between the three of them; it was enough to make you
feel out in the cold!"

One morning in June 1959 James A knocked at the
door in Tara Street and was admitted by Mrs Doyle who
showed him into the parlour. There he asked her
opinion on a selection of diamonds. Mrs Doyle went
into the kitchen to her daughter and said: "You'd better
go in there, he's bearing diamonds." Ursula couldn't
think straight—*diamonds*, she imagined he had a fistful
loose in his hands. "Which one do you want?" asked
James A. But she was so confused that she couldn't
judge, and making a choice in those circumstances was
out of the question. In the end Jimmy said that they
could both go up to West's where he would return his

samples and she could make her own selection. Ursula selected a solitaire and they were officially engaged.

The wedding was planned for 24th September, 1959 in Westland Row Church but as the date drew closer special permission was granted by the Archbishop of Dublin for the ceremony to be held in St Kevin's in the Pro-Cathedral because a quiet wedding could not be guaranteed in Westland Row. A newspaper photograph exists showing a crowd waiting at Westland Row for a bride and groom who never arrived! The best man was Ursula's second brother JP "Chick" Doyle, and the bridesmaid was Maureen Potter. The reception in the Gresham Hotel was arranged personally during visits to the Gaiety by the greatest "Mine Host" of his day, Toddy O'Sullivan. The honeymoon was spent in Paris and Barcelona before Jimmy and Ursula returned to London in order for Jimmy to fulfil his engagements at the Metropolitan.

Back in Dublin, Jimmy and Ursula moved into the house in Herbert Avenue but Ursula was unhappy there: the housekeeper kept referring to the ways in which the former Mrs O'Dea liked to do things but Ursula was of an independent frame of mind and was determined to conduct her marriage according to her own style. She was not without a sense of humour about the situation as she found it and described it as something similar to what she had read about in *Rebecca*. So Jimmy sold the house and took an apartment at 75 Pembroke Road, which they furnished largely from the house in Merrion. Apart from the furniture there was also Jimmy's fairly extensive library and the bric-a-brac, including some old china tea-cups and saucers inscribed in gold "Kyron Dea, Kilkenny." Ursula expressed a preference for remaining at home in the traditional role of housewife but Jimmy was anxious to have her in the shows with him, so she did not sever her connection with the stage: in the 1960 Gaiety revue she had a nostalgic reunion with her brother Noel in a revival of their old double act. Dubliners remembered them as children with their slick routines, bubbling over with *joie de vivre* and personality.

Jimmy often laughingly told friends: "I love being bossed and managed by Ursula. I can make myself feel like a piece of stewed rhubarb being gently pushed around a plate. And she is a grand gentle pusher." In a more serious moment Jimmy told his friend Fr J T Kennedy in Waterford how very much he loved Ursula and admired her courage in marrying him when he was past middle age. He also confided that she made his declining years happy ones.

The happy relationship with Ursula's parents in Tara Street was not neglected by Jimmy. At times if he felt like some home cooking he would take it into his head to buy supplies of meat in the butcher shops in Chatham Street and take them down to Tara Street where he would dine with the Doyles. He would jokingly threaten Ursula that he would report her to "Eamonn Seamus" (her father, Edward James) and did in fact tell tales on her: "I've never seen so many pairs of shoes before in all my life," was his comment on her weakness for buying new shoes. Apart from this, marriage did not alter his life very much. There might be the usual late session in the Green Room with intimate friends or visiting artists during the course of which he would invariably make a point of collecting money from everyone present to pay for taxi-fares for the bar staff. If there was no one present in whom he was particularly interested he ignored everyone and said to Ursula:"I think we should go home dear—now!"

In June 1961 Jimmy was advised to consult a medical specialist. On the way to see him, Ursula reminded him that if this doctor required him to go to hospital it would more than likely be Dr Steeven's Hospital which did not particularly appeal to her, and she got the distinct impression that it did not appeal to Jimmy either. The hospital wasn't exactly fashionable, situated as it was between a brewery and a railway station. The medical man told Jimmy that he would have to go into hospital for exploratory tests—to Dr Steeven's. Jimmy, adept as ever at blaming someone else, explained that his wife did not greatly fancy that hospital. A confused and embarrassed Ursula was ushered into the consulting room where the doctor assured her severely that apart from the fact that there was absolutely nothing wrong with Dr Steeven's Hospital his medical team was resident there, should her husband require surgery. So it was agreed that Jimmy would go to Dr Steeven's but ironically it transpired that Dr Steeven's Hospital did not want Jimmy—at least not at first, to the extreme embarrassment of doctor and patient. When the surgeon tried to arrange a booking for a private room for Mr Jimmy O'Dea he regarded it as a routine matter but the hospital matron wasn't at all keen to accept a "temperamental theatrical" as a patient. But in the end the matter was settled and Jimmy was accepted with instructions, in accordance with hospital procedure, to check in at 4 p.m. on a particular day. Jimmy arrived at the appointed hour by taxi, left the meter running and went inside. He signed all the relevant documents and gave any information that was required, and deposited his bags as if he were checking into a hotel. He informed the hospital authorities who were so shocked that they forgot to protest that he was going out for dinner that evening and would be back at some time around noon on the following day. He then tipped his hat courteously and departed. The ignorance of hospital rules and procedures and the innocence with which they were broken was, in retrospect, almost endearing. It is proof also of the power of his personality; no one else would have succeeded in such an apparently brazen flouting of the rules. He returned the following day to face, eventually, a colostomy operation. This was a tragedy for so fastidious a man. He won the heart of the matron, Miss Mary Carey, who had been doubtful about accepting him in the first place, by showering compliments and jokes upon her and her staff. He regarded the hospital at times more or less as he would an hotel, and when Ursula came visiting he would ring the bell, as one would for room service, and ask the nurse who responded for tea and biscuits, and please to instruct the chef that Mrs O'Dea would be staying for

lunch. He also noticed that there was space for a second
bed in his room and this gave him an idea but his charm
failed him and he was genuinely upset and couldn't
understand the reasoning when the hospital management refused his request to install a second bed so that
Ursula could spend the night with him and he could see
her, as he was accustomed to, if he awoke in the night.
The matron hadn't been entirely wrong in her
assessment of possible developments where "temperamental theatricals" were concerned!

During the period of his recovery Jimmy was prone to
relapse into short spells of coma or deep sleep. Vernon
Hayden went to visit him one afternoon and found the
patient in a comatose condition. Vernon sat by the bed
for a time until Jimmy suddenly sat bolt upright. He had
one eye shut and surveyed his surroundings through the
other great staring eye, more or less in the dramatised
manner of Long John Silver, glanced severely at Vernon
and relapsed into coma. Vernon alerted the medical staff,
who assured him that the behaviour was normal in the
circumstances and there was nothing to worry about.
Vernon resumed his vigil by the bedside, and after an
interval Jimmy repeated his performance of sitting up
and scrutinising everything with one eye open. This time
Vernon decided to address his boss and asked: "Is there
anything you want Jimmy? Can I get you anything?"
There was no response to this but Vernon suddenly
remembered that Jimmy liked fruit, particularly peaches.
"Would you like me to fetch some nice peaches?" he
suggested, and was rewarded by a slight nodding of the
head. Vernon left the hospital, wondering where he
might obtain peaches in that area, but he managed to
obtain some in a small huckster's shop along the quays.
When he returned to the hospital Jimmy was still in
coma so he sat for fully an hour before the patient once
more roused himself and fixed just the one big hazel eye
on Vernon. He beckoned weakly as he settled back on
his pillows and his lips moved soundlessly. Vernon rose
and placed his ear close to Jimmy's mouth: "What is it
Jimmy? Speak up a little and tell me what I can do for

you." There was a slight pause as the patient drew on his reserves of strength, then: "What happened to the bloody peaches?"

By Christmas Jimmy was back in pantomime at the Gaiety playing the title role in *Mother Goose*. The operation was a success although this wasn't apparent in his work he had lost a lot of his vitality,. He worked as hard as he had ever done and made every effort to give his audiences their money's worth. He was extremely lucky to have Ursula's help and support at this time, and she did everything possible for his good. She tried to restrict his drinking and that effort wasn't without its amusing moments. Out in Montrose one morning Jimmy was video-recording an episode of *O'Dea's Yer Man* and James Plunkett called a coffee break. In the canteen, Ursula asked Jimmy if he would have a cup of coffee. He told her: "No, it wouldn't agree with me." A glass of milk was similarly rejected. Jimmy of course knew from experience that Ursula had a baby bottle of Haig whiskey in her handbag in case of dire necessity but she wasn't going to give in so easily. "What about a nice cup of tea?" said Ursula brightly, "You had one this morning and you enjoyed it." Jimmy fixed Ursula with a look and said: "Would you notice it on me?" He got his glass of Haig.

The Montrose self-service canteen attracted a cross-section of people, and one morning as Jimmy was sitting with James Plunkett and some of his crew four nuns joined the queue at the coffee counter. This was before Vatican Two and they were dressed in the old style full-length black habits and wimples. Suddenly one of them raised her habit at the side exposing a long shapely leg encased in a black stocking from the top of which she retrieved a packet of cigarettes and a box of matches. She offered cigarettes to her companions and the four of them lit up. Jimmy was shocked and remained speechless until he managed to mutter lamely, something about "very advanced behaviour." His equilibrium was restored only when Plunkett explained that the "nuns" were actresses working on a TV production for Chloe Gibson.

In 1963 during the run of his last panto *Goldilocks and the Three Bears* Jimmy began to show visibly that was in pain. His old friend, Cecil Sheridan remarked:

Jimmy O'Dea was the greatest artist. It is easy to be good while things are going well with you but I have seen Jimmy rehearse while in drastic pain. There was that Punchinello quality about him which urged to give his best while in sheer agony. I have seen him turn away and grit his teeth thinking that nobody would witness his pain.

Ill himself, Jimmy went to visit one of his earliest colleagues Connie Ryan who had a long-term illness. Connie said of his visit:

I was sitting talking to him and I saw a great change. And, of course, I spent so many years in and out of hospitals myself that I am very quick to know anyone that has suffered, and I said to him, "How are you?" He said, "Connie, I don't have to tell you." I said: "I don't think you're well Jimmy" He said: "I'm not, but I felt, you'll know what pain is, so you know." I said: "I thought so, and I *do* know. And it made me very sad."

And still he was in demand. In 1964 London beckoned once more just before a strike was threatened in Independent Television. They offered him a programme with all the resulting financial rewards and prestige but hearing of the strike, he turned down the offer.

In April 1964 Jimmy was honoured at a luncheon in the Metropole given by the Variety Club of Ireland, on behalf of which he had helped to raise funds for charity for ten years. He was presented with a pair of gold cuff-links inscribed with the club's insignia. The attendance included his old friend, Jack, now Sean Lemass, Ireland's Taoiseach, and Mrs Lemass. Jimmy, he said, and himself had been neighbours in the long ago—and were still very close friends. Jimmy had been the best man at his wedding, and though later both went different roads in their careers he followed his old neighbour's success closely; envied him for the way he had with people, and admitted he was still Jimmy's most ardent fan. Harry O'Donovan, who perhaps knew Jimmy best, remarked: "He is the kind of fella that says what he thinks—and that sometimes got him into trouble." Lorcan Bourke, who had managed several theatres in Dublin and was Eamonn Andrew's father-in-law since the latter was married to Lorcan's daughter, Grainne, (or Grace as she was better known as a member of the Royalettes dancing troupe), spoke of difficult early days with Jimmy when stage props were hard to come by and when scripts were written more or less to suit the scenery that was available. Louis Elliman took the listeners from 1937 when he and O'Dea set off on the first of their 60 shows together. He was pleased now that Jimmy was being honoured, "that he could have flowers from his friends now so that he could enjoy them." A rather strange yet prophetic remark.

Privately, Jimmy was of the opinion that when you get such acclamation from your fellow human beings you feel they've placed you on a pedestal and you often wonder if you are worthy of that. So when he rose to speak he was embarrassed. He said: "It is embarrassing to hear people talking about me when all my life I have been talking about somebody else." He tried hard to switch the focus of attention: he asked for applause for the Taoiseach, "who had hooked two fine salmon on a fishing expedition recently," but he could not divert attention from himself. For once, the running order of a show starring Jimmy O'Dea was not his to dictate, although it must have been one of the most memorable for him, in a long career that was sadly very nearly at an end. At the end of July he appeared in his last show, the revival of *Finian's Rainbow*. A section of the press was unkind about his performance, and if they had been aware of his physical condition they might have shown a little more understanding towards a man who had devoted a lifetime to making people laugh. W D Peirce, critic and correspondent on the profession's own paper, *The Stage,* had written: "To me, Jimmy O'Dea was the greatest comedian ever to come out of Ireland and I can honestly say no artist has given me more pleasure and afforded me more moments of laughter than he, and from a stage critic of many years experience, this is a major statement".

At the end what was needed was not charity—Jimmy would have hated that—but repayment of some of the debt to him.

James Plunkett planned a series of six autobiographical television shows about Jimmy to be called *The Life and Times of Jimmy O'Dea* and he recorded the first and only episode around this time. Written and produced by James Plunkett, it contained details of Jimmy's life interspersed with some of his stage sketches. It was screened on Christmas night 1964 and it ran for 90 minutes. Many of his regular company supported him, but there were a few newcomers like Brendan Cauldwell, Eamon Kelly, and Martin Crosbie, a tenor who had been resident in the Capitol Theatre and could never leave the stage without singing "The Miller's Daughter." Jimmy's regular musical director from the Gaiety, Thelma Ramsey, was the accompanist and the Radio Éireann Light Orchestra was conducted by Robert Murphy.

At the end of October, Jimmy had been readmitted to Dr Steeven's Hospital. He had been there seven weeks when against doctor's orders he left his sickbed in order to be present at a Variety Club Luncheon in honour of "an old colleague," Dr Micheál MacLiammóir. Jimmy insisted on attending, saying: "I must be talking to my friends," echoing the title of one of MacLiammóir's one-man shows. Brought by wheelchair to the porchway of the hospital, Jimmy looked pale and wan but he said: "The doctors told me they felt I should not come out but I feel grand. I think there is nothing like proving you can do something." After being whisked through lunch-hour traffic in Louis Elliman's Bentley, he had a bright smile for hundreds of onlookers as he stepped into the Metropole Banqueting Suite. It was a frosty afternoon, but as Jimmy said: "You could not let down an old colleague." MacLiammóir had no idea that Jimmy would be attending the luncheon and only heard about it as he was himself entering the Metropole. "I am deeply grateful to him for his gesture," he said. "When I heard he was here I nearly burst into tears and just controlled myself in time." In his speech of thanks, Dr MacLiammóir made special reference to Jimmy and thanked him for "his graceful, courageous and beautiful gesture in leaving hospital to attend the luncheon."

Later MacLiammóir was to write of his first sight of Jimmy in pantomime at the Olympia in 1932:

> Incredible is the word that springs to mind for that dauntless diamond-bright, beetle-black, razor-sharp yet strangely benevolent little demoness of an Ugly Sister. Of course he wasn't ugly at all: he was ravishing; one couldn't for a moment understand why Prince Charming didn't fall head first for such impish impudent enchantment; what had a thousand Cinderellas to offer in place of this dazzling radiance? Jimmy remained for me, and will always remain, in the centre of the very front row of the comics of magical spells...whether he skimmed across the stage in apron and shawl as the Pride of the Coombe, or smirked his way towards you as some nameless gorgeous Godforsaken blonde, reconstituted by some wizard's beauty pills, or leered at you from the brisk shadow of a relentlessly combed fringe with eyes like midnight gooseberries, brazen lips, a cavernous mouth and a voice that roared from the darkest depths of the Dodder.

After the luncheon Jimmy returned briefly to his Pembroke Road home where he did some recording for the forthcoming Christmas show, *The Life and Times of Jimmy O'Dea*. Then it was back to the hospital, where, incidentally, he had already been recording some of the sound track for the show. He had an endless stream of visitors including the Taoiseach, Sean Lemass, and the President and Mrs De Valera who had been kept informed of his condition. The street sellers of Moore Street sent him bouquets and when it all became a little too much he would tell Ursula to discourage some visitors while he pretended to sleep. Dr Cyril Cusack, another old friend, remarked after a visit:

> He is a great man of the Irish theatre, yet he is a very humble man. He seemed to think there was a difference between him and those of us in what we call the legitimate theatre but we always felt that if we could be of the same standard as he was we would be very proud of ourselves...because O'Dea knows his theatre, knows his audience, by which I mean audiences everywhere.

Fancifully, this generous tribute could, perhaps, have been inspired from beyond the grave by the man to whom O'Dea had been compared—Dan Leno! Because Dr Cusack's mother claimed some kinship with Leno, and he remembered that once as a child he stayed with Dan Leno junior.

Vernon Hayden, who was a frequent visitor, said that Jimmy was an actor to the last:

> He never once complained of pain, and every time I asked him how he was he replied "Fine, fine, fine," and went on to discuss the progress of rehearsals for the Gaiety panto, *Sinbad the Sailor*. Jimmy had genuinely believed that he would be fit enough to appear in that show but during the run of *Finian's Rainbow* it was obvious to us that it would be out of the question. Still, in order to keep up his heart and to conceal our concern for him I had some showcards printed which I let him see. They read: "Jimmy O'Dea in *Sinbad the Sailor*," but of course, it was not to be.

He was once more under the care of Matron Mary Carey. She said she was speaking for all the nurses in saying that he was "an excellent patient, a most lovable character, and a fun-maker to the end. He never complained and was always trying to make others happy." Miss Carey accompanied Jimmy to the dress rehearsal of *Sinbad* and he spent the following day, Christmas Day, at home with Ursula. He sat beside a huge fire in his apartment reading the greetings he had received from the President, the Taoiseach, scores of theatrical personalities, and hundreds of fans throughout the country. Hundreds of greetings also arrived at the hospital from people who did not know that he had been allowed home for Christmas. On Christmas night they watched the first episode of his biography on television.

The scene was set in the apartments with Jimmy sitting beside Ursula at a big coal fire with a Christmas tree in the background. A replica, in fact, of the scene in which they were now watching the programme. Jimmy read some of the verses from the greeting cards and then reminisced about life at Christmas during his childhood. (The narration which James Plunkett wrote for Jimmy was true to the facts of Jimmy's life, and performing it must have been a nostalgic experience for him).

JIMMY: The candle in the window pane,
Young carols in the snow,
All fill the heart with memories
Of Christmas long ago.

(He places the card on table)

That's what it says here, anyway, and I believe it, Because I've been thinking here to myself of Christmas long ago, the Christmases of childhood and all the simple things that had such a wonder about them; things like the big Christmas candles you'd see in the shops, the iced cakes with Happy Christmas on them, and—the youngest memory of all—the smell of cloves and nutmeg and cinnamon when you sneaked into the kitchen to see if there were any titbits going...unnoticed! And I was remembering the excitement on Christmas Day when the time came to pour the whiskey over the plum pudding—and the blue flame set fire to the sprig of holly on top. That was at the beginning of the century, in a room over my parent's shop at No. 11 Lower Bridge Street—the house I lived in as a child. I can see it now; the mottoes over the fireplace with their greetings and simple messages; the Christmas tree dressed with tinsel and chains and crackers that exploded when you pulled them and had paper hats inside them; the table we played at on long winter evenings; the wide window that looked out on a strange and still unfamiliar world.

The wheel was inexorably completing its full circle.

On St Stephen's Day, Jimmy was guest of honour in Louis Elliman's private box to watch the curtain go up on *Sinbad the Sailor*. It was the first time since his childhood that he had come to see a Gaiety panto from in front of the footlights. During the interval he went backstage and met the cast, and as music and singing filtered through to the greenroom he chatted with the latest generation of juvenile panto performers—a troupe of 12-year-old dancers. One wonders if he had any fault to find with their make-up or other such important details of stagecraft.

A columnist from the *Evening Press* reported on the following day:

> I walked backstage with the little man, then looking more frail than he had ever done when he brought laughter to generations of panto fans. He smiled nostalgically and said "Of course I would like to be going on again." Then he spoke to me about the stage. It was to be his last interview—not that talking with Jimmy was ever an interview as such. The quick joke, the ready smile and the famous laugh were never absent for long. "It becomes part of your life," he explained, "but the doctors told me they couldn't give me the OK to go on with the show. They said they didn't think I would be able for it. I suppose when

you can't do a thing you can't do it. You have to try and bring yourself to realise that, sooner or later. You have to try and realise you may be on the way out." Yet when he spoke about his television programme of the previous evening he said, "We have more work to do on that programme. And then I have to get down to doing some more of the children's programmes for television. I got letters in hospital from hundreds of children who had been watching the story programmes. They all said they were praying for me. I am very grateful to them all. I had no idea the programme was going over to so many of them and that so many of them were enjoying it."

The following, addressed to Ursula, is an extract from the type of letter the children were sending to Jimmy:

> Dear Mrs O'Dea,
>   I called to see Mr O'Dea (with my friend) but the man on the hospital door wouldn't let me in, and I said I knew Mr O'Dea well on TV, and he told me to go home, He was a cheeky man and said he'd get the guards if I didn't go home at once, and I had sweets for Mr O'Dea but I didn't leave them. We pray every night for him. Won't you tell him I went in and I wouldn't be let in by the man on the hospital door...

Jimmy appears to have been a lifelong recipient of sweets from young admirers. One visitor recalls him pointing to a small black object on his dressing-table. "You'd never guess what that is," said Jimmy.

> The other night I was pushing my way through the usual crowd of youngsters round the stage door—they always say "Good-night" to me you know—when one very small boy ran up to me. "Jimmy," says he "I've got something for yer; h'yar." and he pressed that into my hand. I was a jujube, which by the feel of it he'd just removed from his mouth. Of course, I had to

keep the offering, which was made in deadly seriousness.

Jimmy returned to the hospital on December 29, and almost immediately his condition gave cause for anxiety. Ursula rang the hospital at 8 a.m. every day and was always assured that he had a restful night. She rang as usual early on the morning of January 7 and was reassured as to his condition but later in the morning she received a call from the hospital advising her to come immediately. Ursula, Vernon Hayden and Louis Elliman were with Jimmy for a short time before he sank into a coma and died at 11 a.m. The cause of death was gastro-intestinal haemorrhage.

The remains were taken at 5.30 on that evening to St Mary's Church, Haddington Road.

Chapter Fifteen

That evening all the Dublin theatres paid tribute to Jimmy. At the Gate Theatre where David Kelly—his partner in *O'Dea's Yer Man*—was appearing in *See How They Run*, he had difficulty in expressing his grief. After the performance of *Aladdin* at the Olympia Theatre, Jack Cruise said that it was at the Olympia in the 1930s that Jimmy O'Dea had started the career which brought him to such wonderful heights. Now, by his death a gap had been created in the Irish theatre which could never be filled. He asked the audience, as a mark of respect, to stand for a minute's silence. There was a minute's silence also at the Eblana Theatre where Cecil Sheridan was starring in *The Good Old Days,* and he said that it was superfluous to say Jimmy was a great artist—he was original and was born with talent. Cecil concluded with a thought which had occurred to many: "Jimmy would like to be remembered by the joy he gave to people when he was alive rather than by the sadness of his death."

The funeral in driving rain was attended by the President and Mrs De Valera. The Taoiseach and Mrs Lemass, and a huge gathering from the theatre world and public life were in the mile-long cortège to Glasnevin Cemetery. Hundreds failed to gain admission to the Requiem Mass at which the Bishop of Nara, Most Rev Dr Dunne presided. The Mass was celebrated by Rev O'Nolan, O Carm, Gort Mhuire (nephew) who also recited the prayers at the graveside.

Hundreds gathered at vantage points along the route, while others gathered in groups in doorways or at windows as protection from the rain, and there were many who travelled from the country to pay their last respects. The hearse, preceded by a Garda motor-cycle escort, made its way along Baggot Street, through St Stephen's Green to South King Street, where outside the Gaiety Theatre a 30-second pause was made to commemorate Jimmy's more than 60 appearances there in revue, pantomime and plays. At Glasnevin, in spite of the downpour, the route to the grave was lined with people, and some huddled for shelter behind tombstones as the coffin, almost hidden under the floral tributes, passed by. Tributes had arrived from all over Ireland and the United Kingdom; the Grand Order of Water Rats was represented by Mr Roy Lester of Blackpool. The tributes included many from County Councils and The Anti-Apartheid Movement, of which he was a supporter, and those from private citizens included one from Senator Margaret Pearse, who wrote from St Enda's, Rathfarnham: My deepest regret at the passing of Ireland's greatest comedian. "He gave me great pleasure all down the years. God rest his noble soul."

Jack MacGowran had sent a message from London:

His name has been on the lips of all of us who knew him here in London's theatreland. We have raised many a glass together, and now, Jimmy —
Since it falls unto your lot
That you should go and we should not,
We gently rise and as you pass
We raise to you a parting glass.

The famous and the unknown stood huddled beneath umbrellas or soaking hats and caps around the O'Dea family grave. On the headstone the date of the first inscription is 1875, and strangely there is also etched the address where it all began—10 Lower Bridge Street (not No 11 which has since been widely noted and recorded in official documents.)

At last when everyone had gone there was nothing left but a bright, colourful mound of wreaths on which the rain continued to fall:

> "Happy Memories Darling Jimmy, 'Boo' London" (Evelyn Laye).
>
> "To dearest Jimmy with love, Ethel and Louis" (Elliman).
>
> "See you in Gloccamorra Jimmy, from the cast of *Sinbad the Sailor.*"
>
> "In loving memory," from Deirdre.
>
> "With endless memories, admiration and love." Shelagh Richards.
>
> "In remembrance from Alice, Babs and the Royalettes."
>
> "To dear James A from Laurie and David Kelly."
>
> "In fond memory, from Brendan and Beryl Smith."
>
> "Good night, Sweet Prince—Vernon."

Dr Cyril Cusack immortalised it all in his poem dedicated to James A O'Dea, better known to millions as Jimmy O'Dea.

TO A DEAD COMEDIAN

> It was a rough day
> a rough day for the burial,
> wet, blustering wind, rain
> left small time for sentiment. Pain
> of a lost merriment—unusual—
>
> attended the comedian's funeral,
> his going down. Our man
> of our town, turning his head away
> from tedium in game refusal
> had ended much as he began.

God knows his creature,
knows the uncommon clown in each of us.
But is it not a tough old station
where laughter may be medium for grief
and Death be seen, a common thief,

stealing the tag and leaving us—
on-stage—the rag for compensation
and a chief player with no line to say.
It was a rough day,
a rough day for the theatre.

On the afternoon of Jimmy's death the train from Belfast arrived at Amien's Street Station and the passengers included a new long-haired British pop group called "The Rolling Stones" who were to give two performances in the Adelphi Cinema that evening. It signalled a new era in entertainment. Out with the tradition and simple innocence of the old and in with the brash, often short-lived, but self-perpetuating new elixir of the very young. Performers like Maureen Potter in her *Gaels of Laughter* shows, and Jack Cruise in his *Holiday Hayride* fought a rearguard action for a little while, but in the end variety retreated back to what had been its beginnings in the early music-hall—entertainment in pubs and special cabaret venues where food and drink were available. One of them even rejoiced in the name of The Biddy Mulligan, and in faraway Kilburn, London, the revelry continues in a hostelry named with a view to instant recognition by the local Irish residents—"The Pride of the Coombe."

Appendix

No.   *Date*

Radio Éireann Singers, the RELO (con. by Dermot O'Hara). Script and production by H L Morrow. Fictionalised version of the founding of O'D Productions. Songs & Sketches: "Look Who's Here" (Chorus), "Buying The Furniture," "The Last Drink," "Sixpence Each ay," "Mrs Mulligan In Court," "Brighter Broadcasting," "Dolores and Rosie," "The Lost Railway," "Biddy Mulligan" (Coombe Song).

8/01/64   *Conversation with J O'Dea S256/68 (John Bowman)*

7/01/65   *Tribute to J O'Dea S136/68 (H. O'Donovan)*

21/03/76 *From Val Vousden Till Now, 50 Years   of Irish Radio S 95/76*

26/04/78 *Máire Ní Scolaí Remembers SAA453*

7/03/81   *Profile in Happiness S AA1864 (Documentary)*

29/09/81 *Scenes that are the Brightest SAA1914 (Tribute to J Linnane)*

13/12/84 *Appraisal13.12.84: 3.1.85 S BB3240*

22/01/85 *Homage to Jimmy O'Dea S BB2199*

22/02/86 *Spice of Life, Curtain Raiser SAA3804*

8/03/86   *Spice of Life, The Queen's Theatre*

15/03 86 *Spice of Life, Olympia & Capitol SAA3807*

22/03/86 *Spice of Life, Oh, Hadn't We The Gaiety SAA3808*

5/04/86   *Spice of Life, Royale Finale SAA3810*

17/05/86 *Spice of Life, Maureen Potter Story SAA3816*

14/08/88 *SOUNDSTAGE Variety Cavalcade SAA3997*

Jimmy O'Dea Material on Visual Television Archives

Radio Telefís Éireann:

1 02/01/82 R *Late Late Show* Inserts-Compilation A LB683

2 04/09/59R *Gael Linn*, Newsreel showing J. O'Dea and Noel Purcell entertaining orphans at Mosney for Variety Club of Ireland. A GL013

3 01/07/62 *Royal Years, Theatre Royal Dublin* A P88/62

4 01/01/63 *O'Dea's Your Man*—"*Stampede*" A P89/63

5 01/01/63 *O'Dea's Your Man*—"*The Electric*" AP90/63

6 01/01/63 *Once Upon a Time—The Little Fawn"* A P91/63

7 17/10/63 *Once Upon a Time—"Aladdin"* A P59/63

8 21/11/63 *Once Upon a Time—"Jack and the Beanstalk"* A P41/63

9 24/11/63 *O'Dea's Your Man—"The Horse Show"* (A) A LB125

10 5/12/63 *O'Dea's Your Man—"The Holliers"* (B)A LB125

11 22/12/63 *O'Dea's Your Man* ALB125

12 01/01/64 *O'Dea's Your Man—"Changed Times"* (B) A LB126

13 02/02/64 *O'Dea's Your Man—"False Colours"* (H) ALB125

14 16/02/64 *O'Dea's Your Man—"Stampede"* (E) A LB126

15 19/04/64 *O'Dea's Your Man—"Playing The Game"* (D) A LB126

16 30/04/64 *O'Dea's Your Man—"Is TV a Good Thing"* (E) ALB125

17 10/05/64 *O'Dea's Your Man—"The Meaninbg of Malt"* (C) A LB126

18 24/05/64 *O'Dea's Your Man—"Keeping Your Feet"* (A) A LB126

19 27/05/64 *ODea's Your Man—"The Language Question"* (D) ALB125

20 25/12/64 *Life and Times of Jimmy O'Dea—Biography Sketches:* "Mine's A Pint"; "The Plumbers"; "Mrs Mulligan's Party" ALB019

21 25/12/64 *Life and Times of Jimmy O'Dea—Film Inserts* A P77/64

22 11/05/66 *O'Dea's Your Man—"Playing The Game"* AA60/218

23 12/05/66 *Once Upon a Time—"Jack The Giant Killer"* (C) AA60/218

24 15/04/68 *O'Dea's Company—*A tribute to O'Dea which was produced by James Plunkett. The cast incl. Harry O'Donovan, Danny Cummins, Frank O'Donovan, Maureeen Potter, Vernon Hayden, Thelma Ramsey and filed before Jimmy's death included: "Seeing Him Off"; Dolores and Rose in Egypt"; "Maureen's Pub" ALB030

25 14/10/74 *Féach—21st Anniversary of Gael Linn,*(Uses section of No. 2, above) AP282/74

26 31/12/82 *Should Aul;d Acquaintance* (Insert) ALB704
27 24/12/83 *Anything Goes—Christmas Show* incl. insert of
    No. 7, above – "Aladdin" AP536/83
28 07/01/85 *Remembering Jimmy O'Dea—Documentary*
    A P9/85 Produced by Donald Taylor Black (Poolbeg
    Prod) to commemorate 20th Anniversary of Jimmy's
    death Contributors were: James Plunkett, Ursula Doyle
    (Mrs O'Dea), Maureen Potter, Vernon Hayden, Noel
    Purcell, Connie Ryan, Rita O'Dea, Joe Dowling,
    Eamonn Morrissey, Michael Sheridan, Séamus de Búrca,
    Dermot Tuohy, John Jordan, Gerry McCarry, Chas.
    Roberts, Kevin Rockett. Uses some rare material
29 31/12/86 *It's A Hard Auld Station*—Inserts
    AB60/1538
30 08/05/87 *Late Late Show Parts 1 2 3* AB90/1355
31 02/03/88 Evening Extra, Maureen Potter Special
    ABP30/2759
32 28/06/88 *News Bulletin—I/V Maureen O'Hara in
    Galway* ABN180/88

Jimmy O'Dea Films

Prod Co.	Year	Title
Irish Photoplays	1922	*Wicklow Gold*
		The Casey Millions
	1924	*The Cruiskeen Lawn*

Note: These were silent, full-length features but it is not
known if copies survived.

Baxter & Barter	1935	*Jimmy Boy*
O'D Productions	1938	*Blarney*
ATP (Ealing)	1938	*Penny Paradise*
Ealing	1939	*Cheer, Boys, Cheer*
Ealing/Warner	1939	*Let's Be Famous*
4 Provinces	1957	*The Rising Of The Moon*
		(Also known as *Three Leaves In A Shamrock*)
USA/Walt Disney	1959	*Darby O'Gill And The Little People*

Columbia/Viceroy   1960   *Johnny Nobody*

Discography

Key to catalogue number prefixes:

78 rpm Records

A	–	Henecy (Ireland)
A	–	Dominion (Britain)
A	–	Parlophone (Australia)
BD	–	His Master's Voice (Britain)
C	–	Dominion (Re-issues)
E	–	Parlophone (Britain)
F	–	Decca (Britain)
FB	–	Columbia (Britain)
G	–	Columbia (USA.)
IFB	–	Columbia (Ireland)
IM	–	His Master's Voice (Ireland)
IZ	–	Regal Zonophone (Ireland)
MR	–	Regal Zonophone (Britain)
U	–	Rex (Northern Ireland)
W	–	Decca (green label - Ireland)
Z	–	Ariel

45 rpm Extended Plays
45-BE –   Decca, Beltona Label

33 rpm Albums
ACL   –   Ace of Clubs (Decca)
STAL –   Talisman (EMI, Ireland)
GAR   –   EMI, Ireland.

Henecy Records

Recorded in Dublin, September, 1926
10221 –
10222 "A Bargee's Barcarolle," Monologue A 109
10223 "Parody on Dublin Bay," Song A 112
10224 "Ballad of the Medical Student" A 109
10225 –
10226 "Mrs Maher's Little Shop," Monologue A 112
10227 "Cinderella up-to-date," Monologue A 110
10228 "The Foggy Dew" A 110 (Featuring Fay Sargent)
Note: It is not known if Matrix Nos 10221/25 are by Jimmy
O'Dea.

Jimmy O'Dea and Harry O'Donovan are featured on the following recordings with the exceptions of some solo items which are so noted. O'Dea and O'Donovan are identified as A and B respectively, and supporting artists are noted where known.

Dominion Records

Recorded April, 1929. Released, June, 1929
1209-3   "The Two TDs" A 115 (A & B)
1210-1   "A Romance Of Ireland's Eye" A 115 (Solo A)
1211-2   "When Magee Draws His Pay" A 116 (Solo B)
1212-3   "The Next Train" A 116 (A & B)
1212-3   There was an unissued pressing backed with "Hoops and Sawdust" featuring Cyril Lidington – No. C 327

Parlophone Records: (Red & Black Labels)

Recorded July, 1929 (Dublin)
WE 2609-1   "Bridget Donohue"   E 3633 (Solo A)
WE 2610-1   "I'll Slip Out The Back" E 3633 (Solo B)
WE 2611-1   "Sixpence Each Way"   E 3634 (A & B)
WE 2612-2   "The Irish Schoolmaster" E 3634 (A & B)
         E-3634 also issued on IZ-759; IFB-356; Z-4724; USA-G 33468F; Australia, A-2967

Recorded October, 1929
WE 2856-2   "The Irish Jaunting Car," Part One E 3661 (A & B)
WE 2857-2   "The Irish Jaunting Car," Part Two E 3662 (A & B)
WE 2858-2   "Mrs Mulligan at the Telephone" E 3663; MR 1367 (A & B))
WE 2859   "The Waiter" E 3661 (A & B)
WE 2860-2   "Mrs Mulligan at the Pawnshop" E 3662 (A & B)
WE 2861-2   "Vitamens" (sic) E 3663; MR 1368 (A & B)

Recorded June, 1930
WE 3338-1   "Mrs Mulligan in Court," Part Two E 3680; FB 265 (A &B)
WE 3339-2   "Mrs Mulligan and the Motor Car" E 3681 (A & B)

WE 3340-2   "Mrs Mulligan in Court," Part One E 3680; FB 265 (A & B)

WE 3341-2   "Mickie at Ellis Island" E 3681 (A & B)

Recorded November, 1930

WE 3693-2   "Mrs Mulligan at the Racecourse," Part One E 3763 (A & B)

WE 3694-2   "Mrs Mulligan at the Racecourse" Part Two E 3763 (A & B)

WE 3695-2   "Mrs Mulligan at the Talkies" E 3764; MR 1367 (A & B)

WE 3696-1   "Mrs Mulligan in the Tram" E 3764; MR 1368 (A & B) Tom Dunne

Recorded March, 1931

WE 3978-2   "Biddy Mulligan (Coombe)" E 3817; MR 1369 (Solo A)

WE 3979-1   "Ireland's Eye" E 3817; MR 1369 (Solo A)

Recorded May, 1931

WE 3991-1   "The Lord Mayor's Song" E 3823 (Solo A) (from *Babes in the Wood*)

WE 3992-1   "The Lady Sachauna" E 3823 (Solo A)

WE 3993-1   "Mrs Mulligan's Mother-in-law" E 3839 (A & B)

WE 3994-2   "The Next Train" E 3839 (A & B)

Recorded July, 1931

WE 4195-1   "Mrs Mulligan Nearly Wins the Sweep" E 3894 (A & B)

WE 4196-1   "Mrs Mulligan In London "E 3895 (A & B)

WE 4197-2   "Interviewing Mrs Mulligan" E 3894 (A & B)

WE 4198-1   "Mrs Mulligan on Weddings" E 3895 (A & B)

Recorded September, 1931

WE 4264-1   "The Queens of the Bucket and Brush" E3912 (Solo A)

WE 4265-1   "A Topical Song" E 3910 (Solo A)

WE 4266-2   "The Belle of Grafton Street" E 3910 (Solo A)

WE 4267-1   "Mrs Mulligan and Charlie" E 3911 (A & B)

WE 4268-1   "Mrs Mulligan Buys a Turkey" E 3911 (A & B)

WE 4269-2   "Mrs Mulligan's Motor Car" E 3912 (A & B)

Recorded December, 1931

WE 4392-1	"Wait 'Till We Win the Sweep" E 3939 (A & B)	
WE 4393-1	"Crossing the Border—north side" E 3940 (A & B)	
WE 4394-1	"Crossing the Border—south side" E 3940 ((A & B)	

WE 4392-1   "Wait 'Till We Win the Sweep" E 3939 (A & B)

WE 4393-1   "Crossing the Border—north side" E 3940 (A & B)

WE 4394-1   "Crossing the Border—south side" E 3940 ((A & B)

E-3940 also issued on MR 2367; IZ 521; IFB 342

WE 4395-1   "Vote for Bachelors" E 3939 (A & B)

Recorded 23 March, 1932

WE 4482-2   "Evicting Mrs Mulligan" E 3955 (A & B)

WE 4483-1   "Mrs Mulligan Wins the Sweep" E 3956; IZ 761 (Solo A)

WE 4484-1   "McGilligan's Youngest Daughter Maggie May" E 3956; IZ 761 (Solo A)

WE 4485-1   "The Copper and the Lad" E 3955 (A & B)

Recorded 9 August, 1932

WE 4694-1   "Home With the Milk" E 3979; IZ 757 (A & B)

WE 4695   "The Mulligans and McGilligans"—1 E 3978 (A & B)

WE 4696   "The Mulligans and McGilligans"—2 E 3978 (A & B) (from the revue *Laugh Irish*)

WE 4697-1   "Mrs Mulligan Takes a Lodger" E 3979; IZ 757 (A & B)

Recorded 25 October, 1932

WE 4809   "Evolution" E 4023 (A & B—Connie Ryan)

WE 4810   "Legal Separation" E 4022 (A & B—Connie Ryan)

WE 4811-1   "Plumbers-amateur" E 4021 (A—Connie Ryan)

WE 4812-1   "Plumbers-professional" E 4021 (A & B—Connie Ryan)

WE 4813   "Mrs Mulligan Is Bitten" E 4023 (A & B)

WE 4814-1   "Marrying Mary" E 4022 (A & B—Connie Ryan)

WE 4815-1   "Football & Wives" Part 1 E 4020 (A & B—Connie Ryan)

WE 4816-1   "Football & Wives" Part 2 E 4020 (A & B— Connie Ryan)

Recorded 28 February, 1933
Although the Matrix Numbers refer to Parlophone Masters the records were issued on the Regal Zonophone label.

WE 4954-1   "The Dublin Fusilier" MR 921; IZ 200 (Solo A)

WE 4955-1   "The Vamp of Inchicore" MR 922; IZ 201 (Solo A)

WE 4956-2   "Mrs Mulligan's Sheiks" MR 923; IZ 202 (Solo A)

WE 4957-1   "The Baby Elephant" MR 921; IZ 200 (A & B)

WE 4958-1   "The Matrimonial Bureau" MR 922; IZ 201 (A & B)

WE 4959-1   "Mrs Mulligan Records Her Vote" MR 923; IZ 202 (A & B)

Regal Zonophone Records:

Recorded 31 May, 1933 (London)
CAR 2008-1   "The Last Drink" MR 1098 (A & B—Noel Purcell)

CAR 2009-1   "The Irish Way"—Part One MR 1027 ((A & B—Connie Ryan)

CAR 2010-1   "The Irish Way"—Part Two MR 1027 (A & B —Connie Ryan)

CAR 2011-1   "Selling a Dog" MR 1098 (A & B)

CAR 2012-1   "The Barber and The Sweepstake" MR 1099; IZ 216 (A & B)

CAR 2013-1   "Mrs Mulligan Smuggler" MR 1099; IZ 216 (A & B)

Recorded 15 November, 1933
CAR 2369-1   "Mrs Mulligan at the Abbey Theatre"—1 MR 1202 (A & B)

CAR 2370-1   "Mrs Mulligan at the Abbey Theatre"—2 MR 1202 (A & B)

CAR 2371-1   "The Mayor Proposes"—Part One MR 1145 (A & B)

CAR 2372-1   "The Mayor Proposes"—Part Two MR 1145
             (A & B) (from pantomime *Mother Goose*)
CAR 2373   "A Shakespearean Sixpence Each Way" MR
             1146 (A &B)
CAR 2368   "I Am the Mayor" MR1146 (Solo B) (from
             Mother Goose)

Note: Dominion A-115 and Parlophone, E-3817 (Ireland's
Eye) and Dominion, A-116 and Parlophone, E-3839 (The
Next Train) are, in each case, virtually the same sketches.

Decca Records:

Recorded 10 July, 1934 (Thames Street Studio, London)
TB 1369   "Cruising" Unissued (A & B—K. Drago)
TB 1370-1   "Buying The Furniture" F 5147; U466
             (A & B—K. Drago)
TB 1371-1   "The Charladies' Ball"—1 F 5120; USA-
             15009 (A & B—K. Drago)
TB 1372-1   "Hands Across The Border"—Part One F
             5127; USA-15013 W 4167
TB 1373-1   "Hands Across The Border"—Part Two (with
             O'Dea, O'Donovan, Richard Hayward)

Recorded 20 July, 1934 Thames Street Studio)
TB 1402-1   "Everybody Wants to Win The Sweep" F
             5147; U 466 (Solo A)
TB 1403-1   "The Charladies' Ball"—2 F 5120; USA-
             15009 (Solo A)

Recorded 30 May, 1935 (Chenil Galleries Studio, London)
GB 7176   "Proposing" W 4192; U 209 (Solo A)
GB 7177-1   "Flying"—Part One F 5579; U 468 (A & B
             —Richard Hayward)
GB 7178-1   "Flying"—Part Two F 5579; U 468 (A & B
             —Richard Hayward)
GB 7179-1   "Smuggling" F 5632 (A & B—Richard
             Hayward)
GB 7180   "Mulligan v. McIllhagga" W 4192; U 209
             (A & B—Richard Hayward)
GB 7181-1   "Brighter Broadcasting" F 5632 (A & B
             —Richard Hayward)

His Master's Voice Records:

Recorded 9 May, 1938 (London, OEA denotes British Matrices)

OEA 6461	"The Irish Navy" BD 608; IM 544 (Solo A)
OEA 6462	"Orange And Green" BD 608; IM 544 (Solo A)
OEA 6463-1	"Sweet Daffodil Mulligan" IM 543; MR 3109 (Solo A)
OEA 6464-1	"Danny Doogan's Jubilee" IM 546; MR 3052 (A & B)

Recorded 10 May, 1938

OEA 6631-1	"America Hasn't Changed" IM 545 (A & B)
OEA 6632-1	"Fresh Fish" IM 543; MR 3109 (A & B—Noel Purcell)
OEA 6633-1	"After The Ball" IM 546; MR 3052 (A & B)
OEA 6634-1	"The BBC Takes Over Radio Eire" IM 545 (A & B)

Recorded 7 September, 1940 (Dublin, OEL denotes Irish Matrices)

OEL 186-1	"Murphy's V.C." IM 774 (Solo A)
OEL 187-1	"Non Troppo Largo" IM 774 (A—Josie Day)
OEL 188-3	"Rathgar" IM 825 (Solo A)
OEL 189-1	"Men" IM 809` (Solo A)
OEL 190-1	"Mrs Mulligan Joins the ARP" IM 809 (Solo A)
OEL 191-3	"Double Crossing the Border"—1 IM 752; MR 3462 (A & B & Co.)
OEL 192-3	"Double Crossing the Border"—2 IM 752; MR 3462 (A & B & Co.)
OEL 193-1	"Cinderella up-to-date" IM 825 (Solo A)

Beltona 7" x 45 rpm (Decca Record Co.)

Transferred January, 1957
"Hands Across the Border" Parts 1 & 2 45-BE 2654
(With O'Dea, O'Donovan, Hayward)

Compilations Albums (33 rpm)

ACL 1185   *Irish Night Out* (Featuring Richard Hayward)
(Decca)
Side One: "Hands Across the Border"
(O'Dea, O'Donovan, Hayward)
Transferred 4th December, 1964

GAR 1002   *The Golden Years Of The Theatre Royal,*
Dublin (EMI)
Transferred 1986
Side One: "Mrs Mulligan Joins the A.R.P."
(featuring Jimmy O'Dea)

STAL 8005 (Stereo) *Memories of Dublin*
Transferred 1984
Side One: "Biddy Mulligan, The Pride of the
Coombe"—Jimmy O'Dea
Side Two: "Fresh Fish," with Jimmy O'Dea,
Harry O'Donovan, Noel Purcell.

Albums

EMI (Ireland) Talisman Transferred 1973
STAL 1037—Vol. One *Jimmy O'Dea and Harry O'Donovan*

Side One	Side Two
Biddy Mulligan (Coombe)	Sixpence Each Way
Mrs Mulligan In The Tram	Fresh Fish
Non Troppo Largo	Crossing the Border (North Side)
Football And Wives Part 1	Crossing the Border (South Side)
Football And Wives Part 2	Mrs Mulligan, Smuggler
Mrs Mulligan Records Her Vote	The Next Train
The BBC Takes Over Radio Eire	Sweet Daffodil Mulligan

STAL 1044—Vol. Two *Jimmy O'Dea and Harry O'Donovan*

Side One	Side Two
The Dublin Fusilier	Orange and Green
Mrs Mulligan and Charlie	Double Crossing the Border Pt. 1
A Shakespearean 6 pence	Double Crossing the Border Pt. 2
Each Way	Mrs Mulligan Buys a Turkey
After the Ball	Mrs Mulligan in Court Part 1
Danny Doogan's Jubilee	Mrs Mulligan in Court Part 2
Mrs Mulligan's Shieks	Mrs Mulligan in the Pawn Shop
The Irish Navy	Reprise of "Biddy Mulligan The
The Mayor Proposes Part 1	Pride of the Coombe"
The Mayor Proposes Part 2	

Bibliography

We have quoted, briefly, from the copyright material of the following authors and publishers to whom we are extremely grateful.

Barr, Charles. *Ealing Studios*. New York: The Overlook Press, 1977.

Clissmann, Anne. *Flann O Brien*. Dublin: Gill and Macmillan, 1975.

Feeney, William J. *Drama in Hardwicke Street*. London and Toronto: Fairleigh Dickinson University Press, 1984.

Gorham, Maurice, *Forty Years of Irish Broadcasting*. Dublin: The Talbot Press, 1967.

Green, Benny ed. *The Last Empires*. London: Pavilion Books, 1986.

Hickey, Des and Gus Smith. *A Paler Shade of Green*. London: Leslie Frewin, 1972.

Holloway, Joseph. *Irish Theatre*. California: Proscenium Press.

La Rue, Danny. *From Drags to Riches*. London: Viking Press, 1987.

Rose, Clarkson. *Red Plush and Greasepaint*. London: Museum Press, 1964.

Watters, Eugene and Matthew Murtagh. *Infinite Varieties*. Dublin: Gill and Macmillan, 1975.

Young, Jordan R. *The Beckett Actor*. California: Moonstone Press, 1987.

BBC DATA, Written Archives Centre, Reading, to whom we are especially grateful for material relating to the radio series *Irish Half Hour*.

Taylor Black, Donald, *Remembering Jimmy O'Dea*. TV documentary made by Poolbeg Productions in association with RTE, 1985.

King, Steve. A biography now in preparation of Arthur Lucan and Kitty McShane

Index

Note: Plays, pantomimes, revues, broadcasts and films featuring Jimmy O'Dea, and referred to in this book, are listed separately in the **Index to Stage Plays, Broadcasts and Films** which follows this Index.

abbreviations: "J" in an index entry refers to Jimmy O'Dea; "Harry" refers to Harry O'Donovan. The method of alphabetisation used is word-by-word.

Index of
Stage Plays,
Broadcasts
and Films

Note: This Index lists (in alphabetical order) the titles of plays, pantomimes, revues, broadcasts and films featuring James O'Dea (Jimmy O'Dea) and referred to in *The Pride of the Coombe.*

Year of production, theatre and name of production company (where given) are also included.

2. BROADCASTS
(Radio and Television shows)

Our thanks is due to the following organisations for kind permission to reproduce cinema photographs:

United International Pictures: *Jimmy Boy*

Weintraub Screen Entertainment: *Penny Paradise*
Cheer, Boys, Cheer
Let's be Famous

Walt Disney Company Ltd.: *Darby O'Gill and the Little People*